P9-DFR-274

Critical Studies Series

ERNEST HEMINGWAY:
New Critical Essays

ERNEST HEMINGWAY:
New Critical Essays

edited by
A. Robert Lee

VISION
and
BARNES & NOBLE

Vision Press Limited
11–14 Stanhope Mews West
London SW7 5RD

and

Barnes & Noble Books
81 Adams Drive
Totowa, NJ 07512

ISBN (UK) 0 85478 474 8
ISBN (US) 0 389 20284 3

Printed and bound in Great Britain by
Unwin Brothers Ltd.,
Old Woking, Surrey.
Phototypeset by Galleon Photosetting,
Ipswich, Suffolk.
MCMLXXXIII

Abigail E. Weeks
Memorial Library
Union College

presented by

Contents

Introduction

by A. ROBERT LEE

All good books are alike in that they are truer than if they had really happened and after you are finished reading one you will feel that all that happened to you and afterwards it all belongs to you; the good and the bad, the ecstasy, the remorse and sorrow, the people and the places and how bad the weather was. If you can get so that you can give that to people, then you are a writer. Because it is the hardest thing of all.
—'Old Newsman Writes: A Letter from Cuba', *Esquire*, December 1934

A writer's job is to tell the truth. His standard of fidelity to the truth should be so high that his invention, out of his experience, should produce a truer account than anything factual can be. For facts can be observed badly; but when a good writer is creating something, he has time and scope to make it an absolute truth.
—Introduction to *Men at War* (1942)

Both these observations belong to Hemingway's occasional work, the first a commissioned and no doubt well-paying magazine piece, the second his collection of favourite war writing. Although less well-known than those parts of *Death in the Afternoon* (1932), *Green Hills of Africa* (1935), and latterly his *Selected Letters* (1981), which also speak of the kinds of 'truth' writers should aim to achieve, they again emphasize the un-abating, utter seriousness with which he always (surprisingly to some) regarded both his own and literary craft in general. For though Hemingway no longer arouses the spectacular controversies he did for an earlier generation of readers—one has only to recall the Hemingway of the headlines and publicity or of Lillian Ross's 1950 *New Yorker* Profile, for instance—he as often as not still tends to get thought a writer for whom serious

7

fiction lay beyond his grasp, that he belongs foremost with an engaging but always lesser order of journalists and travel-writers. He is to be granted the relative success of *The Sun Also Rises* (1926) and several well-turned stories, even something by way of the celebrated style and his aptitude for landscape and action scenes, but to think him a major literary Modern and a fiction-writer of genuine overall better standing betrays almost wilful slackness of taste.

In this, the weight of past adverse publicity has continued to resonate down into our own time, Hemingway less as a serious writer than a roving public stuntman and maker of headlines. Those dismayed by precisely this 'public' Hemingway, even while the novels and shorter fiction were being published, insisted that he acted at almost every turn as a species of child-man, the incorrigible attention-getter and impresario of his need to be situated always centre-stage. Even to the less censorious he amounted often to a kind of twentieth-century dandy, orchestrating in public his well-known rules of mascu-line conduct, flirting with death, and hooked into an irre-fragably American vision of heroism and his celebrated 'separ-ate peace'. His evident true bent, the argument runs, lay manifestly in the narcissistic playing out of roles, the 1920s young Paris expatriate recalled in *A Moveable Feast* (1964), the frontline war correspondent, the Hispanophile and lover of the *corridas*, or the photogenic adept in matters of fishing and big game hunting, whether in Africa, his Idaho ranch or, in his last years, on the *finca* in pre-Castro Cuba. He thus fell short of the man for all seasons dreamed up by his proponents, the exemplary 'life' figure who offered a way—a code—by which to endure against the malaise of war and deepest sexual and existential uncertainty.

Nor, it continues to be asserted, can Hemingway claim major status as a writer. He wrote, essentially, as the literary mannerist trapped inside his own too familiar stylistic habits and procedures. If Hemingway became the victim of his own publicity, translating human experience into some static or infinitely too reductive virility code, so his famous declarative style led less to genuine distinctiveness of idiom than to a pseudo-style which could do only certain limited things in a limited way. *The Old Man and the Sea* (1952) notably came in for this kind of indictment. Fortunately, we can now begin to see that both his detractors and his card-carrying supporters, between them, in fact unwittingly conspired to deflect the focus away from what Hemingway did most achieve in his fiction. Whether one still judges him far less than the modern American master whom well-wishers thought the rightful heir to a Nobel Prize in 1954, or the novelist and short-story writer better in almost every particular than detractors allow, the point two decades on from his suicide and a welter of exegesis later might belatedly be recognized that he was never wholly to be accounted for by either case. The *Letters*, at least, and comments like those quoted above (albeit made *en passant*), enable us to discern an altogether more painstaking, writerly Hemingway, one who despite everything remained unyieldingly the authentic creative professional.

Which is not to suggest, as this collection bears witness, that there has emerged some final consensus as to the balance of Hemingway's strengths and weaknesses. But Hemingway as an altogether more patient craftsman—serious as to the intentions and means of his art—has begun to show through, especially as the memory of 'Papa' recedes in common with the glamorous litany of his marriages, the gossipy affair with Marlene Dietrich, the strange ritual of the New York visits (usually to Scribners) from Florida or Cuba, the drinking bouts and the safaris and his eye-catching several plane crashes. A Hemingway disinterred from all this mystique and media folklore has helped immeasurably, his art perceived at a distance from his life. Hemingway, too, as everyone's favourite case-study (and who among his critics beginning from Philip Young in 1952 has not been tempted to speak of his neuroses and wounds, his apparent compensations?) has begun to run its course. Despite all the psychobiography and guesswork, Hemingway—one is tempted to say thankfully—still hasn't been comprehensively explained, however much his fiction time and again has been pressed to do duty in confirming his supposed emotional fissures and fears of inadequacy. It ought, however, to be acknowledged that, together with successors like Norman Mailer, he has been returned to that fray to some extent by the advent of feminist criticism in the mould of Kate Millett's *Sexual Politics* (1970) or Germaine Greer's *The Female Eunuch* (1970).

If these essays share a common purpose, and they have all been commissioned with that end in mind, it is to help re-see, and to an extent re-site, Hemingway. To be sure, his essential themes of Death, War, the Hunt, the power of Place and his uneasy male vision of sexual relationship, all come into focus, though not, I hope, in the manner of some dutiful listing. One objection to Hemingway has always been that his interests run too narrowly, and indeed recur to the point where familiarity with them brings on contempt, or if something less rebarbara- tive, a real degree of impatience. To the extent that Hemingway doesn't range widely (as, say, Faulkner?), he doesn't, either, simply mine the one single theme. The stories, the best of his longer fiction, his considerable range of non-fictional writing, all contribute to the supporting evidence. Nor does the custom of imagining him to write unvaryingly in the one style—usually characterized as declarative and hard-boiled, tight picto- graphic phrases strung together by a succession of 'ands' and 'buts'—do anything like relevant justice to his writing. To re-read and ponder, for instance, the cryptic closing dialogue of *The Sun Also Rises*, or the celebrated portrait of soldiers march- ing through the dust which begins *A Farewell to Arms* (1929), or the killing of El Sordo in *For Whom the Bell Tolls* (1940), to name but three occasions from the novels, can't but sharpen aware- ness of Hemingway's skills as a stylist. In each, the narration gathers into itself a fine complexity of tone and nuance. His great themes, in other words, are encountered precisely through Hemingway's command of voice, his ability to render what he calls 'absolute truth' through his distinct, transforming accent. This amounts to a great deal more than mere management of syntax, or adjectives; it bespeaks precisely the 'truer account than anything factual can be', a dimension of Hemingway's fiction which still merits considerable analysis.

The volume opens with David Seed's account of the genesis and local stylistic energies of *In Our Time* (1925), Hemingway's momentous first story-collection. He calls attention to the influence of Hemingway's early newspaper apprenticeship in Toronto and Kansas and the detail of how the impressionistic fragments published in Paris as *in our time* (1924) became the basis of the later text. Colin Nicholson then develops a profile of the stories which came after *In Our Time*, an imagined fictional landscape, as he sees it, inhabited by figures whose lives, to adapt Robert Frost's line, amount to the barest of stays against confusion.

Each of the major novels is given a separate essay. Andrew Hook, after arguing for the separation of Hemingway's art from his life, interprets *The Sun Also Rises* (issued in Britain as *Fiesta*) as foremost a novel of place, its Jazz Age damaged expatriate American colony seen against the touchstones of Paris, Pamplona and other European cities and as the contrast of transience with both 'the earth' and the dense historicity of Europe. In his account of *A Farewell to Arms*, William Wasserstrom blends a purposive note of autobiography into an argument that what finally distinguishes this novel is Hemingway's luminous power of style, an eventual resonance which reaches beyond the ostensible story of Frederic Henry and Catherine Berkeley and the waste of war and speaks to our purported 'post-Modern' sensibility with uncanny prescience. My own reading of *For Whom the Bell Tolls* looks to the generally underregarded design of his Spanish Civil War epic, the subtle, exact way in which its dialectical play of centre and circumference 'knits' (Hemingway's own word) the novel into an imaginative whole. James Justus selects as his focus Hemingway's last 'Book of the Sea', *Islands in the Stream* (1970), setting it in the context of *The Old Man and the Sea* and *A Moveable Feast* and arguing its case as an anthem to the human complexity of defeat and as the best of his later writing.

The four concluding essays range more widely. Brian Way takes the uncustomary line of arguing for Hemingway as a writer of striking creative intelligence (though less so in the later work), an artist in whom thought weighed far more importantly than it is usual to acknowledge. Faith Pullin develops a considered feminist view of Hemingway, contending that his mystique of the loner reveals in him a dark hostility to relationship itself as much as to women. For Eric Mottram, by contrast, Hemingway offers the altogether more heroic example of the writer committed to a philosophy of duty and risk which goes beyond the received (and generally hostile) view of him as unable—or unwilling—to confront the full nuance of human relationship. Frank McConnell's concluding essay examines Hemingway's influence as a modern titular presence to whom,

11

favourably or not, attention has had to be paid, whether in the form of Saul Bellow's aspersions, or the perceivable residue of style at work in Norman Mailer and the classic American writers of detective fiction, or latterly in the vision of such resolute post-Moderns as Vonnegut, Barth and Pynchon, overall the mark of an unignorable progenitor upon a succeeding generation of fabulists.

This collection was almost ready for press when the untimely death of Brian Way occurred. Those contributors who knew him and held him in the esteem I did would wish this volume to be something of a tribute both to his own unfailing warmth and intelligence and to his wife Josephine who, given Brian's fading eyesight, played so vital a role in ensuring that he could always get his work done. I hope she will allow this work to be dedicated to both of them, a truly exemplary collaboration.

1

'The Picture of the Whole': *In Our Time*

by DAVID SEED

It is common knowledge that Hemingway began his career as a journalist. Originally he planned to go to the University of Illinois where he would have majored in journalism. In the event he began working for the *Kansas City Star* in Summer 1917, interrupted this activity to enrol in the American Ambulance Corps where he was wounded during service on the Italian front (1918), and on the eve of his return to Europe in 1921 began a series of articles for the *Toronto Star Weekly* and *Toronto Daily Star*. While Hemingway was writing these pieces he was also experimenting with short stories, sometimes written in the self-consciously colloquial style of Ring Lardner. The phenomenon of a writer producing both fiction and journalism is not unusual in American fiction of this period. Theodore Dreiser began his career similarly on the Chicago *Globe*, and Stephen Crane produced a series of war dispatches from Cuba and Greece shortly before writing *The Red Badge of Courage* (1895). Although in later life Hemingway claimed that his 'newspaper stuff' had nothing to do with his other writing, this early journalism played a crucial role in developing his fictional method.[1]

The *Kansas City Star* style sheet contained injunctions such as 'Use short sentences. Use short first paragraphs. Use vigorous English'; or, again, 'Avoid the use of adjectives, especially such extravagant ones as *splendid, gorgeous, grand, magnificent,* etc.' In an interview of 1940 Hemingway commented: 'Those were the best rules I ever learned for the business of writing.'[2] Apart from disciplining his style, Hemingway also found the stance of reporting useful once he began to experiment with prose vignettes. The earliest of these experiments was a series of statements which he entitled 'Paris, 1922'. They were not, however, news items so much as exercises in disciplining his own descriptive method. The last of these six sentences reads as follows:

> I have watched two Senegalese soldiers in the dim light of the snake house of the Jardin des Plantes teasing the King Cobra who swayed and tightened in tense erect rage as one of the little brown men crouched and feinted at him with his red fez.

This is a very early example of Hemingway's ambition to 'eliminate everything unnecessary to conveying experience to the reader'.[3] He places his main stress on the visual (every sentence begins with either 'I have seen' or 'I have watched') and concentrates his attention on fixing the postures of snake and men as accurately as possible.

The fact that Hemingway began such experiments in Paris indicates how crucial were his contacts with writers such as Gertrude Stein and Ezra Pound. Gertrude Stein read some of his early writings with evident disapproval and told him to 'begin over again and concentrate'. Circumstances more or less forced this advice on Hemingway since in December 1922 a suitcase containing virtually all his manuscripts up to that date was stolen in Paris. Gertrude Stein's injunction must have been very similar to the advice Pound gave Hemingway and there is a striking resemblance between the rules of the *Kansas City Star* style sheet and Pound's 'Don'ts for an Imagiste', especially 'Use no superfluous word, no adjective which does not reveal something.' In *A Moveable Feast* Hemingway was to note that Pound 'taught me to distrust adjectives'.[4] Journalism, Gertrude Stein and Pound thus seem to have exerted an important cumulative influence on Hemingway, tightening up his prose and sharpening his descriptive method. The style sheet alone would not necessarily have pushed Hemingway far enough in the direction of economy

14

which is a surprisingly rare quality in his newspaper dispatches of this period. In 'Refugees from Thrace' (*Toronto Daily Star*, 14 November 1922), for example, Hemingway was reporting on the Greek evacuation but his article contains anecdotal details (meeting a camera-man, sleeping at a brothel, getting covered with lice, etc.) which pull against the main subject. The article is far more discursive and far less focused than anything which appears in *In Our Time*.

As a result of his contacts with the American expatriate circle in Paris Hemingway's first book, *Three Stories and Ten Poems*, appeared in 1923. His next work, however, is more startlingly experimental. Hemingway had published six prose miniatures in the 'Exiles' Number' of *Little Review* (Spring, 1923), under the title 'In Our Time' (v. Appendix). He kept this title for an expanded collection of eighteen pieces which were issued by the Three Mountains Press in 1924. This work was one of a series supervised by Pound whose purpose, according to his postscript, was 'to tell the truth about *moeurs contemporains*, without fake, melodrama, conventional ending'. We shall see that the stance of truth-teller was an important one for Hemingway. The cover to *in our time* was probably the work of William Bird of the Three Mountains Press and consisted of a collage of newspaper cuttings dealing with such themes as warfare, American expatriation, Greek politics and revolutions. In other words, the cover makes a brilliant summary comment on the themes and circumstances of this book, as well as indicating its possible method of organization.

It has been conventional in Hemingway criticism to treat *in our time* as a trial run for the later work of the same title, or to ignore it completely.[5] Hemingway's attachment to the title, which he kept for three published works, suggests what sort of perspective he is adopting. It comes from the Episcopalian Order for Morning Prayer—'Give peace in our time, O Lord.' Hemingway ironically implies a general sense of peace as well as a specific contrast with warfare here. The response to this prayer is also directly relevant to Hemingway's work: 'Because there is none other that fighteth for us, but only thou, O God.' Here man's helplessness is stressed in order to make him put more trust in God. Hemingway keeps the first emphasis but blocks his characters' access to any spiritual consolation. In the seventh vignette of *in our time* ('Nick sat against the wall of the church') (VI) the religious institution has become a mere building; it offers Nick a temporary physical relief (he has been wounded) and nothing more.[6] In the eighth vignette (VII) a soldier prays desperately as his trench is being bombarded. No answer comes, simply 'the shelling moved further up the line', and the prayer becomes a matter of private shame which he hides from everybody. These and other examples indicate the kind of detached vantage-point which Hemingway adopts as well as the pessimistic values which go with it.

The work uses collage to assemble its materials around central themes and subjects. There are obvious groupings such as warfare and a limit of sequence in the bull-fight vignettes, but in general Hemingway makes a use of fragmentation and discontinuity which is similar to that of Pound or Eliot. The reader must be constantly on the alert for cross-references and parallels as, for instance, between vignettes V and XV. Both begin in a rhetorically similar way—'They shot the six cabinet ministers', 'They hanged Sam Cardinella.' In each case the pronoun 'they' suggests anonymous but irresistible forces and thus fits into a general emphasis on man's vulnerability to circumstance. Hemingway certainly knew 'Hugh Selwyn Mauberley', a poem which makes extensive use of collage, since he used it in some of his own poems, and even retitled the last vignette 'L'Envoi' when he placed it at the end of *In Our Time*.[7] It is not really necessary to demonstrate too specific a source for Hemingway's use of collage. The term first appears in an exhibition of Max Ernst's work which took place in Paris in 1920. When he was being interviewed in 1958 Hemingway stated that he respected a lot of painters at this time and named among others Picasso and Braque who had been experimenting with *papier collé*. Given Hemingway's interest in the visual arts and literary modernism, it is almost certain that he was familiar with it.

in our time was reviewed by Edmund Wilson in a particularly complimentary way. Wilson drew attention to the bull-fight vignettes which had the 'dry sharpness and elegance' of Goya's lithographs. Although he does not expand on this comparison it sheds useful light on Hemingway's method and he himself confirmed the connection with Goya in *Death in the Afternoon* where he praises him for seeing directly, for honesty of vision. Thinking back to the Greek flight from Smyrna when they broke the legs of the pack-animals, he comments that it would have needed a Goya to describe them.[8] He has in mind the series of lithographs called *Los Desastres de la Guerra* (The Disasters of War) where Goya adopts an alternating humanitarian and satirical perspective in order to exclude the possibility of glamour. The lithograph entitled 'Yo lo vi' ('I saw it') divides spatially into three areas. In the right background we can see the dim outlines of the town which people are fleeing from; in the middle ground we see a line of refugees carrying bundles of possessions; and in the foreground we see two men together, the one looking back in terror and a mother with one child over her shoulder turning to help a second child who has stumbled and who is also looking back in terror. The foregrounding of these figures forces one to 'read' the picture towards the background and yet it does not show what the people are fleeing from. The third vignette of *in our time* ('Minarets stuck up in the rain') (II) reverses the direction of Goya's picture. The minarets set up a perspective focused towards these distant objects; Hemingway then puts a heavier stress on the sheer scale of the evacuation—there is far more middle ground than in the Goya—by sketching in the lines of cattle and people. Finally in the foreground is a woman in labour and a girl helping her. Like Goya Hemingway packs the emotional force of his picture into a foregrounded figure, in this case the girl crying; and, again like Goya, Hemingway implies that this is a generic scene as well as a concrete one. Hemingway almost certainly drew on Goya for the arrangement of his scenes. The vignette of the evacuation is literally graphic as are those dealing with bull-fights which, like Goya's *Tauromaquia*, suspend dramatic moments or catch the grotesque nature of the contest in hard-edged prose.

In these prose vignettes we can see the first examples of what was to become Hemingway's characteristic prose style. Adjectives are reduced to a minimum; the passages work through a series of consecutive statements which generally avoid subordinate clauses and which give a superficial impression of naïveté. There is a general stress on what can be observed which gives many of the passages a physical actuality. The absence of abstractions does not of itself prove that Hemingway is not interpreting what he presents; rather he does this through ordering and placing his materials with the utmost care.

Thus the sixth vignette ('They shot the six cabinet ministers') (V) immediately locates the scene in time and place; it is half-past six in the morning and we are outside a hospital. One of the ministers who is being executed has typhoid and sinks down to the ground, whereas 'the other five stood very quietly against the wall.' As before the vignette concentrates its attention on one figure in a seemingly impassive way, the passage ending 'When they fired the first volley he was sitting down (51/111) in the water with his head on his knees.'⁹ Hemingway's dead-pan statement sets up a very strong tension between the prose surface and its subject. It is naïve to conclude that, because Hemingway avoids explicit narrative comment, he has no moral perspective on the event. Instead of discursive comment Hemingway uses a rhetoric of selection and arrangement in order to show the barbarity of the execution. The source for this vignette was an uncensored report on the execution of the Greek cabinet ministers who were responsible for the war with Turkey. Hemingway changed the time, weather, place and erased any identifying details which might have motivated or specified the execution too closely. The focus on the sick man sets up an ironic contrast with the hospital whose shutters are 'nailed shut', which suggests secrecy in turn. It is raining and, in these early vignettes just as in *A Farewell to Arms*, rain is associated with death or disaster. The wet dead leaves on the courtyard anticipate the death of the ministers, help to establish a sombre tone, and in fact are probably borrowed from one of Pound's imagist poems—'Liu Ch'e', which evokes absence through the image of a deserted courtyard.¹⁰ The vignette has a scrupulous and disciplined rhetoric which implies far more than it says. In that sense it is absolutely typical of *in our time*. It is also indicative of Hemingway's generic interest in events that the Greek identity of the ministers has been suppressed. They could be any victims of turbulent post-war politics.

Partly thanks to such favourable reviews as Edmund Wilson's, Boni and Liveright published an expanded collection of Hemingway's work in 1925. *In Our Time* intercalated the earlier vignettes between stories, achieving a more complex

structure than the 1924 book. *In Our Time* is unique in
Hemingway's career in being a unified collection of stories. The
main changes which he made from 1924 to 1925 confirm that he
had a particular order in mind. The tenth and eleventh
vignettes were re-classified as stories ('A Very Short Story' and
'The Revolutionist') because they had fuller narratives than the
other passages. The second vignette ('The first matador') was
shifted forward to begin the bull-fight sequence instead of being
isolated awkwardly in the pieces about war (cf. Appendix).
Hemingway wrote to Wilson in October 1924 to explain his new
method. It was designed

> to give the picture of the whole between examining it in detail.
> Like looking with your eyes at something, say a passing coast
> line, and then looking at it with 15x binoculars. Or rather,
> maybe, looking at it and then going in and living in it—and then
> coming out and looking at it again.[11]

The stress on seeing is absolutely characteristic, but the use of
double perspective would distinguish *In Our Time* from two
possible models—*Dubliners* (1914) and *Winesburg, Ohio* (1919).
Hemingway was certainly familiar with *Ulysses* which he
admired greatly, even bringing it into a coda for 'Big Two-
Hearted River' which was eventually discarded; so he very
likely knew *Dubliners* too. There is even less doubt about
Anderson who Hemingway read extensively before he left for
Europe. Indeed, Hemingway told Scott Fitzgerald in 1925
that *Winesburg, Ohio* had been his first model. Both possible
models, however, are unified by place which would not have
suited Hemingway's scope. The characters of *In Our Time* are
constantly in motion, either for warfare, travel or evacuation.
Hemingway studiously avoids any comfortably fixed location
in order to make a general comment on the political and social
instability of the period from 1914 to about 1923.

Exactly how *In Our Time* is unified has been a problematical
issue of Hemingway criticism for years and has led to a variety
of simplistic explanations. Psychological repression has been
proposed as its basic concern; or that it is preoccupied with
periodicity, the 'rhythmic interplay of life and death'; or more
baldly that its theme is death. And so the list could go on. The
problem with these explanations is that they fail to do justice

to the complexity of *In Our Time*. In his review of the book
D. H. Lawrence declared that it was a 'fragmentary novel' and
this points to one of its main differences from the 1924 volume.
Several of the stories centre on the character of Nick Adams
and follow a rough chronology from youthful innocence to
mature disillusionment. These stories give *In Our Time* a much
stronger individual focus and sense of sequence, so that the
collage analogy is far less applicable. Clinton Burhans has
argued that the vignettes follow a pattern of war ('On the
Quai', I–VII) to crime (VIII) to bull-fighting (IX–XIV)
back to crime (XV), finishing with war ('L'Envoi') (cf.
Appendix B). The stories begin and end with Nick Adams,
'and the stories in between concern either Nick, a central
character like him in all but name, or themes introduced and
developed in these stories.'[12]

We can locate four main methods of unifying *In Our Time*;
reference to a central composite character, common themes,
common locations, and quasi-poetical links through recurring
figures or verbal details. Thus 'A Very Short Story' follows on
logically from the wounding of Nick in the preceding vignette
(VI) since the protagonist (who is not named) is recuperating
from war-wounds. Late in the story he goes home to America
and the narrative at that point anticipates the next story
'Soldier's Home'. The theme of 'A Very Short Story', romantic
betrayal, looks back to Nick's youthful affair with Marjorie
and introduces a short series of stories revolving around
marital dissatisfaction. The context of this theme is warfare
which binds the story to the earlier vignettes and the fact the
protagonist's prayer in Padua cathedral fails to stave off
betrayal links the narrative with similar ironic references to
religion in the framing vignettes (VI and VII). The main
location of the story is Italy although it concludes in Chicago,
once again linking the narrative with vignettes VI and VII as
well as the later stories 'Cat in the Rain' and 'Out of Season';
and the shift back to America anticipates the final story 'Big
Two-Hearted River'. On the level of details, the story begins
in darkness like 'The Battler'. The soldier's lover Luz sits on
his bed, thus anticipating Krebs's mother's identical action in
the next story. In vignette VI Nick sees an iron bedstead
hanging out of a war-damaged house. At that point it seems

like an incidental detail, but the story converts it retrospectively into a metaphor of the destructive effects of war on love.
In every story in this collection Hemingway uses similar
details to weave them together into a whole entity. Vignette V
ends with a minister sitting on the ground against a wall. 'The
Battler', which follows it, establishes a continuity of posture
when Nick gets up from the side of a railway track. However,
in the next vignette (VI) he is sitting wounded against a wall.
The recurrence of images and verbal references means that *In
Our Time* has to be read very closely indeed. One of the most
impressive things about this work is the way in which
Hemingway charges apparently trivial details with significance either to bind the stories together or reinforce their
themes metaphorically.

Burhans's analysis of the structure of *In Our Time* has one
weakness: it separates the stories from the vignettes into
parallel sequences in a way which underrates their interaction
on each other. The first vignette, for instance, is narrated by a
soldier who is presumably both young and going into war for
the first time. He notes two main details—the fact that his
lieutenant is drunk and that his adjutant is worried about their
field kitchen being spotted by the enemy—and comments 'it
was funny going along that road' (13/86). The adjective
implies that war has not yet made any real impact on him and
this same theme of youthful innocence is taken up in the first
story 'Indian Camp'. Here Nick Adams goes with his father (a
doctor) to help an Indian woman to give birth. There is a
heavy emphasis on learning, especially in the doctor's clinical
explanation of the process of birth. Although the story is
narrated in the third person, the perspective is virtually Nick's
and that is why Hemingway gives us details of the doctor's
preparation for an improvised Caesarian and nothing at all
about the operation. Nick was looking away. But the story has
a sting in its tail since, unable to stand his wife's screams, the
Indian's husband has committed suicide, and Nick gets a very
clear view of this:

> The Indian lay with his face toward the wall. His throat had
> been cut from ear to ear. The blood had flowed down into a
> pool where his body sagged the bunk. His head rested on his left
> arm. The open razor lay, edge up, in the blankets. (18/89)

21

The hard-edged objective prose captures the scene with a visual immediacy which denies the reader Nick's earlier option of looking away. Indeed seeing takes on a positive moral force in this book in so far as it represents a direct confrontation with the horrifying aspects of life.

Nick is not yet capable of digesting his experience. Death is either just a word or an unpleasant sight, and the story ends with him feeling a naïve confidence that he will never die. The Thrace vignette (II) ironically underlines his child-like lack of reaction in repeating the act of birth, this time with a girl watching and crying in terror. The fact that she is watching and the objectively descriptive prose repeats Nick's vision of the dead Indian, but denies any kind of alleviating context (in 'Indian Camp' the beauty of nature offsets the events in the cabin). Hemingway uses the metaphor of a log-jam to describe the refugees, which leads into the logs that form the ostensible subject in the second story, 'The Doctor and the Doctor's Wife'. Here Nick's father has an argument with an Indian who insists that he is stealing logs which have drifted away from booms. The doctor euphemistically calls them 'driftwood' whereas 'stolen' is repeated again and again in the text. The quarrel is inconclusive and the subject shifts to a contrast between Nick's parents. His mother (like Krebs's in 'Soldier's Home') is nervously religious and naïvely unaware of any unpleasant sides to human nature. Nick only appears at the end of this story when he decides to go into the woods with his father rather than home to his mother, but he is an implied focus to the story. It reveals the differences between his parents in a way which paves the way for his adult engagement with life. As in *A Farewell to Arms*, *In Our Time* erodes any associations between 'home' and pleasure or domestic stability. Krebs feels more disorientated at home than at war, and in 'Big Two-Hearted River' Nick can call his camp 'home' only because he has made it himself. The second story of the book begins this erosion of domestic stability.

The next two stories show the end of Nick's love-affair with a girl called Marjorie and his attempts to console himself with male companionship, and are counterpointed against two naïve reactions to warfare. Vignettes III and IV reduce battle to a grotesque game, the latter particularly which is cast in an exaggeratedly English public-school idiom. Similarly Nick makes adolescent heavy weather of his separation from Marjorie and in 'The Three-Day Blow' gets drunk with a croney called Bill. During their conversation they wander from literature (which to them means Chesterton and Walpole), to more prosaic matters like coal and Hemingway makes one of his few ironic narrative comments—'They were conducting the conversation on a high plane' (45/106). As the whisky they are drinking takes effect they begin to speak in a pompously English idiom, an idiom which resembles the preceding vignette. These earlier vignettes set up what one critic has called 'an ominous parallel between his [Nick's] personal development and that of world events', but 'parallel' does not strike the right note.[13] Vignettes I, III and IV relate by analogy to Nick's naïve reactions. Vignettes II and V are framed in a stark visual description which contrasts with Nick's ignorance of experience. They are certainly ominous in hinting at the sort of experiences which are characteristic of his time and increase the ironic direction of these stories which is towards deflating Nick's indulgent emotionalism. 'The Battler' continues this process. Nick has been knocked off a freight train by the brakeman and is silently vowing revenge with private bravado: 'That lousy crut of a brakeman. He would get him some day' (53/111). It seems at first as if Nick is the eponymous 'battler', but then he comes across a punch-drunk ex-boxer camping in the nearby woods. The man is horribly disfigured which is Nick's first shock. His second is when he tries to pick a fight with Nick. The boxer's companion tells Nick that he has declined ever since his lover deserted him, a story which by implication contrasts very strongly with Nick's limited experience of love. 'The Battler' is a transitional story, showing Nick travelling literally and metaphorically towards adult awareness. Through the shock of his encounter he is confronted—directly and grotesquely—with the violence which, the vignettes imply, is characteristic of the contemporary scene.

A short poem of Hemingway's which appeared in the *Double-Dealer* in 1922 begins 'He tried to spit out the truth' and this line encapsulates his general stance in *In Our Time*. Hemingway is particularly scathing towards any attempts to

23

evade experience as can be seen if we contrast two stories, 'Mr and Mrs Elliott' and 'Soldier's Home'. The first of these ironizes a certain kind of gentility. Mrs. Elliott is a super-annuated Southern belle and her husband an amateur poet of private means. Hemingway particularly mocks their sexual purity, presenting it as a kind of wilful ignorance which sus-pends the couple in a permanent adolescence (Cornelia tells Hubert that he is a 'dear sweet boy'). Sometimes Hemingway mimics the way they speak, sometimes he mocks their sexual efforts through an ironic refrain ('they tried to have a baby'), and sometimes he exploits repetition: 'They did not try very often on the boat because Mrs Elliott was quite sick. She was sick and when she was sick she was sick as Southern women are sick' (85/132). In Gertrude Stein's *Three Lives* (1909), which Hemingway read with admiration, repetition evokes the dogged fixed mentality of the main characters without patronizing or dismissing them. Hemingway is trying to make the epithet 'sick' do too much work for him—to describe a physical state, imply an attitude towards sexuality, evoke fixity of character *and* pinpoint Hemingway's own indigna-tion. It is not a particularly successful story but important to the general theme of confronting experience. Hubert Elliott's final obsession with writing poetry and incipient alcoholism are two predictable results of his evasive idealism.

'Soldier's Home' deals more explicitly with this central problem of the authenticity of experience, the word 'lies' running through the story like a refrain. The story opens by juxtaposing two photographs of the protagonist Krebs, one before the war where he fits into the stereotype of his fellow-students, and one from the war where his uniform seems too big for him, a hint of the unsettling effect his experiences have had on him. From the very start Krebs is a victim of circumstances. He comes home too late to be fêted with stories that are unimpressive compared with anti-German propa-ganda. Ironically he finds that he can only communicate with others by conforming to the roles they expect of him, but, since in terms of personal honesty these are lies, he finds that his actual memories of the war are eroded. He gradually sinks into a kind of limbo where all action has lost its authen-ticity. Not surprisingly in view of the similarity between

24

Krebs's desire for honesty and Hemingway's general fictional enterprise, the perspective is quite sympathetic. The first half of the story emphasizes Krebs's solitude by summarizing his thoughts: 'He did not want any consequences. He did not want any consequences ever again. He wanted to live along without consequences. Besides, he did not really need a girl. The army had taught him that' (71/124). We seem to be witnessing a kind of inner debate where Krebs is confronting and then rejecting life in his home town. The verb 'taught' harks back to the way Nick Adams learns in the earlier stories except that now the bleak conclusion to Krebs's knowledge is to incapacitate him for ordinary life.

The second half of the story consists of two passages of dialogue between Krebs and his sister and mother. Both use the term 'love' and draw explicit attention to a theme which runs throughout *In Our Time*. Romantic attachment is presented as fleeting and unreliable, a constant source of dissatisfaction rather than the opposite. Nick's affair with Marjorie peters out. Luz in 'A Very Short Story' changes lover according to circumstances and, in an ironic coda similar to Maupassant's *points*, the protagonist catches gonorrhoea from a casual contact in a Chicago taxi. None of the characters in *In Our Time* are given access to any kind of substantial idyll like Frederic Henry's period in Switzerland or Robert Jordan's love for Maria in *For Whom the Bell Tolls*. If circumstances thwart the possibility of love it is appropriate for Hemingway to draw ironic attention to the term itself. Krebs's sister and especially his mother use it as a means of compelling emotional allegiance to them. His mother's insistence on love goes hand in hand with a parallel insistence on religion which, Hemingway implies, muffles her capacity to respond directly to life.

In this story Hemingway brilliantly draws attention to the way in which words can be an obstacle to reality. Krebs begins compromising by repeating the sort of expressions he knows will satisfy his mother. Similarly in the introductory sketch which Hemingway added in 1930 and in vignettes I, III and IV, he contrasts the narrative voice with the events which are being described. 'On the Quai at Smyrna' deals with the Greek evacuation of 1922 and right from the beginning draws attention to the voice of the main narrator: 'The strange thing was, he said, how they screamed every night at midnight' (11/84). Hemingway distinguishes himself from the captain although, as he does elsewhere in *In Our Time*, he recounts the story in the third person while retaining the original speaker's idiom. Here we can see, for instance, mere curiosity going with an intense verb like 'screamed'. The captain wanders anecdotally from the agony of the refugees to a story about a Turkish officer. Everything exists on the same trivial level. One of the few critics to comment on this sketch, Daniel Fuchs, has noted that there is a 'tension between the comfortable, genteel English of the English captain who is narrator and the war experience which it cannot seem to contain'.[14] The corpses floating in the harbour become 'nice things' in this idiom which screens the speaker from the experiences he has had. Similarly in vignettes I, III and IV the narrative idiom becomes progressively more noticeable and more absurd. The last of the three (originally entitled 'Mons' (two) to link it with the preceding one) piles up words such as 'frightfully', 'absolutely', 'priceless' and 'topping'. Hemingway is here drawing on conversations he had with an English friend, Captain Eric Dorman-Smith, but it is doubtful that he intended a personal parody since Dorman-Smith was one of the dedicatees of *in our time*. Nevertheless a verb like 'potted' suggests a country hunt rather than modern warfare and the vignette closes on a note of annoyance as if changing circumstances had spoiled the speaker's fun: 'We were frightfully put out when we heard the flank had gone, and we had to fall back' (37/101).

This sort of idiom distorts the reality of warfare by screening the user from its full impact and stands in marked contrast with vignettes II, V and XV where Hemingway draws on his dispatch-writing to good effect. Here he adopts a semi-journalistic role to convey evacuation, political execution and a hanging as directly as possible. The very term 'vignette' carries inappropriate connotations of belles-lettres, whereas nothing could be further from Hemingway's concentrated visual images which imitate the immediacy of an eye-witness and which use precise composition to imply their moral perspectives. In 'On the Quai' the primary narrator functions literally as a reporter, conveying the English captain's words to the reader. Similarly in 'L'Envoi' Hemingway draws on an interview with the Greek king which he had heard about from a friend. Although Hemingway puts the report in the first person there is a hint of dramatic detachment when the interviewer comments 'it was very jolly' (157/185). It is, if anything, grotesque rather than jolly. The Greek king is under house arrest and yet welcomes the interviewer as if he is a social visitor, gives him a whisky and soda and—most important of all—uses an English speech idiom ('frightfully', 'chaps', etc.). His vocabulary strains against the actual dangers of revolutionary politics and transforms the king into an imitation gentleman. The fact that Hemingway keeps a reportorial stance in several of the vignettes is one of the many indications that his years of journalism had a beneficial effect on his early fiction.

Hemingway's letter to Edmund Wilson states that there are two broad perspectives in *In Our Time*, one distant and generalizing, the other immediate and particular. In fact there is a far greater variety of perspective, a variety which reveals an important side of the book's experimentalism. The alternation between objective and 'English' vignettes has been mentioned. The general perspective of the Nick Adams stories is close and sympathetic. By contrast 'A Very Short Story' recounts the failure of a wartime romance in a bald linear narrative which suggests the ironic inevitability of events. The protagonist—significantly denied a name—emerges as a pathetic marionette of circumstances. This story partly anticipates the plot of *A Farewell to Arms*, but nothing could be further from the reader's emotional engagement with Frederic Henry. Again in contrast, 'My Old Man' is the only first-person narrative in *In Our Time* and dates from an earlier stage in Hemingway's career when Anderson was still an important influence. Critics have noted similarities between this story and Anderson's 'I Want To Know Why', but *Huckleberry Finn* (which Hemingway subsequently praised extravagantly in *Green Hills of Africa*) could equally well lie behind its interplay between the perspectives of a child and of an adult. Joe Butler evokes the idyllic early years he spends with his jockey father through a language full of colloquialisms and full of pride at using the jargon of the turf. He describes a race at St. Cloud as follows:

27

> Kzar came on faster than I'd ever seen anything in my life and
> pulled up on Kircubbin that was going fast as any black horse
> could go . . . and they were right dead neck and neck for a
> second but Kzar seemed going about twice as fast. . . .
>
> (123/159)[15]

On the surface this is an authentic child's-eye description. The
absence of punctuation and the repetition of 'faster', 'fast',
'fast' catches the speed of a commentary. But inevitably a
question arises: if Kzar was going so fast, why didn't he win?
The answer is that the race was fixed and there are several
points in the story where Joe doesn't understand what is
happening, but where Hemingway gives the reader enough
information to recognize that Joe's father is in a racket. At the
end of the story Joe's father dies in a racing accident, their
horse has to be shot, and he overhears two men saying what a
thief his father was. It is a very moving ending because Joe has
articulated his love for his father so clearly. 'My Old Man' is
long enough and discursive enough for the reader to take an
emotional purchase on the narrative.

The stories and vignettes examined so far have revolved
around suffering, betrayal and death. It thus seems rather
surprising that critics should try to find moral positives in *In
Our Time*. 'The Revolutionist', for example, could be read
superficially as an endorsement of naïve idealism. The text,
however, would not justify such a reading. The fact that the
protagonist is a Hungarian links him ironically with vignette
VIII which describes the wanton shooting of two thieves by
American policemen. One of the latter insists that they are
'wops' (and so, presumably, fair game), but in fact they are
Hungarians. In 'The Revolutionist' Hemingway adopts the
persona of a fellow socialist but does not commit himself to his
younger companion's enthusiasm. There is an implied contrast between *his* mature scepticism and the naïve idealism of
the other. When the boy insists that revolution will build up in
Italy Hemingway inserts 'I did not say anything' (81/131)
into the 1925 text. This is in effect an inverted narrative
comment. Whenever the same formula occurs in 'The End of
Something', 'Soldier's Home', and other stories, it always
indicates a character's tacit disagreement with the speaker.
'The Revolutionist' is, in other words, ironic towards the boy

28

who predictably ends up in a Swiss jail.

Perspective and context supply two factors in determining the general sceptical temper of these stories and even the bull-fighting vignettes and the final story, 'Big Two-Hearted River', prove on examination to deny any moral positives. Vignette IX begins the series by employing a colloquial American idiom to give us the illusion of hearing a step-by-step commentary:

> The second matador slipped and the bull caught him through the belly . . . and the bull rammed him *wham* against the wall and the horn came out, and he lay in the sand, and then got up *like crazy drunk* and tried to *slug* the men carrying him away. . . . (83/132: emphasis added)

'Slug' is terse and expressive but too isolated to demonstrate a 'hard-boiled' style. That comes later in a story like 'The Undefeated' where Hemingway uses this American idiom in conversations between aficionados. The commentary method here is appropriate because the bull-fight sequence imitates the progressive initiation of a spectator into the sport from the first excited view of a newcomer through closer and closer observation and finally moving into the consciousness of a leading matador.

Thus the first vignette stresses the voice of the describer and was in fact written before Hemingway attended his first bull-fight in Pamplona. The second vignette concentrates on the possible reaction of physical disgust which a newcomer might feel in focusing on a gored horse whose entrails are hanging out. The terminology of bull-fighting has also begun to appear now (Hemingway carefully substituted 'wall' for 'barriera' in revising vignette IX). Vignette XI introduces more technical terms and the concept of honour through a matador who performs badly and whose pigtail is symbolically cut off. By the next vignette we have moved down close to the edge of the bull-ring to witness a performance by one of the leading matadors, Villalta. Now the stress is on elegant orchestrated movement and the sketch finishes with an image of Villalta triumphant gesturing proudly to the crowd. The fact that he is a historical character limits the generalizing force of this vignette. Indeed he seems the exception rather than the rule even within the bull-fight sequence since the next vignette (narrated now by a matador) presents the contempt which Maera (another historic matador) feels for contemporary bull-fighting. Maera and Villalta are two rare heroes of the bull-ring and it is significantly pessimistic that the last vignette of this series shows Maera's death. Hemingway's alternating internal and external perspective denies any heroism or grandeur to the event which is interestingly fictionalized. Maera in fact died of tuberculosis and pneumonia as Hemingway noted in 'A Banal Story' (collected in *Men Without Women*). Certainly Hemingway was fascinated by the sport and wrote in 1923 that 'it symbolizes the struggle between man and the beasts.' But that does not mean that it 'provides one model of how to die, and therefore of how to live, fittingly', nor does it dramatize 'the attitudes and qualities through which man can face the human condition'.[16] Critics who make such assertions are retrospectively reading Hemingway's later writings on the sport back into these sketches and not paying enough attention to the ways in which he blocks any generalizing force. These vignettes move through visual observation of the sport, through greater and greater understanding to the final and unconsoling actuality of death.

'Big Two-Hearted River' appears to offer final relief from the general emphasis on suffering in the book. When Nick treks into the wilderness he is reacting against the cumulative experiences of all the earlier stories. Critics have noted the symbolism which is used here. The burnt out town Seney resembles the damage of war, the river offers him a possibility of healing his psychic wounds. Indeed the whole fishing trip is therapeutic. Nick is positively obsessed with cleanliness and orderliness, and Hemingway uses a prose style which imitates Nick's concentration of physical action in a sustained effort to avoid thought and memory. This sets up an internal tension in the story between the relaxing soothing effects of nature and Nick's willed concentration. Thus his struggle with the trout becomes charged with a significance greater than a simple event because it tests his powers of control. Also memory does creep in towards the end of Part I when Nick thinks back to a former friend. Nick's idyll is, in short, precarious and temporary since he has mental and practical ties with civilization (examples of the latter would be the railway, his cigarettes, his camping equipment). Not only that, the story, the only one in the book to be divided into two parts, is interrupted at its calmest point (Nick has fallen asleep) by a vignette describing a hanging. The juxtaposition of individual comfort with individual terror jerks the reader out of any easy identification with Nick. A concentration on equipment, which goes logically with the subject of his story, now becomes shocking; the scaffold is 'heavy, built of oak and steel and swung on ball bearings' (143/174). And, even though the reader returns to Nick's story, the coda to the book is an ironic reminder that political events are continuing despite Nick's withdrawal.

The startling shift from calm to the bald statement 'they hanged Sam Cardinella', and from Nick's satisfaction with his camping to the interview with the Greek king are only two of the many cases where the vignettes play against the main linear thrust of the stories. This to-and-fro movement constantly disrupts the reader's desire to identify with Nick and the vignettes invite comparison between the composite protagonist's private destiny and the larger scale of contemporary public events. *In Our Time* is thus an interrelated narrative similar in its technique and preoccupations to Dos Passos's *U.S.A.*, which weaves news reports between its narrative sections; and similar also to Thomas Pynchon's *V* (1963) which regularly suspends its narrative to insert sections dealing with recent political crises. In all three cases the method is directed towards defining the contemporary situation.

The characteristic progression of *In Our Time* is a stripping away of moral, social or political supports. Joe Butler's final and despairing comment 'they don't leave a guy nothing' (129/164) applies to the book as a whole, providing we interpret 'they' as internal forces as well as external ones. In 'Cat in the Rain' an American wife wants a 'kitty' because she feels so dissatisfied with her married life. The cat is at once an object of petulant desire (treated like a child by her husband, she behaves like one) and a substitute for the child she lacks. In 'Out of Season' a young couple have quarrelled for an unstated reason and an expedition to go trout fishing collapses. In 'Cross-Country Snow' a skiing trip turns sour because Nick must return to domestic obligations. Hopes fail; ideals crumble

31

before reality; romance proves to be unattainable. Hemingway enacts these themes against a background of wanton violence and suffering through a variety of perspectives which weave them inseparably together. In *Death in the Afternoon* he declares:

> Let those who want to save the world if you can get to see it clear and as a whole. Then any part you make will represent the whole if it's made truly.

The moral positive of *In Our Time* is seeing in the sense of direct and honest confrontation with experience and its cumulative perspective is of a sceptical detachment which looks forward to the use of the book of Ecclesiastes as an epigraph to *The Sun Also Rises.*[17] Hemingway insists that we recognize the primary data of experience before organizing it morally.

NOTES

1. In a letter to his bibliographer, Louis Henry Cohn, quoted in *By-Line: Ernest Hemingway*, ed. William White (1967; Harmondsworth: Penguin Books, 1980), p. 11.
2. Charles A. Fenton, *The Apprenticeship of Ernest Hemingway* (1954; New York: Octagon Books, 1975), pp. 33, 34.
3. Carlos Baker, *Ernest Hemingway. A Life Story* (Harmondsworth: Penguin Books, 1972), p. 137. L. W. Wagner (ed.), *Ernest Hemingway. Five Decades of Criticism* (East Lansing, Mich.: Michigan State University Press, 1974), p. 36 (from the 1958 *Paris Review* interview).
4. *Literary Essays of Ezra Pound*, ed. T. S. Eliot (London: Faber and Faber, 1960), p. 4. Pound's general influence is discussed in Harold M. Hurwitz, 'Hemingway's Tutor, Ezra Pound', *Modern Fiction Studies* 17 (Winter, 1971–2), 469–82. *A Moveable Feast* (New York: Scribner's, 1964), p. 134. Gertrude Stein's advice is from *The Autobiography of Alice B. Toklas* (London: John Lane, 1933), p. 229.
5. A rare exception is Keith Carabine's 'Hemingway's *in our time*: An Appreciation', *Fitzgerald/Hemingway Annual* (1979), 301–26. Bruccoli Clark published a facsimile of *in our time* in 1978, and of *Three Stories and Ten Poems* in 1977.
6. To avoid confusion the 1925 numbering of the vignettes is given in Roman numerals (cf. Appendix).
7. 'The Age Demanded' (1925) obviously derives from poem II, and 'Captives' from poem IV (as does 'Soldier's Home', partly).
8. 'Mr. Hemingway's Dry-Points' (1924), collected in Edmund Wilson, *The Shores of Light* (London: W. H. Allen, 1952), p. 121. *Death in the*

Afternoon (London: Jonathan Cape, 1950), pp. 10, 131. The definitive study of Hemingway's interest in the arts is E. S. Watts's *Ernest Hemingway and the Arts* (Urbana: University of Illinois Press, 1971).

9. Page references in the text are to the Scribner's reprint of *In Our Time* (New York, 1970) and *secondly* to *The First Forty-Nine Stories* 2nd edition (London: Jonathan Cape, 1962) which does not number the chapters. *The Essential Hemingway* (1947) does not include 'On the Quai at Smyrna'. The Penguin edition of *The Snows of Kilimanjaro and Other Stories* (1963) contains misprints and does not include 'L'Envoi'. For full details of the complicated textual history of *In Our Time* the reader is referred to Audre Hanneman's *Ernest Hemingway. A Comprehensive Bibliography* (Princeton, N.J.: Princeton University Press, 1967) and the 1975 Supplement.

10. Michael S. Reynolds, 'Two Hemingway Sources for *In Our Time*', *Studies in Short Fiction* 9 (1972), 81–6. The relevant Pound lines are 'Dust drifts over the court-yard,/ . . . and the leaves/ Scurry into heaps and lie still . . ./ A wet leaf clings to the threshold.'

11. Wilson, pp. 122–23.

12. G. H. Muller, '*In Our Time*: Hemingway and the Discontents of Civilization', *Renascence* 29 (1977), 185–92; E. D. Lowry, 'Chaos and Cosmos in *In Our Time*', *Literature and Psychology* 26 (1976), 108–17; R. M. Slabey, 'The Structure of *In Our Time*', *South Dakota Review* 3 (August, 1965), 38–52. D. H. Lawrence, *Phoenix* (London: Heinemann, 1936), p. 365. Richard Hasbany takes up the influence of imagism on Hemingway in his 'The Shock of Vision: An Imagist Reading of *In Our Time*' (Wagner, 224–40). Unfortunately his critical vocabulary is incapable of dealing with the sequentiality of the book, which he describes as 'one vast image'. Clinton S. Burhans, Jr., 'The Complex Unity of *In Our Time*', in J. J. Benson (ed.), *The Short Stories of Ernest Hemingway: Critical Essays* (Durham, N.C.: Duke University Press, 1975), pp. 15–29.

13. Carl Wood, '*In Our Time*. Hemingway's Fragmentary Novel', *Neuphilologische Mitteilungen* 74 (1973), 720. A more serious mistake is to rearrange the materials in chronological order, as E. R. Hagemann does with the vignettes in his article ' "Only let the story end as soon as possible": Time-and-History in Ernest Hemingway's *In Our Time*', *Modern Fiction Studies* 26 (Summer, 1980), 255–62.

14. Daniel Fuchs, 'Ernest Hemingway, Literary Critic', in Arthur Waldhorn (ed.), *Ernest Hemingway. A Collection of Critical Essays* (New York: McGraw-Hill, 1973), p. 95.

15. Hemingway changed the names of the horses in his revisions of the text. *The First Forty-nine Stories* retains the earlier names of War Cloud and Foxless. For comment on the Anderson connection v. J. T. Flanagan, 'Hemingway's Debt to Sherwood Anderson', *Journal of English and Germanic Philology* 54 (October, 1955), 507–20; Paul P. Somers, Jr., 'The Mark of Sherwood Anderson on Hemingway: A Look at the Texts', *South Atlantic Quarterly* 73 (1974), 487–503. In *The Green Hills of Africa* (London: Jonathan Cape, 1954), p. 29, Hemingway states: 'All modern American literature comes from one book by Mark Twain called *Huckleberry Finn*.'

16. *By-Line*, p. 103. Carabine, 315; Burhans, p. 20. For discussion of the symbolism in this story v. Baker, *Hemingway. The Writer as Artist* (Princeton, N.J.: Princeton University Press, 1972), pp. 125–27 and Paul V. Anderson, 'Nick's Story in Hemingway's "Big Two-Hearted River"', *Studies in Short Fiction* 7 (Fall, 1970), 564–72. James L. Green, 'Symbolic Sentences in "Big Two-Hearted River"', *Modern Fiction Studies* 14 (Autumn, 1968), 307–12. J. V. Hagopian discusses the sexual symbolism of this story in 'Symmetry in "Cat in the Rain"', Benson, pp. 230–32.

17. *Death in the Afternoon*, p. 261. Hemingway originally put Ecclesiastes I.2, 3–7 as the epigraph. Cf. Philip Young and Charles W. Mann, *The Hemingway Manuscripts. An Inventory* (University Park, Penn.: Pennsylvania State University Press, 1969), [Plate 2].

APPENDIX

The contents of *In Our Time* (with dates of original publications of stories, and original 1924 order of vignettes in parentheses)

vignette	story
1 Everybody was drunk (1)[2]	On the Quai at Smyrna (1930)[1]
2 Minarets stuck up (3)[2]	Indian Camp (1924)[3]
3 We were in a garden at Mons (4)[2]	The Doctor and the Doctor's Wife (1924)
4 It was a frightfully hot day (5)[2]	The End of Something (first pub'n.)
5 They shot the six cabinet ministers (6)[2]	The Three-Day Blow (first pub'n.)
6 Nick sat against the wall (7)	The Battler (first pub'n.)[4]
7 While the bombardment was knocking (8)	A Very Short Story (10) (1923)
8 At two o'clock in the morning (9)	Soldier's Home (1925)
9 The first matador got the horn (2)[2]	The Revolutionist (11) (1923)
10 They whack-whacked the white horse (12)	Mr. and Mrs. Elliott (1924–5)
11 The crowd shouted all the time (13)	Cat in the Rain (first pub'n.)
12 If it happened right down close (14)	Out of Season (1923)[5]
13 I heard the drums (15)	Cross-Country Snow (1925)
14 Maera lay still (16)	My Old Man (1923)[5]
15 They hanged Sam Cardinella (17)	Big Two-Hearted River (I) (1925)
16 L'Envoi (18)	Big Two-Hearted River (II) (1925)

1. First appeared as 'Introduction by the Author' in the Scribner's edition of 1930.

2. Originally appeared under the title 'In Our Time' in the *Little Review* 9 (Spring, 1923), 3–5.
3. First appeared as 'Work in Progress' in the *transatlantic review* (April, 1924).
4. Replaced 'Up in Michigan' which was excluded on the grounds of obscenity.
5. First appeared with 'Up in Michigan' in *Three Stories and Ten Poems* (1923).

2

The Short Stories After *In Our Time:* A Profile

by COLIN E. NICHOLSON

The essential—and impressive—cohesion of the stories collected in *In Our Time* rests overwhelmingly upon the way Hemingway directs the emerging overall consciousness of Nick Adams as protagonist. Within the controlling perspective of Nick's induction into adult experience, Hemingway contrives, as Laizer Ziff observes, 'to keep an unemotional face presented to . . . experience and yet communicate sensitivity to it'.[1] Although the style of narration is, as Ziff goes on to suggest, one 'that works effectively only in conjunction with material that supports the view that public ideals are false and truth resides solely in unverbalized private experience',[2] Hemingway throughout manages to suggest a growth in Nick's awareness and an expansion of his feeling self.

If, however, we leave this first collection of tales out of the account, then the characteristic profile which emerges of a Hemingway short story is markedly different in form and temper. Deprived of the ordering principle of a progression through time, however elliptically presented, and lacking the organic and shaping focus of Nick's developing sensibility, the central attribute of such a profile is perhaps most helpfully to be understood through a phrase from Ezra Pound's 'Mauberley'. The world created in the short stories after *In Our Time* evokes an experience of 'consciousness disjunct'.[3]

36

The temporary hiatus of a railway station or a bridge crowded with war refugees; the transience of a hotel room or compartment of a speeding train; a bar in the early hours of the morning or an inn at midday; a coastal journey by car; a drifting from one horse-race meeting to another; a makeshift hospital; a bull- or boxing-ring; a tent in Africa . . . the typical setting of a Hemingway short story calls up enclosure, states of discontinuity or transitoriness. The typical denizens of these fleeting moments and impermanent places are those struggling with frustration or despair: figures variously shell-shocked; or hopeless and dying; the uncommunicative or the diminished and the desolate; and, on rare occasions, the resilient. Central to their experiences, across a range of circumstances and situations, are the recurring pressures of isolation and disconnectedness. A disabling sense of contingency conspires with a pervasive feeling of purposelessness to define an imagined moral order wherein the most to be expected is a momentary stay against disintegration. Few of Hemingway's later short-story protagonists in fact achieve even this.

Hemingway himself offers the best brief description of the general condition of his characters in the epigraph he composed for his third collection of short stories *Winner Take Nothing* (1933):

> Unlike all other forms of lutte or combat the conditions are that the winner shall take nothing; neither his ease, nor his pleasure, nor any notions of glory: nor, if he win far enough, shall there be any reward within himself.[4]

In order to map the literary contours of this later short-story terrain, I want to assemble the most recurrent features in these tales. From there it should be possible to examine the overall larger patterns and configurations which carry both the struggle and the inevitable sense of failure testified to by Hemingway and which, in Robert Penn Warren's words, confirm 'the shadow of ruin . . . behind the typical Hemingway situation'.[5]

Whether it is a bull-fighter's incomplete recovery after hospitalization, a writer dying from gangrene in Africa, an ageing boxing champion in decline, a cuckolded coward on safari, or soldiers recuperating from battle injury, the wounded hero in these stories inhabits a dark, uncomforting world of pain and stress, living always at a level of high emotional intensity. Physical pain thus becomes the outward show of a deeper set of inward psychic afflictions, wounds of the soul as much as of the body. The world thus conjured into being is a cynically punishing and *angst*-ridden place, in many ways a kind of permanent waking nightmare. Indeed, in the closing lines of 'A Clean, Well-lighted Place' the sympathetic waiter offers an image widely deployed by Hemingway to suggest the fearful spiritual desolation of the domain he creates:

> Now, without thinking further, he would go home to his room. He would lie in bed and finally, with daylight, he would go to sleep. After all, he said to himself, it is probably only insomnia. Many must have it. (481)

In these pages many do have it, and one character after another reveals no less than deep terror of sleeping in the dark. In this respect we can refer to Nick Adams as narrator of 'Now I Lay Me', and the protagonist of 'A Way You'll Never Be' as men with virtually no available consolation; indeed in the latter case Nick Adams's searing experiences lead him to express a preference for mind-numbing extremity: 'it should have been trepanned. I'm no doctor, but I know that' (505). The hospitalized Mr. Frazer in 'The Gambler, the Nun, and the Radio' shares the same unmanning fears, while Jack Brennan in 'Fifty Grand' not only confesses 'I got the insomnia' (402), but when asked what he thinks about when he cannot sleep responds with a catalogue of troubles and worries: 'What the hell don't I think about' (403). It appears that sleep as an easeful balm is available in this world only when narcotically induced by the irrecoverable addict, as the last sentence of 'A Pursuit Race' suggests.

Uncomprehending and afraid, and either unwilling or unable to articulate their fears, many of these characters are in flight from their experiences, and many of them take refuge in the easy oblivion of drink. Nick Adams acknowledges his fear of impending battle with the words 'I know how I am and I prefer to get stinking' (504). Brennan and Frazer drink continuously to forget; the dying Harry in 'The Snows of Kilimanjaro' has wasted his talents as a writer by 'drinking so much that he blunted the edge of his perception' (158), and the sprawling structure of 'Wine of Wyoming' seems to resemble nothing so much as the discontinuity of a drunken stupor. 'I wanted to try this new drink', says the pregnant girl in 'Hills Like White Elephants', 'that's all we do, isn't it—look at things and try new drinks' (372). Given this proneness to the easy escape-route offered by drink, it is all the more remarkable that critical acceptance of the waiter's assessment of the old man's despair in 'A Clean Well-lighted Place' should be so widespread.

Cleanth Brooks finds something admirable in the old man's stoicism:

> there, sipping his brandy, he is able, perhaps, to confront with some dignity the invading disorder, and even stare it down. But the order and the light are supplied by *him*.[6]

Far from sipping brandy the old man is consuming large quantities night after night: a preoccupation massively destructive of order and light. Similarly, reacting to the waiter's reflection that

> it was all a nothing and a man was nothing too. It was only that and the light was all it needed and a certain cleanness and order (481),

Tony Tanner comments: 'the Hemingway hero prefers to overcome his horror of vacancy by a ritual of orderliness and cleanness in small things.'[7] But the inability of the waiter to comprehend fully the futility of the old man's despair, even while watching from close-up some of its symptoms, is in fact registered elsewhere, notably in 'The Gambler, the Nun, and the Radio'. There, when Mr. Frazer is ruminating upon 'the real, the actual, opium of the people', he reflects that

> he knew it very well. It was gone just a little way around the corner in that well-lighted part of his mind that was there after two or more drinks in the evening; that he knew was there (it was not really there of course). (584)

The desperate nullity of the old man's plight is revealed, and notions of compensatory rituals of order appear equally destitute.

Yet alcohol does have a limited effectiveness for such

characters in that it offers them escape from cerebration, from thought. For another remarkable constant among those who people the Hemingway short story is the urge to resist thought, the operation of the mind in interpreting experience. Visceral, appetitive or sensory experience is at a premium while introspection is shunned or repudiated. At its bleakest, this tendency presents itself as a psychologically imperative avoidance of the recognition of threat, pain or violence; a turning away from the actualities of experience even as those actualities are inflicting themselves upon the characters concerned. If and when such recognition does occur, it comes too late, as when the dying Harry is compelled to a retrospective acknowledgement of how his life of writing has been a waste of talent: 'You kept from thinking about it and it was all marvellous' (157). For Manuel Garcia, the failing bull-fighter of 'The Undefeated', the diminishing professionalism of his performance is further accentuated by the onset of reflection: 'His eyes noted things and his body performed the necessary measures without thought. If he thought about it he would be gone' (358). In this instance of faltering athleticism it is entirely appropriate that the debilitating effects of thought are expertly caught as the bull-fighter's growing confusion is subtly registered.

> The final stuff with the sword was all he worried over. He did not really worry. He did not even think about it. But standing there he had a heavy sense of apprehension. (352–53)

In common with Manuel and many others in these stories, for Mr. Frazer the active registration of thought is itself a threat, to be deflected if possible or, if endured at all, then unwillingly and suspiciously, and with scepticism. Conceptual engagement with the world beyond the passively sensuous self is a process fraught with further anxieties, and when Frazer realizes that 'he was thinking well, a little too well' (585), he retreats, again, into alcohol and the bland sonorities of popular music from a succession of dimly heard radio stations. Within this territory of radically diminished possibilities, thought is an unwelcome adjunct to individual experience, one which expands the area of pained confusion and deepens the wounds of its inhabitants. Thus the young Nick Adams, distressed and unable to shape a response to the cynical violence threatening Ole Andreson in 'The Killers' confesses:

> I can't stand to think about him waiting in that room and knowing he's going to get it. It's too damned awful. (387)

The advice he receives from those more hardened to brutalizing experience and more practised in the suppression of any involving reflection is deceptively alluring: 'You'd better not think about it.'

A corollary of what has been described as Hemingway's anti-intellectualism[8] is the notorious reluctance of his heroes to put into words private feelings and emotions, particularly when those feelings originate in activities associated with the author's code of male sporting rituals. The irony of 'Today is Friday', for instance, offers a salutary reminder that such encoded toughness can reduce the significance of Christ's crucifixion to a mere celebration of athleticism—'he was pretty good in there today' (455). But more typical is the reaction of the English animal hunter, Robert Wilson, to Francis Macomber's expectant exhilaration at the challenge of killing off a dangerously wounded buffalo:

> Doesn't do to talk too much about all this. Talk the whole thing away. No pleasure in anything if you mouth it up too much. (132)

And these words are themselves a precise echo of the narrator, Jake Barnes, at the close of *Fiesta*: 'you'll lose it if you talk about it.'[9] Such inhibited speech is not confined to athletes or sportsmen. Rather, it is a feature which connects a range of characters in these tales, linking them intertextually beyond their conscious or unconscious isolation. While it remains the case that few writers match Hemingway's ability to reproduce the stunted vernacular of the semi-literate, or to create resonance out of unspoken implications, it is also true that he accords similar speech-patterns to writers as well as jockeys. And because such techniques do connect the disconnected by implicitly comparing the radically unlike, they thereby contribute to the pervasive, overall landscape of feeling in these tales; the atmosphere of emotional and spiritual devastation expertly caught in Harry Levin's remark that his characters, expatriates for the most part, wander through the ruins of Babel smattering many tongues and speaking a demotic version of their own.[10]

Against this ambience, and testifying incidentally to the extraordinary dominance of the Hemingway style during the inter-war years, Saul Bellow's *Dangling Man* reflects that

> on the truest candour it has an inhibitory effect. Most serious matters are closed to hard-boiled. They are unpractised in introspection, and therefore badly equipped to deal with opponents whom they cannot shoot like big game or outdo in daring.[11]

But Hemingway's short stories, in fact, do involve conceptual profundities beyond the comprehension of his perceiving characters. His ability to make his style serve as a way of situating each discontinuity of experience within a steady, implicit point of reference perhaps finds its readiest analogue in the favoured device which situates passive or receptive character in vitally active and frequently hostile circumstance. Whether it is a first person narrator, often a naïve and wondering 'I' who records and registers experience, or the free-floating discourse which allows for narrative 'objectivity' and a more interiorized presentation of impressions, characters in these stories are destined to accept the contours of their world and the fact of their subjection to them. Rarely do they control aspects of their world or their own participation in it. They can observe, register experience, accept the given and endure their lot. In extreme forms this produces the wounded and passive narrator of 'Now I Lay Me' or the blank fatigue of the 'Old Man at the Bridge', 'too tired to go any further' (176). But such cases are paradigms. From the biological fatalism of 'The Sea Change' to the futile inevitability of 'A Pursuit Race' deterministic pressures delimit, and sometimes deny entirely, the possibility of individual autonomy. Nick Adams may decide to leave an environment which allows 'The Killers' such freedom of action, but future optimism in his behalf is hardly justified. 'My Old Man' charts the crumbling of a small boy's world in which he is an entirely passive witness. And the prevalent shaping agency of exterior circumstance is further endorsed by the narrative structure of 'A Canary for One' where the tale is half-told before the first person narrator is revealed. Not until the last line are the actual dimensions of his unspoken discomfort and the scale of the American lady's insensitivity released.

Since, then, individual autonomy is radically curtailed, thought is either impossible or suspect, and speech a potential self-betrayal, a decisive area of release for characters in the Hemingway short story is provided for in a richly-presented life of the senses:

> It was a good morning Wilson thought. There was a heavy dew and as the wheels went through the grass and low bushes he could smell the odor of the crushed fronds. It was an odor like verbena and he liked this early morning smell of the dew, the crushed bracken and the look of the tree trunks showing black through the early morning mist, as the car made its way through the untracked, parklike country. (124–25)

The immediacy of the senses displaces conceptual thought, and celebration of the moment so takes the place of a wider, more ruminative awareness. For Wilson in the present instance, cuckoldry can appear a 'windfall' and personal relationships firstly troublesome and then tragic. The divided selves of Hemingway's short fiction are presented in a mode of writing which registers an extraordinarily vivid attention to the bright surfaces of sensuous experience, and simultaneously delineates a condition of profound disjunction, most explicitly rendered in the opening paragraph of 'In Another Country':

> In the fall the war was always there, but we did not go to it any more. It was cold in the fall in Milan and the dark came very early. Then the electric lights came on, and it was pleasant along the streets looking in the windows. There was much game hanging outside the shops, and the snow powdered in the fur of the foxes and the wind blew their tails. The deer hung stiff and heavy and empty, and small birds blew in the wind and the wind turned their feathers. It was a cold fall and the wind came down from the mountains. (365)

The young men, of course, do not have to go to the war any more; it is permanently with them in their damaged minds and bodies. That experiential continuity is syntactically registered by subtle variations in Hemingway's careful, euphonic repetitions and rhythms. Until they come together sequentially in the last sentence quoted, 'cold', 'fall' and 'wind' invoke precisely those uninterrupted effects of war which the first sentence narratorially denies. Despite that first sentence, the cold wind is a constant, linking the war with their fractured, though apparently perfectly clear perceptions of the city of Milan. Again, Harry Levin has pointed out the filmic immediacy and fluidity achieved in this kind of writing: 'Each clipped sentence, each prepositional phrase . . . has its brief moment when it commands the reader's undivided attention',[12] thereby creating a texture of continuity and inter-connectedness. Yet conversely, as Robert Penn Warren observes,

> the short simple sentences, the succession of coordinate clauses, the general lack of subordination—all suggest a dislocated and ununified world.[13]

It is Nick Adams who offers, in 'A Way You'll Never Be', a psychological justification for the evocative precision of Hemingway's style. Hallucinating as a result of his experiences of war, Nick tries desperately to return things to focus and thus to a form of at least perceptual control.

> If it didn't get so damned mixed up he could follow it all right. That was why he noticed everything in such detail to keep it all straight so he would know just where he was, but suddenly it confused without reason as now. . . . (507)

Scrupulous attention to immediate detail might provide him with some defence, however fragile and fleeting, against the greater horror of disintegration. But such detail is by definition fragmentary, at best providing only a momentary and visceral sense of just where Nick might be. His attempt to establish a coherence in this way necessarily collapses, understandably enough, but for reasons beyond his own powers of comprehension. Nick is driven by the horror at what has happened to him into suppressing memories of his own personal past and towards an attempt to make order of his feelings based upon his sense of the 'now'. The cruel paradox of his condition is that, cut adrift from any sequential principle offered by an historical understanding, his 'now' can at any moment as much confuse as clarify.

Yet the addiction of the Hemingway hero to the immediate moment is itself a characteristic displayed in many of these tales, and one of the most telling examples occurs at the conclusion of 'Fifty Grand'. Jack Brennan, badly injured by a foul blow meant to knock him down and thus cheat him out of the money he has wagered on his opponent's victory so long as Brennan remains standing at the end, returns the foul blow to give his opponent a technical victory and so keep his own winnings. At that moment the narrator Jimmy Doyle, recognizing Brennan's quick-thinking and admiring his courage and tenacity changes the tense of his narrative to end the story in the continuous present, an unmediated celebration of the ex-champion's deviously triumphant defeat. And such devotion to temporal immediacy transcends the dubious morality of 'Fifty Grand'. It also suffuses the texture of 'The Snows of Kilimanjaro' as Harry, approaching death, makes a belated attempt to bestow some kind of order upon his life. Nowhere in Hemingway's writing is the claim that 'the Hemingway hero is committed to "the now" '[14] more fully explored:

> So now it was all over, he thought. So now he would never have a chance to finish it. So this was the way it ended in a bickering over a drink. Since the gangrene started in his right leg he had no pain and with the pain the horror had gone and all he felt now was a great tiredness and anger that this was the end of it. For this, that now was coming, he had very little curiosity. For years it had obsessed him; but now it meant nothing in itself. . . . Now he would never write the things that he had saved to write. . . . Well he would never know, now. (152)

Holding himself in attentive readiness, since 'the one experience he had never had he was not going to spoil now', Harry retrospectively constructs a past sense of temporal relations which is largely characterized by negativity:

> there wasn't time, of course, although it seemed as though it telescoped so that you might put it all into one paragraph if you could get it right. (166)

The hope, however, is illusory as Harry has earlier acknowledged concerning his talent as a writer: 'it was never what he had done, but always what he could do' (158), and the negativity is endorsed by a central image in the narrative.

> Now if this was how it ended, and he knew it was, he must not turn like some snake biting itself because its back was broken. (158)

But self-recrimination is precisely the tenor of Harry's last hours. He cannot help but be aware that, symbol and sentinel of his own death, the hyena eats its own entrails when wounded. Five italicized passages recapture the experiences that Harry 'had saved to write' and now never will, and each of these acts of imaginative memorizing is structured around the immediacy of sensory perceptions:

> Now in his mind, he saw a railway station at Karagatch and he was standing with his pack and that was the headlight of the Simplon-Orient cutting the dark now and he was leaving Thrace then after the retreat. That was one of the things he had saved to write, with, in the morning at breakfast, looking out the window and seeing snow on the mountains in Bulgaria. (153)

From the 'now' of his present imaginings, the past of 'he saw' becomes continuous with 'he was standing' until the first demonstrative 'that' suggests a perceptual recreation of the instant, while the second 'that' returns us to the now of Harry's reverie. Present participles like 'standing', 'cutting' etc. further encode his urge to revitalize that sensation of valued experiential moments. His subsequent memories of war, and of his childhood and fishing, act to precisely similar immediate sensory effect.

But Harry's final imaginative act is not italicized. In his dying reverie, he sees himself being flown towards the summit of Kilimanjaro, away from the self-devouring of the hyena and towards the frozen permanence of the leopard. At this terminal moment of release from time the almost incantatory repetition of the adverbial 'now' is replaced by an equally recurrent 'then'. Only as he escapes from time is Harry able to organize, with the ritual intensity of a drum-beat, a satisfying sequential ordering of events. Paradoxically, his final escape from personal history enables him to make a degree of order of his past:

> Then they were over the first hills and the wildebeest were trailing up them, and then they were over mountains . . . and then the heavy forest again . . . and then another plain . . . and then it darkened and they were in a storm . . . and then they were out. . . . And then he knew that that was where he was going. (174)

For Harry death momentarily substitutes a sense of duration for the effects of intensity which he feels he has betrayed by selling 'vitality, in one form or another' in his writing.

Indeed, sensuous vitality is the mark of Hemingway's own writing as he charts a landscape of failed human possibility. John McCormick has drawn attention to the religious motifs which abound in Hemingway's short stories, and to what he sees as

> a conception of religion common in Spain . . . a conception in which consciousness of death is constant and vivid, together with despair at the human lot.[15]

It might be added that given the severely restricted band-widths, historical, cerebral, verbal and personal accorded to his characters, despair indeed expresses the inevitable human condition. Consciousness of Other, the redeeming transcendence of any single scale of the immediate here and now, seems almost impossible given the very style and overall manner of Hemingway's short fiction after *In Our Time*.

NOTES

1. L. Ziff, 'The Social Basis of Hemingway's Style', *Poetics*, 7 (1978), 417.
2. Ibid., 422.
3. Ezra Pound, *Personae* (London: Faber and Faber, 1932), p. 213.
4. All page references are to *The Short Stories of Ernest Hemingway* (New York: Random House, 1938).
5. R. P. Warren, 'Hemingway', *Kenyon Review*, 9 (Winter 1941), 1.
6. Cleanth Brooks, *The Hidden God* (Yale University Press, 1963), p. 10.
7. Tony Tanner, *The Reign of Wonder* (Cambridge: Cambridge University Press, 1965), p. 236.
8. Warren, op. cit., 7.
9. Ernest Hemingway, *Fiesta (The Sun Also Rises)* (London: Jonathan Cape, 1975), p. 284.

10. Harry Levin, 'Observations on the Style of Ernest Hemingway', *Kenyon Review*, 13 (1951), 592–93.
11. Saul Bellow, *The Dangling Man* (London: Wiedenfeld and Nicolson, 1960), p. 9.
12. Levin, op. cit., 601.
13. Warren, op. cit., 18.
14. Tanner, op. cit., p. 233.
15. John McCormick, *American Literature 1919–32* (London: Routledge and Kegan Paul, 1971), p. 55.

3

Art and Life in
The Sun Also Rises

by ANDREW HOOK

1

Hemingway remains a problem. Has any other modern writer
so divided critical opinion? The difficulty is that there seems to
be less than the usual room for discriminations of the good
with reservations kind. Either Hemingway is a good writer—
who in some novels and stories may well have written better
than in others—or he is a sham, a phony, a charlatan. He
believed that his first book, *In Our Time*, would be praised by
highbrows and read by lowbrows.[1] His fate has been to be
read by all, praised and damned by either or both.

Part of the problem is of course Hemingway the man.
Towards the end of his own career, Fitzgerald came to feel he
had been too much the man, too little the writer; in *The Crack
Up* he suggests he had given too much of himself to life, too little
to art. Hemingway seems never to have felt the need to choose
between the two; unstintingly he gave himself to both. He
worked hard and unremittingly at being a writer; beyond
question he saw writing as discipline and demand. But his
pursuit of life, equally unremitting, was often in danger of
overshadowing his art. The confusion of the two has always
been one of the major impediments to a proper understanding
of his art. Out of that confusion arose the damaging notion of
Hemingway the inspired journalist, his art no more than a

processing of his own life into artistic copy. In fact that problem is partly a result of his own success: how many readers are not surprised to learn not only that Hemingway's brief few weeks on the Italian front in the First World War occurred long after the retreat from Caporetto, but that when he wrote *A Farewell to Arms* he had never even seen the terrain through which Frederick Henry and his men struggle towards the Tagliamento river, and which the novel documents with such strikingly accurate and vivid detail?

Hemingway the artist, and Hemingway the man, have, of course, much in common; Hemingway is no modern master paring his finger-nails, no fabulous artificer wholly detached from the world he creates. Yet man and artist are no substitute for each other; and dislike of the one should not mean rejection of both. It is always possible that the fiction may survive the myth. This is why it is easy to sympathize with the fervent plea of a recent Hemingway critic and scholar:

> Let us declare a moratorium on nostalgia: on the Hemingway-Callaghan fight, the Dôme café, Duff Twysden, on all that public parade.[2]

Michael Reynolds is surely right. The case of *The Sun Also Rises* may be a specially difficult one, but that is all the more reason to adhere firmly to the general principle: it is the fiction, not the life, that is in the end the critic's proper concern.

Hemingway never denied that the characters in *The Sun Also Rises* were based on real people, but he did deny that the novel in any other substantial way transcribed his own or anyone else's life. In 1933 he wrote to Maxwell Perkins: '95 per cent of The Sun Also was pure imagination. I took real people in that one and I controlled what they did. I made it all up.'[3] That he did make it all up is the point to remember. Because once *The Sun Also Rises* has been disentangled from Harold Loeb, Duff Twysden, Pat Guthrie and the rest, it becomes very much easier to see it for what it is: the archetype, the purest and best of all Hemingway's fictions. Michael Reynolds, with whom I have just been agreeing, is on occasion not unwilling to adopt the tone of Hemingway the man. 'I have been told', he writes, 'by old men that after *A Farewell to Arms*, Hemingway is all downhill.'[4] How would he respond to the suggestion: for *A*

Farewell to Arms read *The Sun Also Rises?* Perhaps as Hemingway offered to do to various critics at different times. . . ? In fact
I would not want to suggest that after *The Sun Also Rises*
Hemingway's career was a simple falling-off. There is truth in
the suggestion that *The Sun Also Rises* and the early short stories
go a long way towards defining both Hemingway's characteristic world and his characteristic treatment of it, and that
thereafter Hemingway could only travel through that world
rather than climb beyond it. And perhaps it is even true that in
the '30s the strain was beginning to tell. But, ironically for a
writer who seemed to pay such little tribute to time and history,
Dos Passos's 'murderous forces of history', in the form of the
Spanish Civil War and what came after, gave back his world to
Hemingway. Papa had been right after all, and the sales of *For
Whom the Bell Tolls* soon approached a staggering million copies.

The basic point holds nonetheless. *The Sun Also Rises* is a
definitive statement. At the age of 26 Hemingway outlines to
the attentive reader a vision of the world that he subsequently
develops but never changes. Why it is possible to argue that *The
Sun Also Rises* remains his finest novel depends upon the use of
the word *outlines.* In the first novel outlines have not hardened
into a fixed frame; they are still malleable, susceptible to
pressure. At the end of *The Sun Also Rises* Jake Barnes is a
defeated hero; but he is not defeated in the manner and style
that Frederick Henry and later Hemingway heroes are defeated;
and his heroism is of a different order to theirs. The difference is
a crucial one, but after *The Sun Also Rises* there are no more Jake
Barnes. No more, that is, until Thomas Hudson in *Islands in the
Stream.* (*Islands in the Stream*, or rather Parts I and III of *Islands in
the Stream*, provides the ultimate answer to Michael Reynolds's
old men.) With Thomas Hudson Hemingway ends, after so
many years of holding off, by taking on more than he had even
with Jake Barnes.

2

Hemingway began writing *The Sun Also Rises* in Valencia on
his twenty-sixth birthday, 21 July 1925. Only a month or two
earlier he had been writing to Maxwell Perkins explaining that
the novel form did not attract him:

Somehow the novel seems to me to be an awfully artificial and worked out form but as some of the short stories now are stretching out to 8000 to 12000 words maybe I'll get there yet.[5]

Much later, in 1952, he told Bernard Berenson he had written *The Sun Also Rises* because everyone else his age had completed a novel, and he felt ashamed not to have done so.[6] In any event, once begun, the writing of the novel went on at high speed. On 20 August 1925, he was writing to his father from Paris saying he had completed 60,000 words of a novel, and on 6 September the first draft was finished.[7] On 15 September Hemingway wrote to Ernest Walsh announcing the completion of the novel and telling him that he proposed to 'go over it all' that winter.[8] By December 1925 he was hard at work reworking and rewriting the manuscript. Finally, on 1 April 1926, he writes to Maxwell Perkins saying he has finished working on *The Sun Also Rises*.[9]

The novel that was published in October 1926 differed in only one major way from the completed manuscript version. After discussion with Fitzgerald, who had read and admired the manuscript, Hemingway decided to cut completely his first sixteen pages. 'There is nothing in those first sixteen pages', he wrote to Perkins, 'that does not come out, or is explained, or re-stated in the rest of the book—or is unnecessary to state.'[10] With this excision of what had clearly been an introductory exposition concerning the major characters, Hemingway was satisfied. He was confident he had written a good novel: not as good as he hoped to write in the future, but good nonetheless. To Fitzgerald he wrote: 'Christ knows I want to write them a hell of a lot better but it seemed to move along and to be pretty sound and solid.'[11]

Sound and solid was more or less precisely what the book's initial critics felt it wasn't. Inevitably Hemingway was disappointed by these early reviews, and equally inevitably he tended to suggest that the critics had not understood the book he had written. He was sure that his novel was sad, serious, tragic; hence his irritation at being told he had written 'a jazz superficial story' about unattractive people, or an 'amazing narrative of English and American after-the-war strays running up and down France and Spain in wistful wildness'. 'That's a book', he told Maxwell Perkins, 'you shouldn't miss.'[12] In fact quite a few readers seem unable to miss just that book. In 1940, on the occasion of Fitzgerald's death, Westbrook Pegler, an American columnist not renowned for his liberal views, wrote that the event called to mind

> memories of a queer bunch of undisciplined and self-indulgent brats who were determined not to pull their weight in the boat and wanted the world to drop everything and sit down and bawl with them.

So much for the lost generation. Yet Pegler's view, or one much like it, continues to surface—in my teaching experience at least—in responses to *The Sun Also Rises*.

Hemingway himself, writing defensively to his mother who had been deeply offended by the book, was prepared to concede that the characters in his novel 'were certainly burned out, hollow and smashed'.[13] But he insisted, as I've said, on his book's seriousness of purpose and tragic implications. He was willing to joke about the impotency theme; some subjects, he told Fitzgerald, were particularly good for novels—war is best of all, but love, money, and murder are also good. 'A dull subject I should say would be impotence.'[14] That he was more than half serious though, is proved by a subsequent letter to Maxwell Perkins:

> Impotence is a pretty dull subject compared with war or love or the old lucha por la vida. I do hope though that The Sun will sell a tremendous lot because while the subject is dull the book isn't.[15]

It was to Perkins too, of course, that Hemingway offered his most famous comment on the book's central meaning:

> The point of the book to me was that the earth abideth forever. . . . I didn't mean the book to be a hollow or bitter satire but a damn tragedy with the earth abiding for ever as the hero.[16]

It is a strange comment. A sense of the natural permanence of things, of the earth abiding forever, is not in fact one of the major impressions created by the book. It may well be present, but is it as prominent as Hemingway's comment implies it should be? Perhaps Hemingway should have remembered what he had written to Sherwood Anderson over a year earlier:

> I get something out of bulls and the men that fight them, I don't know what. Anyhow I've got it all, or a big part of it, into the next book.[17]

3

Whether or not the earth abideth in the novel, place is of immense importance in *The Sun Also Rises*. Rather than its formal division into three books, it is place that provides the novel with its basic structure. Paris, Burguete, Pamplona, San Sebastian, in that order, are geographical centres which focus and define the book's central meanings.

Paris, it has become a critical commonplace to insist, is Hemingway's version of the waste land that has emerged in the aftermath of the First World War. And it is true that a sense of sterility, both sexual and more general, of aimlessness and emptiness, of the failure and loss of values, is suggested by these opening chapters. But for Jake Barnes Paris is not all hopelessness and negativity. For Jake life in Paris is problematical; and in the first nine chapters of the novel the nature of Jake's problems is set out and developed: his hurt of course, his relationship with Brett and how he tries to cope with it, his relationship with Mike, Cohn, the Count, and the rest. Problems on every side. But Paris has its sweetness too: coffee and *brioche*, horse-chestnut trees, bridges across the Seine, work. Paris is life as it is: complex, difficult, unfulfilling, but endurable.

Burguete is a different world. The fishing trip with Bill Gorton (and Harris the Englishman) is an idyll, a pastoral interlude. Cohn, Campbell, and Brett, and all the problems and tensions they mean, have been left behind. Here in the hills nothing is messy. The weather is cold and clear like the water in which they fish. Relationships are easy and unforced; there is a purity of friendship and trust. The fishing itself is a delicate ritual. The nature with which the men are involved is approached in such a way as to be always on the point of transformation into sacramental metaphor. At night Jake feels good—in sharp contrast to his nights in Paris.

Burguete is high up, 1,200 metres above sea level. Higher still but visible are Roncevaux and the monastery at Roncevalles, with their suggestions of an heroic, religious idealism. In Hemingway's later fiction such altitudes will recur, always associated with an approach to the ideal. The Abruzzi, for example, in *A Farewell to Arms*, where it is cold and clear and dry and there is good hunting, which the young priest recommends to Frederick Henry but which he is never able to reach; or the mountain above Montreux where Frederick and Catherine live after escaping from the war in Italy. But while Frederick and Catherine find a temporary retreat in the Alps, they are not safe. The war goes on. Similarly, Burguete provides no permanent alternative to Paris. The pastoral interlude can be no more than that. In the classical tradition the pastoral world offers an alternative, more ideal, set of values. For the visitor it provides refreshment, regeneration; but in the end the real world has to be faced again. So for Jake. Paris and its problems have been put aside, but they have not disappeared: the letter and telegram from Mike and Cohn signal as much. They will all meet in Pamplona.

Pamplona means fiesta. In Pamplona the worlds of Paris and Burguete come together and into collision. The festival of San Fermin provides Hemingway with an ideal setting for the crises and climax of his novel. Life during fiesta is extraordinary; colourful, explosive, dramatic. Fiesta is a time of release, of spontaneity and ritual, of passion, excitement, and intensity. Everything is speeded up, raised to a pitch. It is not only the Iruña café that is 'like a battleship stripped for action'.[18] Inevitably, then, the Parisian problems blossom here insistently and violently: emotions spill over, antagonisms flare, frustrations and failures surface uncontrollably. Yet here too are images and experiences of a quite different order. The bull-ring at Pamplona presents a paradigm of ritualized, controlled and disciplined violence. Even more than Jake and Bill and the trout-fishing in the Irati river, Romero and his bulls in the Pamplona fiesta are a positive affirmation, a poised celebration of survival in a hostile and dangerous world. Pamplona juxtaposes Paris and Burguete; but rather than fusing them, fiesta finally blows them cruelly apart.

After the destructive emotional intensities and violence of

Pamplona, Jake returns alone to San Sebastian. He swims in the quiet, cold sea in what is an act of ritual purification and refreshment. Restored, Jake is ready for the Hotel Montana in Madrid, and the renewed acceptance of Brett, his problems, and 'the old lucha por la vida'.

4

Because of his hurt, Jake is a character who knows a lot about life's problems. Because of his hurt, he is also a brilliantly-conceived narrator figure. His two roles as character and narrator fuse admirably in the first person narrative. Detachment, apartness, are imposed on Jake by his condition; but these limitations strengthen his position as a narrator. Unable to be wholly involved, he is in a better position to see things clearly and objectively. Jake's isolation (Hemingway is quite unable to conceive of a satisfactory sexual relationship not involving male consummation) thus contributes both to the method of *The Sun Also Rises* and to its meaning.

The notion of a narrator, at once within and without the story he is telling, Hemingway may have derived from Fitzgerald's use of Nick Carraway in *The Great Gatsby*. Conrad's Marlow, a familiar figure to both Fitzgerald and Hemingway, provides another obvious source. As for Jake's impotency, Hemingway explained in 1951 that the genesis of the idea lay in his own experience:

> It came from a personal experience in that when I had been wounded at one time there had been an infection from pieces of wool cloth being driven into the scrotum. Because of this I got to know other kids who had genito urinary wounds and I wondered what a man's life would have been like after that if his penis had been lost and his testicles and spermatic cord remained intact. I had known a boy that had happened to. So I took him and made him into a foreign correspondent in Paris and, inventing, tried to find out what his problems would be when he was in love with someone who was in love with him and there was nothing that they could do about it.[19]

Hemingway then goes on to repeat that he is not Jake Barnes. Despite these recollections—and it is noteworthy how little the novel is taken up with explorations of Jake's problems—the idea of Jake's impotency may have arisen from another, more literary source. During the Burguete interlude Jake and Bill joke about Jake's problem, referring to the mysterious hurt that kept Henry James out of the American Civil War. Michael Reynolds argues that in the early Paris years, largely through Pound's influence, Hemingway read a great deal more James than has been realized.[20] There is no evidence of his having read *Portrait of a Lady*; but he may have done so, or Pound may have talked to him about the book which was one of his own favourites. The point is that Jake Barnes has not a little in common with Ralph Touchett. Perhaps it was the example of Ralph's debilitating illness, inhibiting a more active expression of his love for Isabel Archer, in association with his knowledge of James's own mysterious injury, which helped to make the impotency theme available to Hemingway.

Hemingway's formal success in *The Sun Also Rises*, however, is not simply a question of the device of Jake Barnes's physical condition. Jake's hurt, as we have seen, defines his character, as well as authenticating his position as objective narrator. And it is this integrity of roles as narrator and character which in turn produces the superbly achieved coherence of form and content, style and meaning, which is perhaps Hemingway's major aesthetic triumph in *The Sun Also Rises*. Jake's hurt has compelled him to come to terms with the pain and violence of living—the First World War has articulated that pain and violence on a grand scale—and his narrative style is the best index of how he has done so.[21] The style is taut, economic, disciplined, unemotional, understated. Living is coped with in identical terms. The aesthetic mode is also a moral one; style is a way of living.

The other main characters in *The Sun Also Rises*, all of them products of the same world that has struck at Jake so damagingly, are judged by how far they approximate or fall short of Jake's style. Bill Gorton and Jake get on famously; Brett and Mike know what is required but lack the self-discipline to succeed; Robert Cohn's is an alternative, rejected style. An admirer of romantic prose, he behaves over Brett in a stereotyped romantic fashion. In the heightened, dramatic world of fiesta, a collision between these styles is inevitable.

But when it occurs this collision does not precipitate the central moral crisis of the book; Cohn's style is not allowed enough force for that. The pressure on Jake's style, which does produce that crisis, has a source other than Robert Cohn.

There has been fairly general agreement among Hemingway critics that the use of Jake Barnes as a first person narrator in *The Sun Also Rises* contributes immensely to the novel's success: the gains in immediacy, dramatic involvement, and the narrative enactment of a code of values, are clear.[22] Nonetheless, it is possible to argue that Hemingway's use of the first person narrative procedure does leave him with some unresolved problems. For instance, he has not chosen to follow the example of James and Conrad, and provide an audience for his narrator's reminiscences—to whom then is Jake talking? (The same question can be asked of Nick Carraway in *The Great Gatsby*.) Much more important is the problem of whether Jake is sufficiently distanced from Hemingway himself. Is Jake given enough independent life as character and narrator, as Carraway is, or does he remain in bondage to his creator? Of course one agrees that Jake is not to be *identified* with Hemingway, but that hardly settles the question. Jake is a working journalist who wants to be a writer; but Hemingway does not dramatize him, say, as a writer with a particular vision which he wishes to communicate. He is presented simply as a man coping with his problems as well as he can, enjoying some aspects of life, unhappy about others. He is silent about *why* trout-fishing in the Irati river matters. About the purity of Romero's art as a bull-fighter, about the dangerous violence in terms of which the bull-fighter orders his art when he works 'in the terrain of the bull', about the moment of death when bull and bull-fighter are locked together in a single image—about all these things he is allowed to be eloquent, speaking either to Brett or directly to us. But about *why* bull-fighting is important in his own life, about the significant link between Romero's art and life and his own, he is silent. In an able essay Terence Doody has argued that it is the tight-lipped morality to which Jake subscribes which makes it impossible for him to be self-conscious about these matters. To talk about them would be to move too far towards Robert Cohn's style. Art and morality, that is, are at odds in *The Sun Also Rises*. But perhaps Mr. Doody expects too much. In his own words, Jake

> does for Romero what Nick does for Gatsby; he sees in Romero more than anyone else does and makes of that insight the definition of a hero, which entails a correlative definition of himself.[23]

Is this not enough? Hemingway's art is always the art of absence, of the unstated. To succeed, such an art demands the collaboration of the reader; it is essential that the reader assent to the meaning Hemingway implies, to reassure him, as it were, that he is right. Hence no doubt his truculent, disbelieving response to those who do not see it his way, who see in *The Sun Also Rises* only the 'after-the-war strays running up and down France and Spain'. If this is true, then the crucial element in the paragraph from Reynolds Price's amazingly resonant essay on Hemingway, which Terence Doody quotes, is not 'I mostly speak as I.' But the sentences which follow:

> What I need from you is not empathy, identity, but patient approving witness—loving. License my life. Believe me.[24]

There is a further difficulty in Doody's position. Like Mark Spilka, in another influential essay, he assumes that Romero is the authentic hero of *The Sun Also Rises*, that it is through his definition of the heroism of the bull-fighter that Jake defines his own.[25] To imply that this is the novel's final statement takes too little account of its closing movement. To that movement I wish finally to turn.

5

One of the finer qualities of *The Sun Also Rises* is its humour. After the scene in which Cohn knocks Jake cold and floors Mike Campbell, Bill's friend Edna asks, 'Does this happen every night at your fiestas?' (p. 219). In this novel, at least, Hemingway does not always take himself too seriously. One recalls the light-hearted exchanges between Jake and Bill at Burguete when, for example, Hemingway makes amusing hay with contemporary American nativist critics:

> 'You know what's the trouble with you? [says Bill] You're an expatriate. One of the worst type. Haven't you heard that?

Nobody that ever left their own country ever wrote anything worth printing. Not even in the newspapers. . . .

'You're an expatriate. You've lost touch with the soil. You get precious. Fake European standards have ruined you. You drink yourself to death. You become obsessed by sex. You spend all your time talking, not working. You are an expatriate, see? You hang around cafés.'

'It sounds like a swell life,' I said. 'When do I work?' (p. 133)

Here the ironies are admittedly directed away from Hemingway himself. But the passage does show that Hemingway understands perfectly well that what he is trying to do can be fatally misunderstood. Jake can be even more self-critical. After one of the few, brief interior monologues that he is allowed, he dismisses his own train of thought comprehensively:

> That was a large statement. What a lot of bilge I could think up at night. What rot—I could hear Brett say it. What rot! (p. 172)

Not even bull-fighting is immune from criticism. After the rain has come, after the facade of fiesta geniality has cracked, and after Brett's destructive desire for Romero has been acknowledged, a Spaniard is gored during the running of the bulls. At this point, one might say, things are not going too well for Jake, but it is now that he has to listen to a Spanish waiter making some simple anti-bull-fighting points:

> 'You're not an aficionado?' 'Me? What are bulls? Animals. Brute animals.' He stood up and put his hand on the small of his back. 'Right through the back. A cornada right through the back. For fun—you understand.'
>
> He shook his head and walked away, carrying the coffee-pots. (p. 227)

Two men passing in the street report that the man is dead. That the earth may abide forever despite the death of Vicente Girones, does not wholly answer the waiter's criticism. That Brett leaves the ear of the bull that killed him, presented to her by Romero, in the drawer of her bed-table in the Hotel Montoya, along with her cigarette stubs, rather reinforces it.

All these may seem somewhat minor points, but cumulatively they suggest that in this first novel Hemingway is prepared to look critically at what he himself holds dear. When one reconsiders the situation in which Jake finds himself in the latter part of the novel, the same point suddenly becomes central to its meaning. Jake is in love with two things: with Brett and with bull-fighting and what it means to him. Brett may not be as unreliable as Daisy Buchanan, but there are hints from the beginning that she could threaten Jake and what he believes in. In the arrow-scarred Count Mippipopolous Brett claims to recognize 'one of us'. But the exchange that follows looks forward very precisely to the crisis in the novel she will in the end precipitate.

> 'You see, Mr Barnes, it is because I have lived very much that now I can enjoy everything so well. Don't you find it like that?'
> 'Yes. Absolutely.'
> 'I know,' said the count. 'That is the secret. You must get to know the values.'
> 'Doesn't anything ever happen to your values?' Brett asked.
> 'No. Not any more.'
> 'Never fall in love?'
> 'Always,' said the count. 'I'm always in love.'
> 'What does that do to your values?'
> 'That, too, has got a place in my values.'
> 'You haven't any values. You're dead, that's all.'
> 'No, my dear. You're not right. I'm not dead at all.' (p. 73)

Brett is wrong about the count. Like Count Greffi in *A Farewell to Arms*, who talks to Frederick Henry in terms very similar to these, he is certainly 'one of us'. But what is truly ominous in the exchange is the opposition that Brett sets up between love and values: because of course that is precisely the opposition she is going to create and act out in her affair with Romero. What Hemingway contrives so brilliantly, then, is a situation in which Jake's two loves—Brett and bull-fighting—come into unresolvable collision.

For Jake, Romero supremely embodies the code in terms of which Jake himself tries to live. Romero does not fake or pose or evade; violence and death are the conditions he has accepted, and in face of them he creates the forms of his dangerous art. His is the ideal which Jake recognizes. Yet the novel at no point questions the depth of Jake's commitment to

Brett. It is not a subject to be talked about—not even with Bill; but it is the primary fact in Jake's emotional life. It underlies his attitude towards all the others, his concern and his revulsion. It explains why he finds it difficult to be hard-boiled at night. It explains, finally, the loyalty which determines his behaviour towards Brett herself.

By forcing Jake to choose between his loyalty to Romero and his loyalty to Brett, Hemingway is putting such pressure on the code of disciplined self-control that there can be no graceful outcome. Whatever course he follows, Jake cannot win; he loses either Brett or something crucial to his sense of his own worth and integrity. The point has just been underlined by Montoya's seeking advice from Jake over the matter of Romero and the American ambassador. Jake, Montoya, and Romero are on the same side—and Hemingway is there too. ('I get something out of bulls and the men who fight them. . . .') Implicated in Brett's behaviour, Jake betrays a precious allegiance.

How does Hemingway expect us to understand this betrayal? What it means is that Jake chooses the impurities of love and life and relationship rather than the purity of moral integrity and personal honour. As we have seen, Terence Doody has argued that in *The Sun Also Rises*, art and morality come into collision. But in another sense art and morality (Romero and Montoya) are on the same side; it is life (Brett) that in the end subverts both. As so often in the endings of James's novels, here it is life which tragically resists the perfection of order which both art and morality strive to impose on it. Seen from this perspective, the definition of heroism in *The Sun Also Rises* becomes less obvious. Romero remains the code hero: knocked down by Cohn again and again, he refuses to admit defeat. But Romero is not the novel's hero. The Jake who responds to Brett's telegram from Madrid is also refusing to accept defeat, is also coming back for more. Jake's heroism, however, is of a more complex, even self-contradictory kind; it is gained at his own expense, and involves a continuing commitment to life and love even on the impossible terms that have been imposed on him. Jake gains or preserves nothing more dignified. Later Hemingway heroes accept defeat too, but they accept it within the logic of their own terms. Only in *The Sun Also Rises* does

Hemingway risk challenging the very codes and values which his fiction as a whole will constantly celebrate. That is why the book is a triumph of art on the side of life.

NOTES

1. Carlos Baker, ed., *Ernest Hemingway. Selected Letters 1917–61* (London, 1981), p. 155.
2. Michael S. Reynolds, *Hemingway's Reading, 1910–40, An Inventory* (Princeton, 1981), p. 28.
3. *Letters*, p. 400.
4. Reynolds, op. cit., p. 30.
5. *Letters*, p. 156.
6. Ibid., p. 792.
7. Ibid., p. 168.
8. Ibid., p. 169.
9. Ibid., p. 198.
10. Ibid., p. 208.
11. Ibid., p. 217.
12. Ibid., pp. 226, 265.
13. Ibid., p. 243.
14. Ibid., p. 177.
15. Ibid., p. 238.
16. Ibid., p. 229.
17. Ibid., p. 162.
18. Ernest Hemingway, *Fiesta (The Sun Also Rises)* (London, 1955), p. 175. All subsequent page references are to this edition.
19. *Letters*, p. 745.
20. Reynolds, op. cit., p. 23.
21. There is some argument over how far it is fair to describe the style as Jake's rather than Hemingway's. (See below, pp. 57–8.) The point remains that the oft-noted characteristics of the style of the novel—its unemotional notations of the external world, its objective registering of sense data, its imagist suggestion of the 'now' of experience—are an entirely convincing mirror of Jake's stance towards the world.
22. See, for example, E. M. Halliday, 'Hemingway's Narrative Perspective', *The Sewanee Review*, LX (1952), 202–18.
23. Terence Doody, 'Hemingway's Style and Jake's Narration', *Journal of Narrative Technique*, 4 (1974), 219.
24. Reynolds Price, *Things Themselves* (New York, 1972), p. 203.
25. Mark Spilka's essay is 'The Death of Love in *The Sun Also Rises*' in R. P. Weeks, ed., *Hemingway: A Collection of Critical Essays* (Englewood Cliffs, N.J.), pp. 127–38.

4

A Farewell to Arms: Radiance at the Vanishing Point

by WILLIAM WASSERSTROM

> I don't see how he could like a phony book like that and still like that one by Ring Lardner, or that other one he's so crazy about, *The Great Gatsby.*
>
> —J. D. Salinger, *The Catcher in the Rye*

1

It was substantially more than a touch chilling to take up that particular copy of *A Farewell to Arms* (1929) so casually removed earlier in the day from the Hemingway shelf. Although such choices often happen less unaccountably than one supposes I confess to not knowing why I picked the copy I'd come away with. I wasn't avoiding a corrupt text and I wasn't hunting a pure one. And I didn't especially care about edition or state. Possibly it was the colour of cloth that had caught my eye: a quiet shade of plum, faded; binding soiled but unstained, not mildewed or fouled. Big print, good paper, unfoxed, clean in the margins. Not at all your standard item of bookstall or university stack, this Scribner's 1952 reissue bespoke a thing well-handled and not ill-used. But the chill, unprepared for, was all the fiercer when at home, book open to its inside cover, there was pedigree of the most unexpected, spectral kind: 'Gift of Eduardo C. Mondlane'. On the facing page his stamp, a facsimile of script, 'Eduardo C. Mondlane', planted an inch below 'Janet Rae Johnson, 1955', handwritten. And an enveloping chill of loss, grief just below the skin of consciousness all these years, merged with a paroxysm of memory.

There's then at least double purpose, a definable scent of personal history, in this reappraisal of Hemingway's *Farewell*. Because presumably it's Eduardo's own copy I have in hand, it's both he and Hemingway I've had in mind during the preparation of these pages. And though I met Mondlane just in passing, knew him as the friend of another colleague, George A. Wiley, himself a barely less notable Movement figure of the '60s, the memory of Mondlane's presence and fate, of Wiley's life and career, cannot be more richly revived than it is by Hemingway's ineffable book. Authentically brave, neither man lusted for glory. Nor was either, even when caught up by events, ever truly comfortable in action, in command. Like the novel itself, however, a work not really responsive to heavy duty lit. crit. or lit. theory, the enduring thing isn't a complexity of character or a revelation of motive but a resonance, a radiance of style.

On earlier readings of *A Farewell to Arms*, those pre-dating the '60s, I'd had no inkling of the rewards in store for a reader who was more kindly disposed to the novelist than Hemingway himself was disposed to the world. And when I was invited to take on the novel for this collection I demurred. Being one whose judgement was fixed at about the time of Salinger's aspersions in *Catcher in the Rye* obviously, or at any rate arguably, I wasn't qualified to do Hemingway justice. Besides my sympathies came down on the side of a writer whose writ Hemingway violated utterly: Chekhov. People don't go to the North Pole to fall off icebergs, said that master of Hemingway's genre. They marry, have children, go to the office and eat cabbage soup.

Had Chekhov lived longer into our century doubtless he'd have amended this protocol. Had Hemingway gone beyond Turgenev he might have solved the problem that haunted his life and art, the problem of fathers and sons, husbands and wives, generation and family. In any event it's Hemingway not Chekhov whose art highlights the short hard life of Eduardo C.

Mondlane. An anthropologist trained at Northwestern University in Illinois, Mondlane's homeland was Mozambique. A man of entirely forthright purpose—to mount and pursue a guerrilla war against Portuguese colonists in Africa—he was an improbable figure on a university campus in Upstate New York, a man quite unprecedented in my own experience until that time. Not only was a person of his extraordinary kind unfamiliar anywhere in the United States twenty years ago but too in that age of innocence very few members of our community had as yet got wind of those great dramas of upheaval which were soon to befall the world at large.

When we first met, Mondlane had just been granted academic leave for field work in his sphere of interest, southeastern Africa. Or that's how Wiley put it to me one evening in spring, 1963. His eyes sent signals I didn't catch. But I put that down to densities of my own, plain ignorance perhaps, or more probably the esoterica of politics I wasn't privy to. 'That's why I wanted you and Eduardo to meet now, before he takes off', Wiley had said as we moved into the lounge for drinks. A company of eight assembled that night, Wileys, Mondlanes and Elliotts—the novelist George P. Elliott and his wife Mary Emma, good friends—a gathering of persons both known and unknown, one to another and to the world. Eduardo, unequivocally black, a man of smiles, of early middle years and middle size; Janet, white, grave, neither cheerful or cheerless; Wileys, he brown and Wreatha stupendously white, lovely, Southern. Greetings, introductions, notice of the usual sort taken all around.

Even on the face of it this sort of dinner party was out of the ordinary course of social occasion on the American academic scene two decades ago. Setting aside a hindsight of lustre, there were cruder and more pedestrian reasons why the evening was exceptional. Middle-class black intellectuals in racially mixed marriages, men and women holding academic posts at predominantly white institutions, were in very short supply. Today, like circumstances are routine. But in that antediluvian age, even in our own midst, even we happy few tended to exert determined effort to transcend unease. Indeed I'd originally met Wiley at luncheon in the faculty club where he and his fiancée sat alone, two at a table for six. I hadn't the least idea who they were. A new boy myself, I knew virtually no one. I did make a point of joining them, was irritated that I felt good about making a gesture of that kind, annoyed to feel virtuous at their expense, grateful that they immediately forgave me the gesture, gratified to learn that they too were new, exhilarated to discover how splendid it was to be with them. ('Have you been around long enough to meet Pat Moynihan?' she'd asked, speaking of the man currently serving in the U. S. Senate as senior member from New York. 'I work for him in the Maxwell School. Hilarious—an Irish pol trying to pass as an okay academic. He'll never make it though he may get to be President!') Three years later self-consciousness remained a chronic though hardly a disabling state.

'Eduardo's just back from Washington', Wiley said. 'Raising money for his war.'

I laughed. 'Everyone runs a war on leave, right? Where's this one going to be?'

'Mozambique.'

'He means it, you know. Just as you arrived, late as usual, Eduardo was telling us who he talked to down there, how much he raised, who gave, who promised, who fumbled, who ducked, who hid. What a crowd.'

'Wait—hold it', I said. All of us had been on the streets, photographed on picket lines by the F.B.I., tailed by the local cops. We assumed that our telephone lines were tapped. Wiley had been gaoled for civil disobedience. In the national arena Martin Luther King Jr. was gathering cohorts. There were sit-ins and marches and murders in the South. James Baldwin had recently vaulted to fame with *The Fire Next Time*. But my sons waved to Kennedys flying low over our summer house, helicopters bound for Hyannisport each Friday. And for all the rhetoric of battlements and barricades real war either at home or abroad wasn't seriously talked about. 'I don't understand.'

'It's all true', Eduardo said. 'Immediately on end of term I'm joining my people and we'll start to recruit in earnest. But I need as much support here as I can put together, so I went down to speak to anyone who'd listen. Talked to lots of government types and you'll be amazed as I was to find that the best by far was Bobby Kennedy. All the liberals say, you know, what a nasty little reactionary backbiter he is but I tell you he heard me out, didn't hesitate a second, said he was with us, whipped out a cheque and wrote me a good-sized sum. Also, may I add, I called on Adlai Stevenson. Quite a contrast. What came from him was mumbles about how as U.S. Ambassador to the U.N. he couldn't jeopardize blah blah but did recognize blah blah blah. Liberal bullshit I got.'

I was stupefied. Is this how guerrilla groups were formed? 'Are you really saying that you Professor Eduardo Mondlane, Syracuse University, picked up money and allies in Washington to support a revolution in Mozambique?'

'All ready started. All planned. Actually my title is President-in-Exile. That's why I could arrange appointments in D.C. Officials there afraid not to see me—politicians cover all bets. Frelimo—watch for us!'

I turned to Janet. 'Are you going too?'

'Yes.'

'But for God's sake people get killed that way.' That's what I said but I didn't for an instant believe that people I knew were likely to be killed that way.

Mondlane, geniality itself, replied, no change of voice, 'Oh yes. I fully expect to be.'

He was. A victim in the rivalries of faction, he died even before the Portuguese smoke cleared.

2

What, one speculates, did Eduardo and Janet make of Frederic and Catherine? On departing for Africa they appear to have left their books permanently behind. Did they also decide to put books behind them once and for all? There's of course nothing idle about either question, merely a presumption of links between their literary taste and their course of political action, between two imaginary lovers who, implausibly, travel a very long distance to fall off an iceberg and two very palpable people whose heroic adventure, at once implausible and matter of fact, was quite prosaic in kind. Compelled by a pure accident of signature to decide what to make of this synchrony of signs, my choice of subject seems almost predetermined. In the event, it does dispose of worry about what fresh or helpful thought will justify still another go at *A Farewell to Arms.*

'A Farewell to Arms': Radiance at the Vanishing Point

It also disposes of any temptation to get into the swim of scholarship by reviewing document by document the material in Mary Hemingway's *Farewell* file at the Kennedy Library, the University of Massachusetts at Boston. Years ago in a review-essay of Hemingwayana then current, I proposed a moratorium on studies in the minutiae of method and career. ('There are some forty-one extant attempts at conclusions in the Hemingway Collection.') No luck. No arrest or decline of spate. What then is there to show for work done in the interim? With allowance made for an exception or two, my recent bout of homework investigating material in print since Hemingway's death accounts for a pennyworth's more pleasure in the text and a considerable store of gossip, to my mind nearly all of it dispensable. In this connection, incidentally, I include ephemera of my own, an essay on *A Moveable Feast* (1964) treating Hemingway's animus against *The Dial*, the distinguished literary paper published in New York from 1920 till 1929. Having taken Mary Hemingway and her literary counsellor Malcolm Cowley at their word about this manuscript— recovered, they said, from that fantastical trunk left in Paris from 1927 until the early '60s and found in the Ritz cellar and published as found—I undertook to sort out matters about which I knew at first hand and which Hemingway had put wrong, intentionally it seemed. Blame of long standing, pique at *The Dial* and its management, recurs in print forty years later as an attack on Ernest Walsh and others by then either defenceless or weary of the bother of parrying Hemingway's thrusts.

Although the pique remains eternally unpurged, its force has been defused by a Canadian scholar, Jacqueline Tavernier-Courbin, who learned that Mary Hemingway, on preparing the manuscript for publication, didn't just fiddle with a word here, a comma there. 'Once in a while she cut a sentence' or 'switched a paragraph' or 'deleted' and 'amended'—all in good faith, one supposes. But the chief effect of tampering was to confirm her husband's reputation for acting in bad faith: she or someone else confounded two distinct magazines, *The Dial* and *This Quarter*, two separate literary awards, two or more editors and proprietors as well as dates, circumstances and practices. And a chapter of *A Moveable Feast* on which Hemingway had pencilled 'too dangerous and libelous to publish' appears in print under

69

Mrs. Hemingway's auspices even more outrageously off.

So much for matter of this kind—of interest only if it turns out that Hemingway's lasting claim on our attention is more a question of American social history than of literary history. Meantime, in part because his literary rank is still undecided, the weight of books that codify, sanctify, reconstruct and annotate his least mutter is lopsidedly heavy against those that don't. It may happen that the annotators will be proved right, that his fascination is less literary than cultural. Born at the very verge of our era, from 1899 to 1962 he visibly waxed and waned in time to rhythms set by the main events of this century. Long before he could have learned anything from Henry James he seems to have instinctively known that he was destined to become a man on whom nothing was lost. Among his many attainments therefore perhaps this must be rated imposingly high, that it was Ernest Hemingway—knowing everyone, doing everything, going everywhere—who invested the vocation of literature with a glamour never before acquired or since surpassed in the United States.

Banal words, peripheral though hardly inconsequential in bearing. But even if they're right, those who find the figure of Papa at once invincibly grand and all too flagrantly louche, nonetheless a permanent state of celebrityhood must not be permitted to displace the effect of reading a few unparalleled books—above all *A Farewell to Arms*. High on everyone's short list of pre-eminent '20s novels, this fiction retains standing sturdy enough to exempt it from the vagaries of taste. Unlike books less long-lived, it possesses the faculty of self-renewal, generated not by its ideas—principal ground of its early fame— but by its force as a work of experiment. Indeed it's said to deserve applause without stint precisely because it unites avant-garde experiments of language with a presiding mode of American demotic speech. A writer who paid 'loving attention to the spoken word', Paul Goodman said in a late essay, Hemingway is also meticulously, 'sweetly devoted to writing well'. Had not his arrival in Europe coincided with that instant when its miracle occurred, when modernism gelled, Richard Bridgman adds, Hemingway would have lost the opportunity which instead he was canny enough to seize. For 'it only required a writer willing to submit himself to the discipline then current'—Joyce's, Gertrude Stein's and Pound's in literature, the post-impressionists' in paint—before inevitably a style would emerge 'holding compressed within it a focused world of experience *and* a series of verbal elements formally arranged' (Bridgman's emphasis). 'In my opinion,' Goodman rounds off his essay, 'Hemingway's work will last, not because of his stoical ethic' but because of the 'sweetness' of his style. Surfacing 'more frequently in books later than *The Sun Also Rises*, especially in *A Farewell to Arms*', his music is heard in 'short sentences that coalesce and flow and sing'.

Among the earliest American novels to exploit modernist theory as well as a classic American tradition of vernacular speech, *A Farewell to Arms* is an accomplishment very near the first order. That it's Hemingway's accomplishment to which we must return in order to comprehend some quintessential functions and radical traits of style in American language and culture, in contrast to British style, is tribute of the most telling kind. 'The ensemble of a people's customs has always its particular style', Lévi-Strauss observes in *Tristes Tropiques* (1955), adding that customs always stem from a finite 'repertory of · ideas' and invariably record those dreams, images, myths which exemplify a culture inside and out. Precisely in these respects *A Farewell to Arms* is a landmark text within the Anglo-American tradition of narrative. And not the least of its splendours is the distinctness with which it dramatizes the opinion of those who hold that twentieth-century American writing and British writing diverge at ever-increasing rates of speed. Consolidating those elements of sensibility and language which differentiate American from British styles of imagination, Hemingway's novel is prodigious indeed.

Perhaps the most pertinacious spokesman of this view, George Steiner, reviewing *The Supplement to the Oxford English Dictionary* (1972) in the *New York Times*, reminded his audience that 'literature is only the surface' of national style whereas language is its centre. Stressing those operations of language which illustrate varieties of cultural style reaching beyond speech to spirit, Steiner contended that modern British letters are marred by a parsimony of attention. Because 'today the dynamics of English are centrifugal' and are 'most evident in America', British readers must listen not just to American accents but must also attune their ears to an inner voice—to a unique 'cadence', as Hugh Kenner said in *The Pound Era* (1971). For it's cadence that enables us all to 'tell which sentence is British', Steiner continued, 'which American'. Hearing it, we can gauge 'what scope of feeling to accord to the words'. When eventually we 'do this so well we do not know we do it' we discover 'how much of what we supposed a dictionary can sort out (it cannot) is controlled by our sense of the voices cadence imitates'. In learning what sorts of sense this dictionary could legitimately be expected to sort out, we find ourselves referred back to Lévi-Strauss's ideas on ideology, society and style. 'Like England itself', the O.E.D. is superbly suited to play what Steiner calls a 'formidably important role in making visible a new equipoise' between Great Britain representing 'genuine civilization' and the United States, representing 'the energies of colloquial' change.

Whether or not Steiner's talk expresses an English parsimony or an American opulence of invention, I'm at a loss to say. More to the point, these musings allow us to reconsider the course of Hemingway's lifelong love affair with the spoken American word. An inconstant man, mainly, he was in this matter utterly constant, ever scrupulous, virtually chaste. Indeed there's no question it was this purity of passion, the fabled style of *A Farewell to Arms*, which presides over all the rest, an entire imbroglio of persons and actions encapsulated in a title that tropes its theme, a tale of love and death. Consummated in a text that unites inner voice and inner ear in cadences of thoroughly original invention, Hemingway's story registers a scope of feeling at once his very own and simultaneously peculiar to compatriots everywhere, exiles of the lost generation. Whatever else Gertrude Stein and he expected to find lurking inside that portentous phrase it drew together a whole host of etiolated waifs, writers whose intercourse with their mother tongue was the last remaining tie of nation. It was the American language in all its variety and elasticity and ineluctable energy which would generate a whole new world of creation—so Stein fancied fifty years ago—despite the wasteland. And it's a transcendent trait of Hemingway's genius that *A Farewell to Arms*, modulating its music, changing keys, accommodates speakers of every human dialect and moral stripe.

It is in this unique respect, let it be said, that his art can be seen to exhibit certain tendencies which captivate post-modern schools of criticism today. Because a national repertory of ideas informs his sweet new American style, it's the orbit of structuralists he's drawn to. For no matter how post-modern he may eventually come to seem, it's not an evasion of meaning his art endorses, not its absence or anonymity, not a caprice but a coherence of *langue* and *parole*. A writer whose fiction resists those anarchic exercises of vanguard literary theory that beset us now, he's naturally more comfortable with a Frenchman of an earlier age. As if chosen to incarnate Tocqueville's prophecy (it's not to the 'written but the spoken language' that 'attention must be paid' if we would 'detect the modifications which the idiom of an aristocratic people may undergo when it becomes the language of democracy') Hemingway straddles the century and a half between 1830 and 1980.

3

It follows from these observations that the full power of his force as a writer cannot be sought in his subject, his disposition of details of plot, his themes and characters, his poses. That is to say, the terms of inquiry favoured by two generations of critics are no longer serviceable. It is also to say that the singular quality of his gift, especially vivid in *A Farewell to Arms*, has little to do with the matter of Catherine's love. A World War I pinup, she's a dream girl at once sedate and indecorous, abandoned. Kid stuff. Nor does his catalogue of spirits, the peasant red wine and the vintage white, the strega, cognac, whiskey, asti, capri, grappa, absinthe, beer, vermouth, champagne—liquids lovingly drunk—satisfy more than a taste in decoration, a flair for interior design. Nor do the ritual, cleansing dive into the Tagliamento, the separate peace, the echoes of Eliot or the tuition of Pound, not the rain and ruin nor the wound and the bow—none of these either singly or collectively invite further evaluation. Although we discard plot at our peril, we run far greater risk of irreplaceable loss if we're distracted by Hemingway's pretty decor. What we're left with first to last is the writer's preoccupation with and command of the act of composition itself. 'Food, drink, sex and writing were intertwined in a continuous circuit of energy', Leo Gurko observes. 'Maintaining this circuit, keeping it going at a high level, engaged his unflagging attention.' To what end neither Gurko nor Goodman nor any others I know of, manage to say. And yet it's the art of prose narrative, the language of art focusing on itself not on a world elsewhere that engenders this writer's immortal longings in book after book which are inherently bookish whatever the battle of the moment may be.

At bottom therefore Hemingway's manly men of derring-do aren't mere bounders of bed and bottle but are positioned in actions which implicate the over-arching concern of modern letters. From Joyce and Proust to Nabokov and Garcia Marquez it's the act of creation which mediates between the uses of imagination and the process of history. Composition as explanation, Gertrude Stein called this central motif of the modernist enterprise. Taken a small step further, composition also can serve as the moral equivalent to war: that's Hemingway's astonishing variant of William James's celebrated proposal. 'The martial type of character can be bred without war', James had written a few years before the start of the Great War. Following the Biblical injunction, to acquire dominion over the fish of the sea, the birds of the air and all things that move on earth, young men will engage in an 'immemorial human warfare against nature' and in this way, according to James's belief, perpetuate 'even in a pacific civilization' those manly virtues which the military party is so afraid of seeing disappear. Paying their 'blood tax' they will disprove the vulgar notion that fear of death in battle is, 'as our military enthusiasts believe and try to make us believe, the only stimulus known for awakening the higher ranges of man's spiritual energy'.

In summoning the spirit of William James, I do not contend that Hemingway literally drew on 'The Moral Equivalent of War' (1910) or took James as found on the page. But it's surely appropriate to suspect that the work of a figure who was ever at the forefront of thought in the mind of a favourite pupil, Gertrude Stein, does recur in Hemingway's reflections on grace under pressure in war and peace, his equation of death and art. At the highest conceivable plane of moral and intellectual and spiritual energy Hemingway placed the art of bullfighting, of painting, of writing. Writing well is thus the simulacrum, the moral equivalent of living well only if the conduct of life and art in the bullring, on the page and on the canvas encompasses the fact of death. 'Now the essence of the emotional appeal of bullfighting is the feeling of immortality the bullfighter feels' and shares with spectators. 'He is performing a work of art and he is playing with death, bringing it closer, closer, closer, to himself, a death that you know is in the horns' because the dead horses prove it. 'He gives the feeling of his immortality, and, as you watch it, it becomes yours. Then when it belongs to both of you, he proves it with the sword.' So too did Goya assume a like burden of art and proof, Hemingway said in *Death in the Afternoon* (1932), a book widely damned for bluff and bluster. But Goya isn't introduced so as to scaffold the tiresome persona of Papa Hemingway. Rather it's Goya's will to unify images of life and death Hemingway conceived himself to share. Deploying 'blacks and grays, in dust and in light, in high places rising from plains in the country around Madrid, in movement, in his own cojones'— out of everything 'seen, felt, touched handled, smelled, enjoyed, drunk, mounted, suffered, spewed-up, lain-with, suspected, observed, loved, hated, lusted, feared, detested, admired, loathed, and destroyed', the painter drew life and light for his dark art.

Whether or not Hemingway's admiration of Goya is simultaneously a form of self-applause it's impossible to know and probably immaterial to decide. That these carefully chosen words are at the very least unconsciously self-referential, however, the famed first paragraph of *A Farewell to Arms* establishes beyond dispute. What is also unarguable is a virtually naked impulse to affirm his own sense of his role, his idea of literary vocation, by way of the matador in Pamplona and the painter in Madrid. 'Bull in the Afternoon', Max Eastman sneered, mistaking Hemingway's nonsense ('the false tough stance and the romantic gush', the tendency to sentimentalize, as Anthony Burgess, too, has said) for his essence. But neither Eastman's derogation of principle in 1932 nor Burgess's confusion of purpose in 1978 ('gratuitous parade of Goya-like images of destruction' mitigated only by the matador's 'pride, dignity and panache'), takes into consideration Hemingway's avowed aim, to wrest proof of potency from performances of the Word. In this glory all humankind is supposed to share.

Forced but not faked, then, those overloaded words from *Death in the Afternoon* are invested with meaning identical to that rendered by the Goyaesque pattern of images—black and grays and dust and light—which three years earlier had set the tone of *A Farewell to Arms*. Looking 'across the river and the plains to the mountains', go the familiar opening lines, we saw troops pass by raising dust that 'powdered the leaves of the trees'. And we saw 'afterward the road bare and white', heard fighting in the mountains and at night we could see flashes from the artillery which 'in the dark was like summer lightning'—and so on, each stroke of prose drawing Cézanne into the ambience of Goya and thus preparing his stark landscape for the play of light and shadow. Add Stendhal and Crane for warfare, Henry James for arabesque and Mark Twain for cadence of conversation, and the tally of ingredients is all but complete. It's only Hemingway's recipe that remains secret at last.

Not until we've included William James, however, do we infuse a proper charge of redemptive creative energy into the discourse of disaster. And unless this is done *A Farewell to Arms* will remain lodged where Carlos Baker left it, 'the best novel by an American about the First World War'. It is James furthermore who assists in rescuing Henry from the niche, similarly secure and narrow, into which he was inserted long ago by Robert Penn Warren. For it's quite out of sync with contemporary taste to dismiss Henry as simply a violent man who takes 'an action appropriate to the fact of nada' so as to recover 'human values in a naturalistic world'. Shades of yesteryear, of Eliot and his epigones of the 'Southern Renaissance'. Far more enlightening, more germane to the state of Hemingway's reputation over the long haul, is a reckoning of the pressure of *nada* on style. If the art of bullfighting can be taken as a moral equivalent of war then the art of literature—its analogue— requires a discourse of substraction adapted to the state of being at ground zero. As each act in the drama heightens the intimacy of death, so too each word keeps movement in motion, movement towards degree zero of life and of art. And finally when there is nothing left to do or say, 'that was what you did, you died.'

'A Farewell to Arms': Radiance at the Vanishing Point

The force that propels this movement, like the means Hemingway used to animate Frederic Henry, all but 'dead from wounds and other causes', is a dying fall of language that parallels the plot and its gamut of mutilation, disease, murder, suffocation and haemorrhage. Unlike Samuel Beckett, however, whose every move is designed to steal a march on silence, Hemingway built a monument to sound and sense. Its foundation does not rise from Frederic's conviction that he was not 'made to think. I was made to eat. My God, yes. Eat and drink and sleep with Catherine.' That may be occupation enough for a besotted lover but it isn't signification enough for an ambitious novel. On the contrary, it's another of his remarks about Catherine that provides the tonal key to the novel as a whole. 'I knew she was going to die and I prayed that she would not', Frederic says 'not very long' before he 'left the hospital and walked back to the hotel in the rain', as the story ends.

In defining the terms of his dilemma, in contrasting what Henry knows is inexorable with what he wills magically to circumvent, Hemingway portrays a man doomed to suffer affliction greater than grief. It's an atavism, a spasm of hope rather than an expectation of Providence that moves him to prayer, for in addition to the obvious reasons why her death is inevitable, there is another, less excruciating but more un-remitting, more commanding. Absolutely fundamental to the scope of *nada* in this novel is the fact that Hemingway has situated his lovers in a region which is beyond the power of Providence: Switzerland. Or said so as to accommodate that Cézannesque design of landscape he was so proud of, living occurs in Italy and Austria, in England and France and Germany—and Mozambique—not in Switzerland. No matter how devoted Frederic is, no matter how tender Catherine may be, their union is a masque of marriage—a masquerade, like his civilian dress—which occurs under dispensation of rarest kind, a suspension of all the rules. Alert to the valence of landscape in *A Farewell to Arms,* we are constantly reminded that real people don't marry in Switzerland. Despite Catherine's cheery chatter about a wedding when she's thin again both she and Henry know in their bones that the prospect of marriage is nil. Were they to carry it off, were they to sanctify their affair, wedlock itself would appear to certify their success in establishing a durable peace not just an interregnum, a lull of annihilation, in a world whose permanent condition is war.

'Life isn't hard to manage when you've nothing to lose', Catherine says a moment before she tells him she is pregnant. That she's dead right geography soon confirms. Once they're forced to abide by the rules of nature, the biological trap as it's petulantly called, once they're compelled to stop playing house, they remember what they've suspected from the start—that their liaison has served to suspend the process of passage from here to eternity. 'Fight or die', Fergy says. 'That's what people do. They don't marry.' Switzerland, an ideal land for confinement, offers asylum only. Exquisite for the short run, months not years, lovely for snow, it provides no shelter at all, is incomparably the ugliest place to be when the rain comes. Once the sabbath is over and the game resumes, time's back in play, years begin again, life's inordinately hard to manage—even to bear—and there's everything to lose.

In a word: an affair that begins in a hospital bed in Milan is foredoomed to end in a hospital bed in Lausanne. Had their infant survived, had he even been baptized before dying—had Catherine recovered—Hemingway's novel would have contrived to conjure Is from *Nada*. But it had been his aim from the start, plotting Henry's return to a Swiss hotel in the rain, to have him arrive there at exactly the right moment. In this final version of nearly two dozen attempts at an ending, the words just stop, a matador's sword to the heart faultlessly aimed and flawlessly timed. Although not all of us are like Catherine 'Scotch and crazy', each of us deep down is 'afraid of the rain'. Along with Cat in the rain and Mondlane in Mozambique we're all 'cooked and know it'. Alive in this century, we've learned that there's no liberation without war, no liberation from an addiction to war, no escape along the route William James envisioned, except in language honed to the sharpness of a blade in Toledo, art that's paid the 'blood tax'. Playing with death coldly, 'not so coldly as clearly and emptily', Hemingway arrived, Frederick Henry in tow, at the vanishing point of speech.

5

'Everything Completely Knit Up': Seeing *For Whom the Bell Tolls* Whole

by A. ROBERT LEE

You see every damned word and action in this book depends upon every other word and action. You see he's laying there in the pine needles at the start and that is where he is at the end. He has his problem and all his life before him at the start and he has all his life in those days and, at the end there is only death for him and he truly isn't afraid of it at all because he has a chance to finish his mission.

But would all that be clear?

—Letter to Maxwell Perkins, 26 August 1940[1]

The most important thing in a work of art is that it should have a kind of focus—i.e. some place where all the rays meet or from which they issue. And this focus should not be capable of being completely explained in words. This, indeed, is the important thing about a good work of art, that its basic content can in its entirety be expressed only by itself.

—Tolstoy as reported by A. B. Goldenweiser[2]

1

In confiding to Maxwell Perkins, the shrewd Scribners editor he shared with Scott Fitzgerald, Thomas Wolfe and others, the hope that *For Whom the Bell Tolls* would exhibit a 'clear' interdependence of all its essential detail—everything 'completely knit up and stowed away ship-shape' as he says earlier in his letter—Hemingway showed himself perfectly acute about what, and what not, ought to count in his novel. The issue he calls attention to, whether Robert Jordan embodies a sufficiently credible and inclusive viewpoint through whom to refract the drama of the Civil War and the Spanish soil itself, offers a most engaging critical point of departure. Does Jordan's three-day *partizan* mission at the bridge begun and ended 'there on the pine needles' serve convincingly as the book's fulcrum, the means through which its widening circle of other concerns is brought to overall imaginative order? More precisely, can we say that Jordan's consciousness and his undertaking behind enemy lines establish a sufficient centre for the novel's moral perspectives, or for its portraits of Pablo, El Sordo and the others as expressions of the human spirit under press of war and beleagured by Fascism, or for Hemingway's long-standing preoccupation with Spain (begun in *The Sun Also Rises* and the shorter stories and carried forward through *Death in the Afternoon, The Spanish Earth* and *The Fifth column*) as an essential arena for the conflict of good and bad faith? If, as he believed, and his letter is cast in characteristic telegraphese, 'every damned word and action' indeed depends upon 'every other word and action', then how well does *For Whom the Bell Tolls* meet Hemingway's own criteria?

Opinion has generally agreed that *For Whom the Bell Tolls* marks a more ambitious effort than both *The Sun Also Rises* and *A Farewell to Arms*, but that equally it falls down in several key aspects. Even among enthusiasts who greeted it on publication as a landmark achievement, the Spanish Civil War at last made over into epic and a work to be put alongside George Orwell's *Homage to Catalonia*, the cavils have been many and frequent. And though Hemingway's comments on the novel don't provide the only measure for its success or failure, they do direct us back to how *For Whom the Bell Tolls* operates as an imaginative whole. The issue has received a degree of attention, notably in their different ways by Philip Young and Carlos Baker,[3] but the full weight of Hemingway's own concern with whether, and in what manner, the novel achieves, in Tolstoy's terms, its 'focus', a 'place where all the rays meet or from which they issue', has not.

False trails were quick to emerge. Lesser sniping, for instance, to nobody's particular advantage, took after Hemingway's supposed politics in the novel. A number of unyielding Stalinists, with apparently untroubled conscience and in plain defiance of what Jordan says to be his own political outlook,[4] pronounced Hemingway soft on Fascism, or at least as having given tacit support to the Fascist cause by his conception of Jordan as the code hero acting only according to the dictates of his own will and by depicting the Loyalist side as dishevelled and both in need of and inevitably giving way to the unrelenting eventual smack of Franco's dictatorship. Conversely, many of more liberalish persuasion, including over time several ex-Party members, thought him duped by the efficiency of the Communist Party machine in the Spain of the 1930s. Hemingway, the argument runs, simply misunderstood long-term Soviet and Comintern operations in the Spanish struggle. Hence Robert Jordan as fellow-traveller, and Hemingway behind him, unwittingly abetted an ideology whose consequences for Europe were ultimately as pernicious as the ideology which produced Francoist authoritarianism. Such views grievously misread both Hemingway and his novel.

Other charges, also pertinent enough at first glance, have similarly hindered the business of seeing the novel whole. Hemingway is tasked with lacking an authentic historical consciousness, a comprehensive grasp of the full nuance of the Spanish past. Too perceptibly he writes selectively of Spain, the incorrigible Hispanophile whose insistence on Spanish peasant values as an exemplary moral way of being blinkered him to the country's infinitely subtler human complexity, not to mention the historic intricacy of its religion and politics. A Pablo, or Sordo, or Anselmo, even the glimpses of the Republican command-structure, simply fail to do full service as the carriers of Spanish identity. One needs a more representative human cast, a sharper sense of other political and regional groups— POUM, the Falangists, the Catholic Church hierarchy, the Catalans, the Gallegos or the Nationalists' Italian allies perhaps—seen across a time-span more appropriate to epic. Here again, however, criticism seems to ask of *For Whom the Bell*

Tolls what insistently it is not, the historical *roman-fleuve*, a full-blown panorama of the Iberian past metamorphosing in all due complexity into the present.

In this connection, too, *For Whom the Bell Tolls* has regularly had to bear comparison with *War and Peace*, a standard which, as Hemingway several times ruefully observed, could hardly not appear rigged to make him come off the loser.[5] For despite apparent similarities of surface—a classic war and armies on the move, individual points of consciousness poised against the larger military operation—*For Whom the Bell Tolls* is not especially Tolstoyan, if by Tolstoyan one means the consciously philosophic depiction of 'war and peace' as recurring dialectical antimonies in the human make-up and set to a suitable scale of time and place. Hemingway's version of the Spanish Civil War in fact differs in almost every major aspect from Tolstoy's massive, Shakespearean conception of Napoleon's attempted invasion of imperial Russia. Simply as battle-terrain the Castilian hill and pine country behind Fascist lines north of Madrid hardly resembles the great set-pieces of Tolstoy's Austerlitz and his other principal battle-scenes. Nor can Robert Jordan, though the novel's central consciousness, be accurately thought the fictional equivalent of Tolstoy's Pierre or Prince Andrei. Unlike them, he is not there to give the longer, deliberated historical view. Which is not to say that Tolstoy isn't a relevant name to invoke. His general observation to A. B. Goldenweiser particularly applies. Though readers may disagree about the success with which Hemingway creates his 'focus', the point of centre from which the rest of the novel takes its imaginative departure, it can't be denied that in Robert Jordan and the bridge a centre does actually exist. No doubt, in part, this can be explained by the less comprehensive span of Hemingway's novel as against Tolstoy's. To invoke, say, Henry James's well-known unease about Tolstoy's 'loose, baggy monsters' in relation to *For Whom the Bell Tolls* would be to deny the kind of novel actually before us.

Then, there is the repeated, and vexed, question of Hemingway's women. Pilar as the incarnation of the earth madonna is routinely judged to lack all credibility, while Maria, adoring and healed of her rape by the Fascists through her too instantaneous love for Jordan, amounts to no more than a cipher, a figure out of barely disguised supremacist male fantasy. Although few readers would make any very emphatic case for either, especially Maria, when remembered within the context of the novel's detail—the local eventfulness of the preparations in the cave and Pilar's relationship with Pablo for instance—they hardly seem the *complete* disasters each has come to be designated almost by rote.

Hemingway's Spanglish has also been the occasion of great complaint.[6] His transliteration of the Spanish *tú* in a succession of thees and thous (though not something he in fact does all the time) irrecoverably mars the novel, giving it the look of near-parody, or at least of unacceptable stylistic clumsiness. This surely is to miss the point. Hemingway clearly wishes to signal something of the acute difference inherent in this Spanish peasant world, especially the argot in which events are understood and the residual habits of thought and speech passed down through generations. His thees and thous and consciously literal renderings of different blasphemies and curse-forms, it might fairly be argued, successfully imply an older ancestral community of usage, a romance or medieval chivalric world recalled precisely in the seeming stilted anachronisms of Anselmo and the other camp members.

The other repeated misgiving lies with Robert Jordan himself, allegedly yet one more of Hemingway's formulaic heroes in the line of Nick Adams (though Adams has rightly been recognized more for the tyro, the shocked initiate), Jake Barnes, Frederic Henry, and latterly, Thomas Hudson, a man who once again plays out the familiar Hemingway scenario of the tough-guy loser vindicated only by the separate peace he has made with what in *A Farewell to Arms* Frederic Henry laconically (and typically) invokes as the 'bitch' nature of History. Again this smacks of the superficial half-truth. Robert Jordan, in fact, is anything but the initiate which is Nick in the early Indian and war stories. Nor is he Jake Barnes, the sexual casualty of war and Jazz Age expatriation unable to achieve love with his ruined and ruinous Lady Brett. And nor is he Frederic Henry, the would-be healer cheated of Catherine and their child as a result of the flight from the Italian 'joke front' of Caparetto. Unlike them, he consciously experiences at close focus the coming of his own death, an event the novel treats with scrupulous tact as a major ceremony of life and which both recalls the American Civil War times of his grandfather and binds him in shared, vulnerable mortality with Lieutenant Berrendo, his fellow combatant and symbolic and opposing *alter ego*, the Nationalist officer from Navarra on whom he has his gun trained while covering the retreat of Pablo and the women. There, as dramatically as anywhere in the novel, the touchstone of 'No man is an island', death as the common democratic human inevitability, is given vivid local force. To be sure, Jordan does share with Hemingway's other main protagonists the need to make his own separate peace against a collapsing international and moral order, but he does so on terms wholly specific to the psychology and situation given him by the novel. Too frequently, especially by adverse critics, Hemingway has been interpreted as though the novels and stories were episodes from a single ongoing serial, barely differentiated variations on the theme of the code.

Nor have these been the only worries to surface. Robert Jordan's interior monologues, for instance, represent an indulgence on Hemingway's part, occasions to re-invoke a partly autobiographical mid-Western American boyhood or engage in semi-documentary reminiscence of Gaylords Hotel in Madrid and Republican notables like Karkov, Golz, Lister, Marty, Modesto and El Campesino. Even the action around the bridge has been thought a weakness, altogether too concentrated and archly symbolic in its echoes of Leonidas and Horatio and its use of the seventy-hour time-span as the measure of a single human life. The different flashbacks, too, from Pablo's taking of the Guardia Civil post and the flailing of the village's Fascists to the train blowing and Maria's rape, betray Hemingway into doing ostentatious set-pieces, easily detachable dramatic vignettes. El Sordo and Pablo, further, have been considered to balance off over-symmetrically as the good and bad *partizan* guerrilla leaders. Finally, the novel's general stylistic manner has about it too ritualized a quality, with the result that the whole reads as if the imaginative life had been rendered down to a point approaching woodenness.

Most of these recurring dissatisfactions, whatever their respective merits, have tended to divert attention from whether or not *For Whom the Bell Tolls* holds up as an imaginative whole, and if so, how that whole is achieved. Both in his letter to Perkins, and in the relevant correspondence of 1939–40 with his publisher Charles Scribner, Hemingway went out of his way to insist on this as the essential test. Furthermore, his standard can hardly be thought other than perfectly exacting in its own right: for how convincingly is *For Whom the Bell Tolls* 'knit up', the integrated and better sum of its contributing parts?

The point, at any rate, was not lost on Edmund Wilson. In one of the novel's earliest reviews, Wilson set the critical pace in handsome, intelligent style, alighting on precisely the same issue which had exercised Hemingway. For him, too, Jordan as consciousness and about his duties at the bridge serves as the novel's inescapable centre of gravity:

> [*For Whom the Bell Tolls*] is Hemingway's first attempt to compose a full-length novel, with real characters, and a built-up story. On the eve of a Loyalist attack in the Spanish civil War, a young American who has enlisted on the Loyalist side goes out into the country held by the Fascists, under orders to blow up a bridge. He directs with considerable difficulty a band of peasant guerillas, spends three nights in a cave in their company, blows up the bridge on schedule, and is finally shot by the Fascists. The method is the reverse of the ordinary method in novels of contemporary history, Franz Hoellering's or André Malraux's which undertake a general survey of a revolutionary crisis, shuttling back and forth among various groups of characters. There is little of this shuttling in 'For Whom the Bell Tolls', but it is all directly related to the main action: the blowing-up of the bridge. Through this episode the writer has aimed to reflect the whole course of the Spanish War, to show the tangle of elements that were engaged in it, and to exhibit the events in a larger perspective than that of the emergency of the moment.

So much, for Wilson, was positive, but he also had his reservations:

> The novel has certain weaknesses. A master of the concentrated short story, Hemingway is less sure of his grasp of the form of the elaborated novel. The shape of 'For Whom The Bell Tolls' is sometimes slack and sometimes bulging. It is certainly quite a little too long. You need space to make an epic of three days; but the story seems to slow up towards the end where the reader feels it ought to move faster; and the author has not

found out how to mold or to cut the interior soliloquies of his hero. Nor are the excursions, outside the consciousness of the hero, whose point of view comprehends most of the book, conducted with consistent attention to the symmetry and point of the whole.[7]

Taken together, both Hemingway's own view of his novel, and Wilson's, usefully suggest how *For Whom the Bell Tolls* might most appropriately be understood and judged. Does it achieve the 'larger perspective', but at the expense of slackness? How true is it to say that the material which lies outside Robert Jordan's 'consciousness' insufficiently ties in with the central drama of the bridge-blowing and Robert's own immediate experience? We return, through Hemingway's first major critic, to the issue of the novel's 'attention to the symmetry and point of the whole', to whether *For Whom the Bell Tolls*, as Hemingway initially put matters, can indeed claim to be 'knit up'.

Before, however, turning to the novel's integration, a further point might be registered, and one not always given due emphasis. One doesn't have to think *For Whom the Bell Tolls* an unalloyed success to grant Hemingway the recognition of having taken on a subject of genuine consequence, the Spanish Civil War assuredly seen as a fiction with its own imagined cast and adventures, but also as depicting the profounder questions of personal allegiance, the moral drama of how to act under duress. The novel thus runs deeper than the oppositions of Republican as against Fascist, existentialist as against Christian values. In this, assuredly to his own design, Hemingway deserves his place alongside Orwell, Huxley, Koestler and Malraux, to number the better-known, in depicting perennial human vulnerability to authoritarian power. Hemingway, whatever else, really ought not to be denied the seriousness of his subject, nor the obvious care with which he has sought to give his story an appropriate form.

2

'*Un callejón sin salida.* A passageway with no exit'[8]: so Robert Jordan judges the predicament of El Sordo and his men trapped on the hilltop by the Nationalist troops and their supporting airpower. As much, however, might be said of his own situation, or at least the reader's emerging sense of his situation. In part, this has to do with the novel's thematic devices, the warning raids of the Fascist bombers, Pablo's well-taken peasant misgivings about the blowing of the bridge, Pilar's reading of Jordan's palm, and Golz's initial forebodings about the counter-offensive. Andrés's subsequent inability to get past military bureaucracy with Jordan's letter adds further credence to the operation's likely failure. But the novel's closing confirmation of a historic human tragedy being played through in small to its inescapable conclusion is also carried by the way Hemingway manages the structure of the novel. For the structure of *For Whom the Bell Tolls* reflects with extraordinary precision its theme, subject and means blended one into another, an achievement which, if not absolutely perfect in execution, merits considerable respect.

In some measure this match of subject and form might be thought to follow inevitably from a story so conceived as to honour almost to the letter the Aristotelian unities, the seventy-hour or three-day rite of passage made to do duty for the assumed norm of a human lifetime, the single locale of the hillside camp within range of the bridge, and the narrative unfolded as an integrated sequence of cause and effect. But it amounts to more than that: Hemingway goes further than simply to unify time, place and action. He keeps our attention as closely engaged as he does by making the bridge (and Jordan's consciousness of it and of his mission) not only the novel's thematic centre, but its structural centre. The different flashbacks and insets, Jordan's interior monologues and the transcription of daily life at the camp underline the bridge's importance as the place where the novel's action will reach its dramatic climax, but also its contribution to the novel's pattern as a species of lodestone, the essential hub of the narrative. It becomes, to use Tolstoy's image again, the place where the novel's 'rays' meet and find their 'focus'.

Whether we move through time-present, as in Jordan's arrival with Anselmo, his love-affair with Maria, Pablo's defection and life as given inside the camp, or through time-remembered, as in the account of Pablo's seizure of the Fascist command-post and the flailing of the village, or through a kind of parallel-time, as in Andrés's abortive endeavour to get the letter to Golz in time and El Sordo's doomed stand against the Nationalists, Hemingway works each of these sequences into the action at the bridge with meticulous timing and calculation. This is equally true of Jordan's monologues, the references back to his Montana upbringing and the memory of his father and grandfather and American Civil War figures like the Confederate grey ghost John Moseby, or the recall of his fellow-dynamiter and expatriate Kaskin, or the Gaylords crowd, Golz, and others in the Republican command. In other words, despite obvious blemishes—Maria or Jordan's occasional too explicit political reflections—*For Whom the Bell Tolls* operates to genuine advantage on its strategy of centre and circumference, nearly every part working towards the whole, the whole securely reflective of each contributing part. I want to redirect attention first towards the novel's creation of its 'focus', then in turn at the flashbacks, the insets, and Jordan's interior monologues.

If analogues for the bridge in *For Whom the Bell Tolls* were to be advanced from other classic American texts, then Hawthorne's scaffold in *The Scarlet Letter* or Twain's raft in *Huckleberry Finn* would be among the most appropriate. For the bridge acts both as an emphatically literal point of reference, an actual thing in an actual war, but also as a larger touchstone for other local stands and battles, in the Spanish War and by implication all wars. It perhaps is not, to be sure, the deific Brooklyn Bridge of Hart Crane's poem—it does not lend of its curveship a myth to God—but it radiates, as the novel says early on, a 'solid flung metal grace' (35), an iconic power which grows in impact as Anselmo, Agustín, Pilar and Fernando (Pablo is the dissenter) come to see that it is here and finally that their stand must be made. They, in turn, speak of it in implicitly religious terms, the place of duty which if it is to cost them their lives must do so with all the dignity of an enterprise worthy of the sacrificial contract. In this, too, the bridge appropriately keeps us mindful of other bridges, other antecedent occasions on the Tiber and at the Concord where earlier legendary hero-warriors have found the final turn of their destiny. Both Jordan and Pilar sense this, Jordan in one of his soliloquies:

> My obligation is to the bridge, and to fulfill that, I must take
> no useless risk of myself until I complete that duty. (63)

and Pilar, slightly more euphorically, by identifying the bridge
with the Republic:

> 'I am for the Republic,' the woman of Pablo said happily.
> 'And the Republic is the bridge. Afterwards we will have time
> for other projects.' (53)

With a keen touch of irony, Hemingway shows, too, that as
the bridge grows in importance for the band, and especially
after Pablo's return from the 'loneliness' of his defection, so
paradoxically at command headquarters, it recedes in tactical
importance, a symptom of the impending larger collapse of the
Loyalist forces. In this respect it becomes, also, an omen, of a
kind with the triads of Fascist bombers which destroy El Sordo
and penetrate into the hills and behind Republican lines. The
appropriate general note is struck by Golz to his French
subordinate Duval: *'Nous sommes foutus, Oui. Comme toujours'*
(428). Though obviously unheard by Jordan, or the band,
Golz's observation, by its confession of frailty, enhances, if
anything, rather than diminishes, the human worth behind
the action at the bridge.

Nowhere does the bridge loom more importantly than in the
novel's closing sequence. To Jordan it becomes 'a dream
bridge. A bloody dream bridge' (437), not only his designated
target, the object planned against, spied upon, easy to dynamite, but the place where finally his boyhood dreams of heroic
Civil War and Western frontier derring-do become for a
moment utterly real, romance literally transformed into historic
actuality. To an extent, thus, the novel aptly offers itself as
slightly ritual in manner, for behind its surfaces lies the appeal
to a discernibly larger, mythic paradigm of heroic action, the
fugitive, shadowy memory of past and recollected other raids
and counter-raids, whether the picture book chivalry of childhood classics, or the epic moments from actual history.
Hemingway hints a number of times, and adroitly, of the
fascination most male childhoods display for heroic lore and
deeds, often enough acted out in games and gang charades. For
Jordan, he has the recall of a younger imagination nurtured

89

both on the West and on his grandfather's stories of the Civil War, as well as his eager adolescent taste for the reading of adventure. In this sense the bridge joins personal memory to fact, an individual American past to the European and war-torn present. It also, as the considerable commentary on the novel has not failed to point out, serves as the place where life is brought up sharp against death, movement becomes stasis, and human connection undergoes split and severance. Without wanting unduly to add to this commentary, it ought to be stressed again how subtly conceived are the bridge's several purposes and resonances throughout *For Whom the Bell Tolls*.

But if the bridge functions as the novel's epicentre, around it Hemingway builds a busy composite human world, at each turn linking the bridge to life in the camp, especially the tangle of energies and tension among Pablo, Pilar, Anselmo, Maria, the gypsy Raphael, and the five others, the brothers Andrés and Eladio, and Augustín, Fernando and Primitivo. Hemingway's detailed evocation of this life—the edgy group loyalty, the stock of curses, superstitions, stories told, retold, and frequently embellished into legend, Jordan's wary relationship with both Pablo and Pilar, the ritual of meals and guard duties and the different spats—amounts to no small tour-de-force, *partizan* life under war vividly excerpted and caught on the page. Part of this life, too, is the monitoring consciousness of Robert Jordan, directing our attention both to the time-present as experienced at the camp, but also directing us backwards into past time and patterns of causation. Thus the bridge becomes dramatically more than some mere static point of reference, it offers a 'focus' in the larger Tolstoyian sense.

Take, at the start, Jordan's arrival at the camp with his dynamite under orders from Golz. In classic declarative style, Hemingway sets before us the essential terrain against which the novel's action will be enacted, 'the brown, pine-needled floor of the forest' (1), the knotty, tree-lined mountainside, the painterly mill and stream which lead on to the bridge. In Anselmo, he establishes the first of the *partizans*, the tough, grainy, companion mentor who guides both Jordan and the reader into the hidden world of Pablo. Anselmo's utterances nicely confirm the simple good faith he has in the Republic's cause, but also suggest a veteran who knows the terms on which he must live. 'I am an old man who will live until I die' (16) is his affecting answer to Pablo's taunts, for instance. He again conveys the human touch when he speaks to Jordan of God: 'Clearly I miss Him, having been brought up in religion. But now a man must be responsible for himself' (41). Anselmo also offers the perfect angle through which to encounter for the first time Pablo, a leader convincingly suspicious of Jordan's arrival, a drinker, and at once shrewd yet beset with contradiction, with a peasant's wary eye upon any disruption of what he knows as the best terms of safety. His general savvy in not being taken in by Jordan's blandishments works especially well:

> 'He is Pablo,' said the old man. . . .
> 'Good. I have heard much of you,' said Robert Jordan. . . .
> 'I have heard that you are an excellent guerrilla leader, that you are loyal to the republic and prove your loyalty through your acts, and that you are a man both serious and valiant. I bring you greetings from the General Staff.'
> 'Where did you hear all this?' asked Pablo. Robert Jordan registered that he was not taking any of the flattery. . . . 'What are you going to do with the dynamite?'
> 'Blow up a bridge.'
> 'What bridge?'
> 'That is my business.'
> 'If it is in this territory, it is my business. You cannot blow bridges close to where you live. You must live in one place and operate in another. I know my business. One who is alive, now, after a year, knows his business.' (10–11)

Hemingway then appropriately locates Pablo within an imagery of the hunter and the hunted, the knowing fox but also the vulnerable hare. As Pablo says, weariness in his tone:

> I am tired of being hunted. Here we are all right. Now if you blow a bridge here, we will be hunted. If they know we are here and hunt for us with planes, they will find us. If they send Moors to hunt us out, they will find us and we must go. I am tired of all this. You hear? . . . What right have you, a foreigner, to come to me and tell me what I must do? . . .
> To me, now, the most important is that we be not disturbed here. (15)

The accent convinces because it has about it the weary ring of experience, and because Pablo's scepticism acts as the right counter to the military planner's abstractions, tactics made at the desk and set down bloodlessly upon army maps, even by so disciplined and well-meaning a general as Golz. The hideaway mountain way of life which Pablo and his band have made for themselves and into which Jordan has intruded, Hemingway then makes into a wholly credible imagined frontline arena, an uncertain provisional place which matches the justified uncertainty of men deeply at risk and with only few and precarious means of survival. That Jordan both sees this and tries to negotiate his way through to Pablo's trust adds further human depth to the novel's creation of a working centre.

The picture is then built up in accretions across the three days and nights Jordan spends in preparation for the attack on the bridge. The venial irresponsibility of Raphael, the gypsy, his mind always on the next meal or snaring a rabbit, is to have more serious consequences when he fails to guard the dynamite properly so allowing Pablo to attempt sabotage by destroying the plungers. Even the first glimpse of Maria, mute and temptingly pretty, suggests an appropriate element, the girl as Spain's vulnerability to the dark, vengeful angers of Fascism. But what most gives dynamic to the world of Pablo and the camp is Pilar and her strange, mesmeric hold over each aspect of daily life, the talk, the orders, the rituals of food and drink, and especially the bombast and cursing. Her first physical appearance confirms not exactly the gorgon conjured up by Raphael and the others, but a woman whose strength of will is expressed in her solid physical make-up:

> Robert Jordan saw a woman of about fifty almost as big as Pablo, almost as wide as she was tall, in black peasant skirt and waist, with heavy wool socks on heavy legs, black rope-soled shoes and a brown face like a model for a granite monument. She had big but nice looking hands and her thick curly black hair was twisted into a knot on her neck. (30)

She it is, too, who in her embrace of Jordan, her nursing of Maria, and above all, her fraught, complex 'marriage' with Pablo, expresses the standard for life and for the human meaning of the Loyalist cause. At the same time, she is not made by Hemingway into some easy emblem of matrilinear strength; she exhibits a gamut of feelings, motherly sentimentality as in the care of Maria, an inclination towards tough, in-the-grain emotion as in her stories of Pablo's role in the attack on the Fascist village and her affair with Finito, the energy of the vixen as in her cursing and direction of the camp's daily rhythm.

Hemingway manages the relationship with Pablo to especially fine effect. Even as she ponders the notion of killing Pablo, the leader gone slack on his past skills and bravery, so Pilar recalls with mixed sentiments a man for whom she has shown love, even though she has come to him from Finito and from other men. Hemingway also catches in their relationship the ambiguous Spanish construction of male and female roles, not to mention the awareness of a Castilian in relationship with a part-gypsy woman. The arguments and bids for authority can hardly be thought other than handsomely authentic. She it is, too, who presides over Maria like Juliet's nurse, over the love-affair with Jordan, and who, at the end, as Jordan is wounded, presides over the escape from Berrendo and his troops. She appropriately is also given the story of the flailing of the village to relate, told en route to the meeting with El Sordo, Pilar as witness and historian to the cruelties which any partisanship can inflict. Her presence touches every aspect of the camp's life, a portrait which allows Hemingway once more to underline the human dimension of his story and to give it a principle of continuity, and altogether a better, deeper creation than he has often been allowed.

The other feature of the camp life as centre has to be Jordan's love for Maria. Even though no convincing case has ever been established for Maria, the childlike submissive lover invented by a Hemingway hopelessly unable to imagine an adult woman according to his rebuking critics, the relationship as such hasn't always been given its due. Given the claustrophobic pressures of war (one recalls Stephen Crane's notion of the American Union army as a moving box in *The Red Badge of Courage*), and Jordan's odd ascetic life in the service of the Loyalist cause, the notion of sexual release through Maria isn't entirely without foundation. Hemingway, to be sure, errs badly in transforming the relationship into some version of a lifetime's love, again the trope of a life lived through in three representative days, but he suggests something deeply convincing in how men at war, their nerves kept sharp to the possibility of death or disabling injury, discover in themselves a more than customary drive towards sexual release. This does not deny that in *For Whom the Bell Tolls* the transaction goes all one way, towards fulfilling Jordan's needs not Maria's, his fantasy not hers. Maria can't honestly be thought other than a mistake, but the complex pressure of Jordan's needs, a man wound tight by his obligation to his mission, might be regarded more sympathetically than it usually has. For as Anselmo, Pablo and Pilar are given in distinctive terms, so Jordan—not only as *partizan*, volunteer Loyalist and Hispanophile, but a man possessed of complex emotional and sexual drives—is given a fuller personality than that merely of the behind-the-lines warrior.

Each of these four, and the picture draws further human detail from the band's other combatants, make up a gallery of types and voices. Their cumulative human weight of presence, and Hemingway's scrupulous observation of food, wine, camp and guard duties, and the constant working in of memory (not to say the ways in which a *partizan* group goes about its business of survival and hit-and-run harassment of the enemy) build into a substantive, credible whole. They provide the novel's continuity, its human time-present. As Jordan transforms them into a fighting unit, the instrument for Golz's policy, so the reader engages with both a representative world and one actively fleshed through by Hemingway. When, therefore, we encounter in turn the flashbacks, the insets and Jordan's soliloquies, we have, as it were, a secure touchstone, a sense of life persuasively imagined against which to set each in turn.

3

Just as Hemingway establishes in the bridge and camp life the novel's centre, so in almost all the dozen or so flashbacks he gives notice of the enclosing larger world of politics and Spanish history against which Jordan's action can be understood. Several deal with Jordan's own reminiscence, and perhaps belong more aptly with his interior soliloquies, but the others give *For Whom the Bell Tolls* its wider embrace of the Civil War and the historic clash of loyalties. The first we encounter, Jordan's meeting with Golz, blends with remark-

able ease into the journey to Pablo's camp with Anselmo. The
transition runs from carrying the dynamite, to Anselmo, to
Golz's dialogue with Jordan:

> 'To blow the bridge is nothing,' Golz had said, the lamplight
> on his scarred, shaved head, pointing with a pencil on the big
> map. 'You understand?'
> 'Yes, I understand.'
> 'Absolutely nothing. Merely to blow the bridge is a failure.'
> 'Yes, Comrade General.'
> 'To blow the bridge at a stated hour based on the time set for
> the attack is how it should be done. You see that naturally.
> That is your right and how it should be done.' (4–5)

Where Golz, however, a portrait done with considerable
sympathy, is all discipline and command, the depiction of
Anselmo guiding Jordan to the camp translates the abstrac-
tion of orders into literal action. Hemingway also shrewdly
shows Golz as a man with his own becoming traits—the jokes
about his and Jordan's names and about their respective
haircuts, the drink he offers—and as precisely the *Général
Sovietique*, in touch with the larger campaign against the
Fascists. The implication is just about right, Jordan as but one
figure of many, his mission part of a more inclusive strategy.

The major other flashbacks, especially those I now want to
call attention to—Pablo's attack on the Fascist village, Pilar's
relationship with Finito and Maria's rape—similarly blend
into the novel's creation of its time-present. Not only are they
managed with great imaginative authority in themselves, but
they contribute to the novel's overall scheme as essential forms
of the past through which to understand the present impasse
of Spanish history. They take their place, too, alongside other
smaller points of recall, each located at appropriate intervals,
reminding us of what was and what now is, past cause and
present effect. These include the memory of Kaskin, killed by
Jordan to prevent capture yet his own secret sharer in doing
the dynamite work, or Joaquin's remembrance of the killing of
his parents in Valladolid for having voted socialist, an event to
set against Pablo's flailing of the Fascists, or the slightly
indulgent remembrance of Karkov and Gaylords, a reminder
among other things of Jordan's own aspirations to write.

Jordan's harping back to his earlier American life also matches events in his Spanish experience. For instance, when he packs with meticulous care the dynamite it recalls for him the care he showed as a boy for his collection of bird eggs (48). His vivid memory of a black lynching in Ohio carries real implications for the barbarisms committed by both sides of the Spanish Civil War (116). Even the memory of the young Belgian soldier from the Eleventh Brigade whose emotional balance has been so disturbed that he cries all the time (136) suggests an analogy with Pablo and his lachrymose, relentless drinking. Similarly, the invocation of Jordan's journeyings, from Billings, Montana, to college, to France and Spain, ties in with the pasts given by the novel of Pilar, Pablo and Maria. The sum effect of both the larger and smaller flashbacks is one of thickening the narrative, so that the central thread within the camp and at the bridge indeed works outward and across time to a larger frame of allusion.

'I will tell it as it truly was' (99): in these terms Pilar begins the account of Pablo's attack on the Guardia barracks and his brute, systematic execution of the village's Fascists. The story is told, we need to be mindful, as Pilar, Jordan and Maria, are on their way to El Sordo's camp, for whom history has reserved an equally sombre fate. Hemingway renders the account with great energetic flair, avenging humanity turned bestial by the sick, self-mutilating nature of civil war. Pablo's fear of what the event has transformed him into, Pilar's comforts to him, and the sad final lament of a crying woman, underline to a fine point the despoiling touch of the war, whether waged from Loyalist or Nationalist assumptions. The episode amounts to drama in its own terms, but also once more as a way of pulling into the novel's present the pressing reality of the immediate Spanish past. Pablo, the others, are the necessary veterans of this event, hunters as well as the hunted, at once killers and yet still vulnerable.

Pilar's recollection of Finito the novel tells in two sequences (Chapters 8 and 14), a story which calls up the Spain of the *corridas*, violence ritually controlled and defeated, and which Hemingway's *Death in the Afternoon* takes such impressive pains to document. Pilar's initial reminiscence refers us to the Spain of good food and wine (85), customs like the *Feria*, Spanish

music and festivity at large. Her account of Finito's eventual
death, a haunted, tubercular matador haemorrhaging from
deep within towards collapse, Hemingway offers both as literal
biography and, if not exactly as allegory, then as an implied
metaphor of Spanish history. The story possesses its own
slightly surreal, Goyaesque sadness, and the bull and *corrida*
materials recall, to good effect, the world of Jake and Romero
in *The Sun Also Rises*. That Pablo, a handler of picador horses
for Finito, should become his successor with Pilar suggests also
how the Civil War has likewise transformed irregulars into
regulars, the handlers into the warriors. Once more, and in
touching particularity, the novel builds before the reader an
appropriate biographical past, the sense of literal prior circumstance, to Jordan's encounter with Pablo and Pilar at the
camp.

Maria's rape (Chapter 31) is recalled as she and Jordan talk
after their lovemaking, a past hurt healed and redeemed
through their present intimacy. Or at least so one presumes
Hemingway would have the relationship understood. The
detail of the Falangist assault on the village, and the hair-
cropping and rape itself, Hemingway relates with the same
dramatic flair shown in the accounts of Pablo's exploits at the
train and in the Fascist village. The lovemaking itself flatly
does not carry imaginative conviction, any more than the
implication of Maria as yet another instance of Spain's mar-
tyrdom, its vulnerability to the self-inflicted trauma of civil
war. Maria's story, however, does refer us again to the broader
historical context of the Spanish past, and of major importance, of the relationship of that past to the present mission at
the bridge. Jordan's reflections point in the appropriate
direction:

> What a people they have been. What sons of bitches from
> Cortez, Pizarro, Menéndez de Avila all down through Enrique
> Lister to Pablo. And what wonderful people. There is no finer
> and no worse people in the world. No kinder and no crueler.
> And who understands them? Not me, because if I did I would
> forgive it all. . . .
> Well, it was something to think about. Something to keep
> your mind from worrying about your work. It was sounder than
> pretending. God, he had done a lot of pretending tonight. And

Pilar had been pretending all day. Sure. What if they were killed tomorrow? What did it matter as long as they did the bridge properly? That was all they had to do tomorrow.

(354–55)

The past links to the present, and from Maria's story, as from Pablo's and Pilar's we pass forward to Jordan's obligations at the bridge. Hemingway's way of keeping his novel 'knit up' is again there to be seen.

4

The two principal insets in *For Whom the Bell Tolls*—the death of El Sordo and his men and Andrés's endeavour to get Jordan's message through to Golz—work, as I have suggested earlier, in a kind of parallel-time. They set the main line of action at the camp and bridge within a context of simultaneous action, the one vintage Hemingway military drama, the other a quite major insight into the petty bureaucratic vagaries of war. The first, as it were, points towards the best of American war fiction, the tradition embracing Stephen Crane, John Dos Passos, Norman Mailer and latterly the realism of a work like *Soldier Blue*. The other hints of a more absurdist dimension, especially the crazed figure of Marty, the domain explored in novels like *Catch-22* and *Slaughterhouse-Five*. There are, to be sure, other insets in Hemingway's novel, the conversation of the Gallego guards at the post near the bridge and the several allusions to the journalist Karkov, but those of El Sordo and Andrés offer the best matching episodes to the three-day drama at the camp.

The story of El Sordo's death begins irresistibly:

> El Sordo was making his fight on a hilltop. He did not like this hill and when he saw it he thought it had the shape of a chancre. But he had no choice except this hill and he had picked it as far away as he could see it and galloped for it, the automatic rifle heavy on his back, the horse laboring, barrel heaving between his thighs, the sack of grenades swinging against one side, the sack of automatic rifle pans banging against the other, and Joaquín and Ignacio halting and firing to give him time to get the gun in place. (307)

The careful, declarative release of detail, and the vivid implicit drama of men cornered but turning to make their stand, carries the same authority as the opening description of soldiers on march through the dust in *A Farewell to Arms*. Their attempt to make their fortification against the superior force of Berrendo's Nationalist troops, and the references to La Pasionaria, the oaths and even the jokes, add reinforcing layers of credibility to the action. The hill, however, despite El Sordo's attempted ruse, indeed becomes a chancre, a lost, infected place once the bombers arrive. The stink of that kind of death—arbitrary and unfair—Hemingway catches in the physicality of his descriptions:

> Keeping a heavy fire on the hilltop, Lieutenant Berrendo pushed a patrol up to one of the bomb craters from where they could throw grenades onto the crest. He was taking no chances of any one being alive and waiting for them in the mess that was up there and he threw four grenades into the confusion of dead horses, broken and split rocks, and torn yellow-stained explosive-stinking earth before he climbed out of the bomb crater and walked over to have a look. (322)

The language works at one with the moral detritus of the action. The hill is chancred, the earth 'stinking', the horses as dead and broken as the baroque beasts in Picasso's Guernica. All of this is picked up at distant earshot, and guiltily, by Jordan and Anselmo and the others, evidence of their limited ability to act, and a reminder that their duty can be directed only at the bridge. The El Sordo episode both parallels, and acts as a commentary on, Jordan's own endeavour with Pablo to strike back at the Fascist assault. Not only does Berrendo's final scrupulosity in turning away from the act of decapitating El Sordo match Hemingway's willingness to grant him his dignity as he approaches Jordan at the end, the whole pattern of strike and counter-strike helps locate the novel's overall movement between hunters and hunted, winners and vanquished.

The portrait of Andrés's attempt to deliver Jordan's letter turns on another tack: the sheer infuriating way bureaucracy works in a war, especially a war fought with volunteer, improvisational military forces against Spain's Fascist *putsch*. Andrés's initial guilt at having left his comrades, the repeated challenges to his identity, and his eventual ride on a motor-bike with Captain Gomez, the ex-barber, to H.Q. and to the crazed, untender mercies of Comrade Marty, might well suggest a species of Catch-22 nightmare, war as a hallucinatory regime of orders, paper, unacknowledged safe-conducts and arbitrary acts of command. The release of Andrés and Gomez, through Karkov's intervention with Marty, however, does no more than confirm that Golz's notion of 'Rien à faire' (428) is indeed the right gloss on events. The whole sequence works wonderfully well: it shows bureaucracy gone awry and contrasts with the *partizan* action in the field. It also underlines how even the attack on the bridge, so carefully prepared for by Jordan, signifies the merest small part in the pending overall collapse in the Loyalist resistance to Fascism. In this respect, it heightens our consciousness still more acutely of what is finally about to occur in 'the thing of the bridge'.

5

Jordan's interior monologues recur at intervals throughout the novel, glossing in precisely the same way as the flashbacks and the insets the general pulse of the action. They build up, in turn, the portrait of the historic, individual figure who is the novel's central consciousness. One line of retrospective contemplation helps us to see Pablo and Pilar and the camp, especially Jordan's wary sense of where and where not he can take command, when best to speak and when not. Another guides us back to his American origins, in Montana, with his father and grandfather, and into the education which eventually brought him across the Atlantic to France and Spain and into an awareness of how his life's necessary commitments to the Spanish Republic have come to be. Then there are his frequent contemplations of Spain itself, a history and for him a destiny, to which everything else would seem to have tended. At least that with justice can be said to be the import of his final soliloquy when, wounded, he attempts his *compte rendu*:

> I have fought for what I believed in for a year now. If we win here we will win everywhere. The world is a fine place and worth the fighting for and I hate very much to leave it. And you had a lot of luck, he told himself, to have had such a good life, You've had just as good a life as grandfather's though not as long. You've had as good a life as any one because of these last

days. You do not want to complain when you have been so
lucky. I wish there was some way to pass on what I've learned,
though. Christ, I was learning fast there at the end. I'd like to
talk to Karkov. That is in Madrid. Just over the hills there, and
down across the plain. . . . There's no *one* thing that's true. It's all
true. The way the planes are beautiful whether they are ours or
theirs. The hell they are, he thought. (467)

The notion of a life contracted into the brief stay at the
camp operates persuasively here because Jordan has demon-
strably earned the right to his views. Whether we see his
action in remaining behind as his last chivalric hurrah, or as
the appropriate act of a seasoned *partizan*, his thoughts bring
back into focus the whole contour of the novel: the arrival with
Anselmo, Pablo's flight, the love of Maria, his warmth towards
Pilar, the wider embrace of the war's planning and command
in Madrid, and above all the motifs of earth and pine which
begin the novel and to which Hemingway alludes in his letter
to Maxwell Perkins. As the novel rounds to its last moment,
Jordan and Berrendo, *partizan* and Nationalist officer, become
a mutual nemesis, men whose shared destiny is to be, in John
Donne's words, 'diminished' by each other's death. Through
this last of Jordan's soliloquies, *For Whom the Bell Tolls* thus
rightly closes on the allusion with which it began:

> He was waiting until the officer reached the sunlit place
> where the first trees of the pine forest joined the green slope of
> the meadow. He could feel his heart beating against the pine
> needle floor of the forest. (471)

It does not have to be argued yet again that *For Whom the Bell
Tolls* displays flaws in plenty. Hemingway has been duly
indicted on a variety of counts: most especially for Maria, his
code material and supposed infantilist intoxication with death,
the Spanglish and the monotonal flavour in stretches of the
style. But if my argument has been at all apt, he deserves to be
granted the success of the overall design behind his novel. Parts
do fit the whole, and the whole, I believe, to a degree far greater
than has generally been acknowledged, acts to carry and unify
the energy of those parts. Hemingway has by no means won his
due as the conscious pattern-maker in his longer fiction. *For
Whom the Bell Tolls*, 'knit up' as it is, suggests he deserves better.

NOTES

1. Carlos Baker (ed.), *Hemingway: Selected Letters, 1917–61*, (New York: Charles Scribner's Sons, 1981), p. 514.
2. Quoted in R. F. Christian, *Tolstoy's 'War and Peace'* (Oxford: Oxford University Press, 1962), pp. 104–8, 124–50, and reprinted in George Gibian (ed.), The Norton Critical Edition of *War and Peace* (New York: Norton, 1966), p. 1456. The original appeared as A. B. Goldenweiser, *Vblizi Tolstogo* (Moscow-Leningrad, 1959).
3. See Philip Young, *Ernest Hemingway* (New York: Rinehart & Company, Inc., 1952), pp. 75–82 and Carlos Baker, *Hemingway: The Writer as Artist* (Princeton University Press, 1952). See the Third Edition, pp. 246–59.
4. Jordan muses as following in one of his interior monologues: 'You're not a real Marxist and you know it. And you never could have. You believe in Liberty, Equality and Fraternity. You believe in Life, Liberty and the Pursuit of Happiness. Don't ever kid yourself with too much dialectics. They are for some but not for you. You have to put many things in abeyance to win a war. If this war is lost all of those things are lost' (p. 305).
5. For an indication of Hemingway's regard for Tolstoy, see his letter to Charles Scribner, 6 and 7 September 1949 (*Letters*, p. 673).
6. Most notably by Arturo Barea, in *Horizon*, May 1941.
7. Edmund Wilson: 'Return of Ernest Hemingway', *New Republic*, 103, 28 October 1940, pp. 591–92.
8. *For Whom the Bell Tolls* (New York: Charles Scribner's Sons, 1940), p. 305. All page references are to this edition.

6

The Later Fiction: Hemingway and the Aesthetics of Failure

by JAMES H. JUSTUS

Man as victim in a world at war is, arguably, the fundamental twentieth-century vision, and its most compelling spokesman is Hemingway. If he was not the first American writer to appreciate this permanent condition—it is already a settled conviction in Dreiser, Crane, and London at the turn of the century—he was the first to articulate it without the pretension of intellectual theorizing, instinctively aware even in the early 1920s that to fit the disturbing truth into a framework of theoretical structures was itself a kind of softening of the truth. And despite the perceptible shift in emphasis from the buttoned-up stoicism of Jake Barnes and Frederic Henry to the acknowledged need for communal co-operation in Harry Morgan and Robert Jordan, the original insights and the usable metaphors remained the same in the work of the 1930s and after: in a life of warfare, man suffers.

Indeed, nothing in the later work can support the contention occasionally voiced that Hemingway's 'growth' can be traced in his sequence of protagonists, that there is a steady ennobling process, from the nihilistic entrapment of man to his victory through tragic transcendence. For all the bathos of one and the noble self-sacrifice of the other, Harry Morgan and Robert

Jordan are linked with the earlier protagonists in trying to fight through delusion and personal inadequacies to some clear picture of the reality of inevitable loss. And lest we accept too readily the notion of a mellow Hemingway in *The Old Man and the Sea*, the rhythms of mythic parallels, the quasi-biblical diction, and the stark Homeric courage of its protagonist cannot disguise the central fact of the fable: the grand victory is brief. Santiago *loses* the great fish, and for all the skeletal proof of his catch, he is still an old man with only residual skills, a failure who must retreat to dreams of youth and vigour. What we learn from Hemingway in the 1920s is what we learn from Hemingway throughout his career: the fact of failure is the one clear-eyed and undeviating purchase on reality in the midst of falsifying stratagems, poses, masks, and those defensive bursts of justification that weave together author and authored, life and art. Man is doomed to failure; he must run a race whose outcome is already known; 'they' who finally 'get you' are often not indifferent but apparently malevolent; man must live with violence and pain in a sustained anguish that comes from a realization of his only temporary survival; fear is a constant, and while courage is possible, heroism is not. There is not a single Hemingway protagonist who is not wounded, sometimes physically so, always psychically. Because loss is their permanent condition, these protagonists are prey to nostalgia and fantasy and reconstituted versions of the self, dodges and substitutionary acts that somehow function as temporary comfort and assurance.

A catalogue of Hemingway's characters from Nick Adams to Thomas Hudson, as well as the narrative situations that document their difficult adjustment to lives that are only minimally self-directed, shows a remarkably consistent record of human failure. In addition to a physical disability that he knows is permanent, Jake Barnes betrays his own best instincts and violates his own carefully devised code of personal conduct. Nick Adams never quite recovers from the traumas of childhood violence, the suicide of his father, and his own wounding in Italy. The rain that symbolizes the death of his lover and child is also Frederic Henry's own symbolic future of unrecoverable loss. Harry Morgan is one of the spiritual and economic Have-Nots whose general failure is merely ratified by his formal death in a hail of bullets. And if Robert Jordan is, according to Philip Young,[1] the first of Hemingway's protagonists to conquer his 'incapacitating nightmares', we should not forget the end of his story; our final glimpse of him, a peripheral figure in the failed struggle for Spanish freedom, is of supine man whose final act is gestural rather than definitive. What he loses are his love, his cause, and his life. While much of Colonel Cantwell's last phase is marked by revaluation, reminiscence, and rewriting of the record to strengthen his place in it, the picture is one of sad depletion and the often quirky energy of the dying. The heart of Santiago's spiritual victory would seem to be sheer endurance of the fact of failure. And the evidence of the short fiction is similar. The protagonists in the most memorable stories—'The Snows of Kilimanjaro', 'The Killers', 'The Short Happy Life of Francis Macomber', 'The Undefeated', 'The Gambler, the Nun, and the Radio'—are caught in a context in which they or a third party engage in a recital of their failures or where victory is brief.

Given such a grimly consistent vision, we may well ask what *are* the possible counters to it? The work of the late Hemingway, like the early, reveals *no* satisfactory alternatives to the vision of failure—indeed, now that we have available the biography of, letters from, and assorted memoirs about this intensely autobiographical writer, we might well suspect even darker hues in that vision in the later fiction. That this is not the case is the triumph of Hemingway the artist over Hemingway the man. In both *The Old Man and the Sea* and *A Moveable Feast*, the writer who always complained of the difficulty of writing invented and managed to maintain the pace of certain rhetorical rhythms which in the first instance dignify and elevate the fable of failure and in the second disarm the reader's instinctive distaste for what the author reveals of his own selfishness, competitiveness, and mean-spiritedness. Style, that is, becomes one strategy for countering content.

In a sense, *The Old Man and the Sea* is now a lesser achievement than it was once thought to be because of the transparency of the device. The choice of a simple old fisherman who is down on his luck but who still proudly exercises his long-used skills is an explicit dalliance with sentimentality, a situation containing a ready-made, built-in poignancy not unlike that found in the pages of *The Reader's Digest* or *Guideposts*: in short, the inspirational value—the human spirit triumphing over adversity—is inherent in the very subject itself. What remained for Hemingway was the manner of telling, a style simultaneously detailed and generalized, calling upon his own specific familiarity with Gulf Stream fishing and a heightened form of the kind of translated English he had brilliantly but sporadically used (mostly for comic effects) as early as *The Sun Also Rises*. It is no wonder that *The Old Man and the Sea* was praised extravagantly when it appeared in 1952, and that the best critics correctly perceived that the victory was one of style. That, of course, had been the single greatest achievement of the early Hemingway, too—the forging of an uncluttered style that became the most influential of the twentieth century. Now, in the Santiago story, the stripped-down diction, the simple syntax, the repetitions, and the use of the conjunctions for rhythmical purposes had been redirected away from the blunt, tough-guy mannerisms into something akin to the scriptural.

But anterior to a famous literary style that gives a patina of success to the sequential fables of failure is an equally famous personal style that provides the illusion of success within a vision in which failure is a given. The story of Hemingway's art is the spectacle of failure both personal and existential. The story of Hemingway's career as man and artist is the search for techniques to neutralize if not to overcome failure. No protagonist wins, since none can win, but the famous dichotomy between the Hemingway hero and the Hemingway code hero, the imaginative splitting apart of The Way It Is and The Way It Should Be, is one obvious means for handling the fact of failure. Figures such as Manuel Garcia, Ole Andreson, Rinaldi, Santiago, Pedro Romero—and the Ernest Hemingway of the public press—are flesh-and-blood exempla who show how, in the face of certain defeat, man's only nobility consists in personal conduct, an integrity that allows him to face his defeat with dignity.

This personal style in its largest sense is anterior and analogous to the crafted precision of Hemingway's literary style. In this respect the competing values of style and vision become an important source of the undeniable vitality that even readers not notably sympathetic to Hemingway admit they find in the best of his work. What we often note in the Hemingway hero is a dramatized instance of that tension between style and vision, a structuring of human responses into aesthetic patterns that constitute creative counters to the gloomy fact of failure. His projected but never completed Book of the Sea is neither the best nor the worst of Hemingway's work, but even in its post-humous, edited state it reveals considerable interplay between vision and craft; and as 'late Hemingway' it may illustrate some final creative statement in that interplay which from the beginning characterizes its author's approach to his art—and to his life.

One measure of the decline in Hemingway's creative energy for the last fifteen years of his life is the gap between the works he ambitiously planned and worked on and those he actually completed. In Carlos Baker's description of the unfinished novel Hemingway called *The Garden of Eden* (some of it canni-balized for *Across the River and Into the Trees*) we find that to the usual difficulty of composition was added the apparent loss of authorial judgement generally.[2] Personal engagement with his subject in *The Dangerous Summer* was no guarantee against slack, self-indulgent writing, embarrassingly evident even in the heavily edited excerpts that *Life* (but not Charles Scribner) saw fit to publish.[3] Embedded in the 'Cuba' segment of *Islands in the Stream* is what may well be the author's own self-mocking gloss on his failure to make anything of another large project. In his preparations for his day off in Havana, after a lengthy time at sea, a fretful Thomas Hudson asks himself: 'What the hell is wrong with you? Plenty is wrong with me, he thought. Plenty. The land of plenty. The sea of plenty. The air of plenty.'[4] For several years Hemingway planned a grand trilogy of novels with the vague rubric of 'Land, Sea, and Air'. Within that plan, the Book of the Sea itself consisted of four independent novels, three of them devoted to Thomas Hudson and a briefer fourth to Santiago. From the testimony of friends and the evidence in the *Selected Letters*, the only piece of writing from the last period that came without agony was *The Old Man and the Sea*, for which Hemingway interrupted the writing of 'Bimini' and 'Cuba'; after completing the Santiago story, intended from the start as a coda for Hudson, he returned to the final sea-chase segment, now titled 'At Sea', which he wrote in the spring of 1951. After editing and cutting by Mary Hemingway and Charles Scribner, Jr., the three Hudson parts of the Book of the Sea were published in 1970 as a single novel, *Islands in the Stream.*[5]

Although the narrative discontinuity between *The Old Man and the Sea* and *Islands in the Stream* is clear, more significant is their thematic and psychological continuity. If, following the author, we consider the two novels as a single work issuing from a common period of composition (irregularly from 1946 to May 1951), and if we remember that Hemingway interrupted his Book of the Sea to write *Across the River and Into the Trees* (1948), what we most dramatically see is the functional interrelation of the author's life and art. That intimate connection is of course the hallmark of Hemingway throughout his career, evident to everybody during his lifetime despite the author's own annoyed disclaimers. But this cluster of work is different. These titles are an old man's books. Though Hemingway was only 47 when he began this work, as the biography sadly documents, he was already a prematurely ageing man. One sign in the fiction is the prominence of nostalgia, the recurrence of dreams, the bouts of reassessments, and the impulse to reshape old mistakes into more acceptable forms. All three heroes are manifestations of a battered lifetime of constant threats, tests, and disappointments, and a few victories that are memorially rehearsed to help shore up defences against a larger defeat to come. Explicitly, Cantwell and Hudson have perceptibly moved beyond the expectations of youth and the accommodations of maturity, from the nagging moral question of how shall a man live? to the starker one of how shall a man die? If Santiago, a simpler man, is not given to such lofty meditations, it is only because his creator is still being faithful to a realist's creed of credible characterization; the fable itself and the modest self-assessments of the old man are implicit articulations of the same thing.

Given the circumstances of Hemingway's creative life during the composition of his Book of the Sea, the wonder is that it possesses what vitality and coherence it does. No other of his works is more consciously *composed* than *The Old Man and the Sea*, the coda segment. It is not merely that, to follow Gertrude Stein's famous observation on Hemingway's early writing, it smells of the museum. In this case, the classical and biblical analogues of epic endurance are retold with austerity and restraint. While its control, its willed perfection, its rigorous excision of anything left to chance are its obvious strengths, they also make *The Old Man and the Sea* finally less interesting than the other parts of the sea story that became *Islands in the Stream.* Unlike the taut structure and the calculations of style in the Santiago story, with its air of a rhetorical exercise, the Thomas Hudson story is *under*written: the shapely but flexible patterns of its structure can still surprise, and the more varied, less processed style accommodates a wider range of human complexity.

Two similar episodes—Santiago's successful struggle with the marlin and David Hudson's unsuccessful struggle with a broadbill—suggest the general differences in the two works. Even though the David episode is the dramatic centre in 'Bimini', it is preceded and followed by other incidents, other characters, other anxieties. Its pacing and its placement meet our conventional expectations of the novel form; that is, it has context. In *The Old Man and the Sea* the landing of the marlin is also central, the first necessary stage in a continuous drama, but it is its own context. While the sense of place is firm, the action seems to occur in some realm of storybook time. Partly because of its rigorous adherence to the old unities, Santiago's drama is fablistic, not novelistic. What passes for its narrative extension is really symbolic, mythic, even allegorical, a characteristic that explains why ordinary copy-editors at *Life*, where it was first published, were instantly able to see something more in this work than a simple, primitive story exquisitely told.[6] Its 'upper' level of meaning is as insistent as its 'lower' level of story. Unlike *The Old Man and the Sea, Islands in the Stream* is complex in its narrative situations, its characterizations, and its sense of a society in a specific moment in time as well as a sense of place. As many readers have shown, *Islands in the Stream* is also shot through with hints of a larger symbolic significance, but they are merely intimations and they remain firmly subordinated to narrative.

Despite its considerable editing—the first by Hemingway himself[7]—*Islands in the Stream* retains enough narrative patterning to make it structurally and thematically coherent. Each of the three-part narrative has its own architecture, and each is designed to display different facets in the drama of human decline. Each book is dominated by the fact of death as Thomas Hudson, without fully understanding his sons, wives, and lovers, undergoes the searing experience of deprivation of those he loves, until, at the end, he himself lies dying. One critic has perceptively commented on Hemingway's technique of representing literally Hudson's progressive narrowing of his life in 'At Sea', in which 'at last in a channel along the Cuban coast, where the mangrove presses close on either hand, he finds his death'.[8] 'Bimini' economically supplies all that we need to know—and the most we will ever know—of the circumstances behind this twentieth-century 'grief-hoarder'. Its narrative rhythm is established by alternating segments of repose and action. The obscure tensions, both cultural and personal, that culminate in the ugly fight on the Queen's Birthday; David's narrow escape from a shark; and David's heroic bout with his fish: these three dramatized episodes reveal the protagonist as spectator. With a stability all too precarious, Hudson is unable to affect events; his is a recuperative sensibility whose major threat is the eruption of the very emotions that make men human: rage, love, remorse. In between these scenes of action are moments of repose, carried mostly by beautifully rendered conversations in which Hudson meditates on his vulnerability and stands exposed to a fate he cannot change.

'Cuba' is an extended segment of repose whose only action—patrol duty—is background. It consists of talk—conversation, story-telling, reminiscence—and functions as the first available, and finally inadequate, counter to suffering. The other available counter is the commitment to duty, the action of 'At Sea', although Hemingway implies that in the overall scheme there is finally little relationship between the purgative and what is being purged. Indeed, the swiftly paced action of the sea-chase in part three, like the sustained talk in the repose of part two, is merely substitutionary. While both telling and acting have their own integrity, they are modes that ultimately make no difference. Grief, loss, suffering are existential, and they are paramount in the emotional structure of the novel. When Hudson and his first wife are reunited in 'Cuba', the happiness is momentary, doomed already by their individual personalities and by the fact of their son's death; being suddenly summoned for sea duty is almost irrelevant in an uneasy relationship that is already spoiled. 'Get it straight', Hudson tells himself. 'Your boy you lose. Love you lose. Honor has been gone for a long time. Duty you do' (326). Patrolling the Gulf Stream looking for Nazis is, potentially at least, an action in the service of a higher cause, the stuff of conventional World War II films, but *duty* here is grimly personal. He does not have to like chasing Nazis, Hudson reminds himself; he merely has to do it well. The emotional state of the protagonist is the consistent focus throughout the novel, and depletion is its most telling note. Texturally, the novel is studded with the diction of defeat: *unhappiness, suffering, loss, sorrows and cries, grief, hopelessness, blankness, wickedness.*

This study of failure is pervaded by a mood of imminent social and cultural collapse, an aura of dread that provides a context for, even as it condenses into, the personal collapse of Thomas Hudson. 'Bimini' opens on the Queen's Birthday, an anachronistic event whose honouring by irrelevant celebrants is noisy, vulgar, and violent; with a sick gusto Mr. Bobby collaborates with Hudson in projecting the painter's masterpiece, 'The End of the World', a Caribbean version of Hieronymus Bosch that will of course never be painted; the wealthy tourists from the yachts are 'trash', but even Hudson's friends are 'a pretty seedy lot', not bad but 'worthless'. Roger Davis, the closest of these friends, is another of Hemingway's walking wounded, a burnt-out case when we last see him looking, with neither enthusiasm nor hope, for a new start in the west. The atmosphere of dread takes on a metaphysical cast whenever Davis and Hudson, brothers in pain, are by themselves. Davis suffers from guilt arising from the failure of responsibility (in the death of his younger brother and with a succession of women) and the prostituting of his talents, but he tends to transfer such personal problems into the public realm. After his fight with an obnoxious tourist, Davis admits his regret in succumbing to violence:

> 'There's a lot of wickeds at large. Really bads. And hitting them is no solution. I think that's one reason why they provoke you. . . . You know evil is a hell of a thing, Tommy. And it's smart as a pig. You know they had something in the old days about good and evil.'

111

'Plenty of people wouldn't classify you as a straight good',
Thomas Hudson told him.
'No. Nor do I claim to be. Nor even good nor anywhere near
good. I wish I were though. Being against evil doesn't make you
good'. (47)

They both agree that the wealthy tourist was an 'awful type',
and as a final comment, Davis observes:

He couldn't have been any worse than the last one on the coast.
The trouble is, Tommy, there are so many of them. They have
them in all countries and they are getting bigger all the time.
Times aren't good, Tommy. (48)

The evils are real, of course. They include natural disasters,
such as waterspouts and hurricanes, sharks, and Nazis as well
as spoiled vacationers and corrupt Hollywood tycoons; but,
more importantly, they include personal demons, the dark
nightmares of nearly all the adult characters in *Islands in the
Stream*. Davis recognizes the principle: 'I was against it and
then I was evil myself. I could feel it coming in just like a tide'
(47). Hudson is not only not exempt; he is Hemingway's prime
example of the fragile remnant, a human being victimized as
much by his own inner deficiencies as by any of those assorted
external evils. Roger Davis is a reminder of his own darker self,
a figure sapped of self-confidence and self-control and occasional
hostage to self-pity.[9] But there is another side to this relationship. Davis has squandered his talent and has made himself
vulnerable by loving others. The poignancy here is that even
in his ruin he may be superior to Hudson. It is not surprising
that a tactful Hudson hesitates to preach too readily or too
directly to his friend; Davis's squandered talent may be
greater than Hudson's husbanded one.
Throughout 'Bimini', the only section in which Hudson's
profession is treated, Hemingway establishes the grounds by
which we can be assured that Hudson is trying to be a good
artist in a bad time. The assurances are not convincing.
Despite his protagonist's early friendship with fellow artists in
Paris—Picasso, Braque, Miro, Pascin—the author gives no
real evidence that Hudson is anything better than a passably
decent artist, commercially successful enough to maintain an
agent but imaginatively deficient. His most admired painting,

hanging behind the local bar, is of three waterspouts and three men in a dinghy; his most heartfelt painting, generated by his son's struggle with a broadbill, tries to capture transient reality in a moment of actual loss; and Mr. Bobby, though his aesthetic judgement may be suspect, gives what is clearly intended to be an unsentimental summary of Hudson's *oeuvre:*

> People paying money for pictures of Uncle Edward. Pictures of Negroes in the water. Negroes on land. Negroes in boats. Turtle boats. Sponge boats. Squalls making up. Waterspouts. Schooners that got wrecked. Schooners building. Everything they could see free. They really buy them? (17)

The professional perfunctoriness of island genre painting is only a part of Hudson's general personal failure. The summary is additionally resonant, coming as it does after Mr. Bobby's exasperated wondering aloud why Hudson and his friends 'stay around this island'. The painter's precise calibration of his island life can also be seen as a tucked-tail retreat, rehabilitation, or escape.

If Roger Davis's other problem is loving too freely, Hudson's is his emotional penuriousness. To love is to make the self vulnerable. That sad truth of human relationships explains both Davis and Hudson: if the first is ravaged by too much giving of the self, the second is desiccated from giving too little. Like the 'carapace of work' he has devised to protect himself, Hudson's stoic imperturbability protects him against further emotional lacerations. While Roger displays all the scars of psychic hurt, Hudson carefully, formally, maintains the disjunction between his equally serious psychic hurts and the external self he shows to the world. We never see or hear him without the full 'Thomas Hudson', an attribution that formalizes the emotional distance between reader and protagonist. He once observes an officer from the Headquarters code room in Havana: 'He looked healthy and his unhappiness did not show' (255). This is the same sort of desperate adjustment that Hudson himself makes, and one that dates not from the time he is massively visited by the disasters of fate—the loss of his two younger sons at the end of 'Bimini' and that of his oldest son in 'Cuba'—but from our initial glimpse of him.

Like many other Hemingway protagonists, Hudson lives a

life of psychic recuperation, remembering fitfully his past disappointments and failures in the midst of the necessary compromises of the present. 'You have to make it inside of yourself wherever you are', he reminds himself, and to Davis, who expresses a need to get away, he says: ' "Geography isn't any cure for what's the matter with you" ' (16, 102). But making it inside, laudably realistic as it is, requires even for Thomas Hudson an almost systematic manipulation of the outside. His chief failure is his first marriage, the breakup of which he mentally returns to again and again. Although we are told that he 'had long ago ceased to worry' about it, having 'exorcised guilt with work insofar as he could' (7), his 'work', though he takes it seriously, is always regarded as an activity just slightly better than therapy:

> He had been able to *replace* almost everything except the children with *work* and the *steady normal working* life he had built on the island. He *believed* he had made something there that would last and that would *hold* him. Now when he was lonesome for Paris he would *remember* Paris *instead of* going there. He did the same thing with all of Europe and much of Asia and of Africa. (7, italics mine)

What is striking about both syntax and diction in this passage, a piece of authorial exposition internalized by the protagonist himself, is its provisional character, Hudson's own awareness that he must rely on surrogates, not to regain anything but simply to keep from losing everything. The make-do stability only barely disguises desperation, and the desperation is disguised not at all by the explicit patterns, order, and rhythm that Hudson arbitrarily imposes on himself. From larger concerns— such as alternating segments of work and reward in a discernible predictability—to smaller ones—such as the little ritual he makes of burning driftwood in his fireplace—Hudson devises and cherishes willed activities 'that would hold him'.

For many of the residents Bimini is a boring stasis; for Hudson the island, a refraction rather than a true reflection of the actual world, is simultaneously an eden, a purgatory, and a refuge. ' "It's a good place for a guy like you that's got some sort of inner resources" ' (25), says an admiring friend, but Hudson's cool surface is hardly an accurate indicator of either the depth or variety of those inner resources. His characteristic position at the Floridita is itself the language of wary defensiveness: 'He took his seat on a tall bar stool at the extreme left of the bar. His back was against the wall toward the street and his left was covered by the wall behind the bar' (258). His heavy dependence upon alcohol and seconal and his insomnia suggest a fragile psychological balance that is threatened as much as it is strengthened by the emotional adjustments he must make for his sons' visit. Although his proprietary airs and patrician condescension instantly establish Hudson as a valued Bimini resident, not a transient, his own internal musings reveal a more ambiguous status. He is still a foreigner living alone, a spiritual alien adjusting as well as he can to the condition of human separation. Every detail of his biography is a reinforcement of his spiritual rootlessness: he is thrice divorced, the father of three sons by two wives, the owner of three houses but no home—the solid, prominent Bimini house that has withstood three hurricanes, a Finca in Cuba, a ranch in Idaho—and a boat with a flying bridge that ranges all over the Gulf Stream, first for fish, finally for German submariners.

Hemingway's extraordinary attention to sensuous details in *Islands in the Stream* functionally underscores his protagonist's need, since they are often his points of stability in a wavering world. The preparation, colour, taste, feel, and smell of his drinks—the Tom Collinses, the frozen daiquiris, the Gordon's gin with lime juice, coconut water, and bitters—are precisely, lingeringly itemized. The description of Honest Lil's complexion—'She had a skin that was as smooth as olive-coloured ivory . . . with a slightly smoky roselike cast . . . [like] well-seasoned *mahagua* lumber when it is freshly cut, then simply sanded smooth and waxed lightly' (273)—comes naturally from a consciousness that has long contemplated the object. The discipline of description, always a hallmark virtue in Hemingway, here is exquisitely fitted to the protagonist, who not only has, literally, a painter's eye but who must also cultivate it compulsively for his own emotional good, for by this practice an indifferent and disparate nature can be spatially disposed, 'a lot of the wickeds at large' can be blocked out or compositionally transformed, and his own griefs and guilts can be exorcised.

' "I've learned how to live by myself pretty well and I work hard" ' (25), Hudson tells a friend, and his hard work is not limited to his painting; he works hard to keep a general routine; to drink, fish, and party in planned segments, and to disallow, if he can, any untoward occasions which would drain his emotional resources. Even little pleasures are planned: Hudson puts away the Mainland newspaper 'to save it for breakfast'. The high point of his summer at Bimini is his sons' visit, but it is potentially the most draining. Knowing the customary disorderliness of youth allows him to prepare for a house disrupted by scattered clothing and fishing gear:

> When a man lives in a house by himself he gets very precise habits and they get to be a pleasure. But it felt good to have some of them broken up. He knew he would have his habits again long after he would no longer have the boys. (52)

But the inevitable results of his sons' high energy and spontaneity and their relational chemistry among themselves and others cannot of course be fully planned. Before the boys leave David narrowly escapes an attack by a hammerhead shark and undergoes a gruelling day trying to land a swordfish; and the emotional toll is greater for the damaged father than for the resilient son. By himself Hudson is unable to fill the customary parental role, which functionally is shared by not only Roger Davis, a kind of shadow version of Hudson and David's tutor in the fighting chair, but also Eddy, the alcoholic cook who kills the attacking shark when Hudson's aim proves faulty. What Hudson *can* do is to paint two pictures of David's fish that got away. This after-the-event tribute is anticipated during the action, when Hudson maintains his distance on the bridge, seeing David's ordeal from a 'foreshortened' perspective, and when, finally, after he descends to the 'same level as the action', his observation of his son's 'bloody hands and lacquered-looking oozing feet' (136) is more painterly than fatherly. Hemingway clearly intends the lack of discipline in Davis and Eddy to be more blatant versions of the disabling flaws that the protagonist only by great dint of effort has managed to control.

The cost is high. A life of enforced habits, of measured pleasures, is also a life of emotional barrenness, as we see in

Hudson's adjustment to the loss of his sons. No amount of self-discipline can fully prepare him for being hostage to fate, but it is the only kind of behaviour he knows. Despite having little 'interest in the game', he tells Eddy: ' "We'll play it out the way we can" ' (196). Aboard the *Île de France* the grief is blunted by drinking, reading, and exercising until he is tired enough to sleep. He also learns that *The New Yorker* is a magazine 'you can read on the fourth day after something happens' (200).

In both 'Cuba' and 'At Sea' the self-discipline is that of a zombie. Whatever bouts of pleasure were possible in 'Bimini' are nowhere in evidence in the second and third segments, but what is even more pronounced is the grim game itself. And although Hudson and his crew play the game reasonably well in their search for the Nazis, they make tactical mistakes that put the chasers at the mercy of the chased, and they impulsively kill rather than take prisoner a German sailor, an act that in Hudson's mind renders all their efforts useless.[10] From small details to the larger structure, most of what Hudson undertakes as action is substitutionary. He carries his .357 Magnum between his legs: ' "How long have you been my girl?" he said to his pistol'. And he uses it to blast a land crab on the beach who, like him, was doing nothing more than 'practicing . . . his trade' (316–17). 'There is no way for you to get what you need and you will never have what you want again', Hudson tells himself. 'But there are various palliative measures you should take' (282). These measures are talking to and sleeping with his favourite cat; long, ritualized drinking sessions at the Floridita; curiously detached sexual acts; and doing his 'duty'—service for the Navy. With his sons he can play the game of rummy for the shocked delectation of the tourists at Mr. Bobby's; without them at the Floridita he plays a cheerless game of the dignified rummy telling 'happy' stories to Honest Lil. To Hudson's credit nowhere does he engage in that most stereotyped palliative—talking out his grief. He tells Honest Lil: ' "Telling never did me any good. Telling is worse for me than not telling" ' (274). Rather his stories—fanciful concoctions—are aesthetic displacements; when he is forced into conversation about direct matters that hurt, the information is as sparse, oblique, and clipped as the speech rhythms.

117

One of Hemingway's devices for showing the desperate nature of these palliatives is the frequency of flashbacks. In 'Bimini', when he has the quiet joy of his sons' companionship, the memories of Paris are collaborative—young Tom remembers, too—but after their deaths Hudson's memories return more compulsively to the past—to happier days at the Finca and the exploits of his cats, to other love affairs, to earlier days in North Africa, the Middle East, and Europe. Despite the 'carapace of work' and doing his duty 'well', Hudson's is characteristically memorial living.

The Book of the Sea is of course about the author just as the most generative energy in all the previous books, fiction and non-fiction alike, had been autobiographical. Hemingway's dismay in 1952 that his simple story of Santiago was immediately read as parable and allegory of the author grown old, harassed by enemies but still equipped with the finest skills of his contemporaries, was understandably half-hearted and ambiguous. *The Old Man and the Sea* accurately, sensitively, depicts the psychological status of its author, whose view of human possibilities and whose devices for countering that gloomy assessment had not been changed by Depression America, Fascist Spain, or an entire World War. The logic behind the aesthetic of contest (big-game hunting, deep-sea fishing, bull-fighting) is precisely the fact that the chaos of living—with violence at its centre—can be mitigated only through human efforts to give it shape and purpose, that is, arbitrarily, by the imposition and acceptance of rules, pro-cedures, and conventions in which the playing of the game itself is its own significance. If there is any 'victory' in Santiago's story, it comes because the old fisherman plays out his given game with whatever determination and energy are left. The 'victory' in the Thomas Hudson story is even grim-mer, and its poignancy lies in the very closeness of protagonist and author.

Gregory Hemingway and James McLendon have shown the extent to which the novelist made use of his Caribbean experi-ences in the 1930s. Following his usual penchant for the techniques of the *roman à clef*, the method in *Islands in the Stream* is even more transparently autobiographical than it is in earlier work, most notably in his frank use of his wives and their sons, but also including the friends, bores, and islanders, even Honest Lil, the long-suffering whore who likes to hear happy stories, and the author's favourite cat that gets the honour of keeping his original name, Boise. Even the episode of the pig that commits suicide by swimming out to sea is based on an incident during 1943 when Gregory and Patrick stayed on Cayo Confites while their father took the armed *Pilar* on sub-scouting expeditions.[11] Commenting on the fact that the episode of David and the shark attack in *Islands in the Stream* stemmed from an incident involving himself, the younger son (rather than Patrick, the middle), Gregory Hemingway adds: 'Papa almost always changed the situation a little and usually improved on it slightly but mainly he used material that had actually happened.'[12]

We are now able to see the autobiographical basis of Hemingway's art with greater clarity than we were thirty years ago, but, more importantly, we are also able to see the logic behind that fact. With more intensity than most writers Hemingway wanted no biography written, no letters collected. He wanted only his published works to be read and admired. In retrospect this may have been an aesthetic instinct as well as personal choice. A biography must have struck him as redundant: he was all there, in better versions usually, in the works themselves. What is bothersome in the later fiction is the apparent loss of authorial judgement generally, such as the garrulous posturing of Hudson in 'Cuba'. But it is a weakness that appears as early as *Green Hills of Africa*, in which dramatic thrust is calculatedly cast aside in favour of an artificial 'interview' situation featuring a straight man and a Papa who knowingly pronounces his judgements on literature, sports, nature, and the meaning of life. It is a posture that recurs in *Across the River and Into the Trees* and, with minor adjustments, in *A Moveable Feast*; and the pattern establishes the basic autobiographical basis of Hemingway's art, so much so that Papa the Hunter, Colonel Cantwell, and Thomas Hudson are merely variations of a single identity; further, the Hemingway of Paris in the early 1920s is a variation, too. All these characters are projections, idealized figures put to the service of a writer whose

119

primary creative energy was necessarily his own life.

The emotional honesty especially evident in Thomas Hudson as self-portrait may not say as much for Hemingway's conscious judgement as for his psychological agony. But even here, at his most transparent, the matter of real life is usually adjusted into more shapely patterns than real life supplied, and the impulse behind the reshaping was aesthetic more than biographical: the need to show, not the need to conceal. Again, we have Gregory's testimony: 'My father had a tendency to improve on even the best of real stories.'[13] Hemingway's early traumatic experiences, his loves and hates, his wars, his sporting exploits, his sensitivity to place are recounted from *In Our Time* to *Islands in the Stream* in ways that are both auto-biographical and aesthetically artifactual. Finally he projected his best version of his own death in *Across the River and Into the Trees*, an event quintessentially Hemingway, since it dramatizes the extent to which man can control, shape, arrange that major moment that, except for suicides, lies beyond human agency.

NOTES

1. Philip Young, *Ernest Hemingway: A Reconsideration* (University Park and London: Pennsylvania State Univ. Press, 1966), p. 114.
2. Carlos Baker, *Ernest Hemingway: A Life Story* (New York: Scribner's, 1969), pp. 454–55, 460, 540.
3. 'The Dangerous Summer' appeared in *Life* in three successive numbers: 5, 12, 19 September 1960.
4. *Islands in the Stream* (New York: Scribner's, 1970), p. 237. Page references to subsequent quotations are included in the text.
5. For a full chronology of the composition, see Carlos Baker, *Hemingway: The Writer as Artist*, 4th edn. (Princeton: Princeton University Press, 1972), pp. 299–400; Baker, *Ernest Hemingway: A Life Story*, pp. 488–94; and Baker (ed.), *Ernest Hemingway: Selected Letters, 1917–61* (New York: Scribner's, 1981), pp. 574, 616, 719, 730–39.
6. Jackson J. Benson calls attention to the 'lacquered design' of the novel and the 'stylized role' of the old fisherman who too perfectly exemplifies the 'game code in action'. See *Hemingway: The Writer's Art of Self-Defense* (Minneapolis: University of Minnesota Press, 1969), pp. 172, 177. For a reading of *The Old Man and the Sea* as successful Christian tragedy, see Chapter 9 of Wirt Williams, *The Tragic Art of Ernest Hemingway* (Baton Rouge and London: Louisiana State University Press, 1981).

7. See, for example, Baker, *Ernest Hemingway: A Life Story*, p. 497.
8. Francis E. Skipp, 'Metempsychosis in the Stream, or What Happens in "Bimini"?' *Fitzgerald/Hemingway Annual*: 1974, 137.
9. The physical resemblance between Hudson and Davis is noted by Mr. Bobby. Hudson says they are no kin: 'We just used to live in the same town and make some of the same mistakes' (155).
10. In a letter of 13 June 1951, Hemingway refers to the fact that in the sea-chase the Nazi crew members 'out-class those who pursue them', who are 'sucked into one perfect, but underarmed, ambush'. See Baker (ed.), *Selected Letters*, p. 730.
11. Gregory H. Hemingway, *Papa: A Personal Memoir* (Boston: Houghton Mifflin, 1976), and James McLendon, *Papa: Hemingway in Key West* (Miami: E. A. Seemann, 1972), *passim*.
12. *Papa: A Personal Memoir*, p. 67.
13. *Papa: A Personal Memoir*, p. 29.

7

Essential History: Suicide and Nostalgia in Hemingway's Fictions

by ERIC MOTTRAM

> Reason is an instrument of thought and not thought itself.
> Above all, a man's thought is his nostalgia.
> —Albert Camus, *The Myth of Sisyphus*

1

Hemingway's fictions now demonstrate a nostalgia which bears the virus of its own destruction within the lingering, sometimes ecstatic death of inherited necessities of manliness in the twentieth century. The plots carry his imagination of figures who hold together configurations of possibility and potentiality—partly realized, partly to be realized—between nostalgia and malingering, triumph and defeat. They research a desire not to be indebted to overwhelming pressures from those ways in which the mass of men have been trained and coerced to live, and now choose to live, joining ruling-class wars and yelling at expensive spectator sports. Gradually, within the Hemingway work, the ageing hero spends his energies, and his money, if he has it, on a safari after beasts who test his remaining terrors, and a *finca* in Batista's Cuba, a resource barely placed within the poverty and tyranny his own

own nation actively supports. If he is to be sacrificed, it will not be in the cause of the ideologically polarized world but because he chooses that end as the only proposition conceivable in the existential world which he has decided to be the pattern and the process.

Gershon Legman's critical scorn was directed back in the 1940s[1] against Hemingway's censored sexual language, publicly expurgated in the texts, his need for 'a great deal of killing . . . before he can take his position as a man among men . . . the infliction of death not life', and his aggressive fear of women: 'women being too strong for him, the Hemingway hero has no other resource but . . . to castrate himself, or turn homosexual, or die and thus punish her. Suicide as revenge. In order to make his loss more deeply felt, however, he must first have had his woman climbing the wall with pleasure in his sexual prowess.' Hemingway reproduces the Christian West's myth that women destroy men and that men destroy women only in reprisal. Edmund Wilson's 1939 essay believes this to be Hemingway's version of Thurber's notorious *New Yorker* 'war between the sexes'—'a terrific fable of the impossible civilized woman who despises the civilized man for his failure in initiative and nerve, and then jealously tries to break him down as soon as he begins to exhibit any.'[2] Neither Legman nor Wilson attempt to organize their insights within the total production of American society's place in the West. The insight of Paul Hoch, for example, forty years later, when the nature of a possible dialectic of sexual liberation is fervently discussed, is not available to them.[3] At least Legman partly understands that the Hemingway male configuration generated his worldwide popularity: he confirms, he does not initiate. The fictions could be read as myths because his readers recognized his issues perfectly. Archetypes may only stand a chance of being destroyed by changes in political and social structure; Hemingway and his fans are not interested, having identified the myth with existence. In Rosenberg's terms for America in 1967: 'the ultimate mark of manliness [is] the readiness to die.'[4] American men '*play* manliness', 'actors in a charade of nostalgia'. By 1967 everyone sees through the performance. Hemingway's novels and stories, on the other hand, propose it as an existential necessity, far from Rosenberg's mocking of 'a new choice of male makeup', and the poem in e. e. cummings's *No Thanks* (1935) which mocks 'little Ernest' endlessly returning to 'the daydreams of boyhood'.

But such criticism misses the facts of propaganda, to use the term in Ellul's sense of social and political training: to masculinity modes.[5] The masculinity 'masquerade' is not nearly as obsolete as Rosenberg believed, even if the sexual polarization in which it is based is obviously 'an ideal of the frustrated, not a fact of biology'. Hemingway helped and helps many men, and probably women, too, to cherish archaic myths through literature, one of the main functions of fiction, television and film in the decaying twentieth century. His revolters, like Fitzgerald's and Faulkner's, do not revolt against society; in Rosenberg's words, they revolt into it. The more it repels them, the more they need to be in it. The popular media reinforce this form of revolt provided it does not take political or existential form: that is, provided the hero does not stand back from his impulses and abstract his conduct as an historical performance. Hemingway's *nada* can be closely related to the Existentialists' *néant*, as Killinger demonstrates,[6] but Rosenberg offers another interpretation, more secure in its political penetration, but still not simply cancelling the existentialist idea:

> The Nothing of the Existentialists represents the presence in the centre of contemporary experience of the proletarianized mass of civilized societies—a cultural proletariat produced by the 'decomposition of all classes'. . . . Is proof needed that the void of the Existentialists and the mystics is an historical phenomenon? Today, anyone who looks into himself is certain to discover there the debris of his class heritage in a desert of freedom and aimlessness without limit.

The Hemingway hero can still look into his needs within limits, the limits of popular masculinity in the current socialization of boys and men, but dignify them. It is as if the aims of dignity in Malraux (which Mailer absorbed as early as 'A Calculus at Heaven') were existentially fused into the kind of historicized view of the social anthropologist, Lionel Tiger, when he writes:[7]

Essential History: Suicide and Nostalgia in Hemingway's Fictions

The generalized conception of maleness, represented in such projective materials as films, advertisements, literature, and in the sexual composition of the controlling organizations of societies . . . suggest that the central concern or capacity of males for toughness, bravery, confident assertion, violence, and related phenomena is probably species-specific. This is understandable in phylogenetic terms, as well as through functional analysis of contemporary societies.

'Invalidation of maleness' recurs; renewing rites are set up. The drinking and smoking suggests to Tiger that 'the ingestion of a mild poison' is still a test of manliness (even when alcoholism and cigarette-induced cancer are commonplace, it must be added) as well as more obvious warrior vestiges. But Tiger omits the capitalist necessity of creating and maintaining addictive substances and activities—the junk, to use William S. Burroughs' accurate terms, to which the consumer is endlessly sold. So that 'invalidation' is never simply existentialist *or* socio-political *or* anthropological. Hemingway's fictions may deal with the junk of maleness but his heroes do not invent their routines, their needs and their groups. Part of his popularity is his identification of non-bonded or aggressionless men as weaklings, vulnerable in the sense that Melville's bachelors so often are, except that they move more rapidly out of the invalidating group towards suicide and other forms of victimization. (It is Hunilla who survives, not Bartleby or Cereno.) The burden of imposed male performance is so great after the first World War that Hemingway can display his plots of nostalgia, survival and suicide without overt psychological and political analysis. They are romances (in Hawthorne's sense) of masculine validations breaking down into the varieties of death. In American romance artists can survive—Ishmael, the hero of 'A Descent into the Maelstrom' and Thomas Hudson. Scarred and grizzled, with the haunted grasp of an Ancient Mariner, they tell survival tales until they, too, yield their lives to a death within validation, hunters and soldiers and sailors whose quarries and campaigns are compulsive work seeking dignification.

Josephine Herbst's beautiful memoir shows Hemingway in Barcelona always slipping away to write (he is also engaged in Joris Ivens's Civil War film). He first greets her with 'How are

125

you Josie? I'll never forgive you for letting that sixty-pound king off your line', with his arms around her and 'a big kiss'. But she knows why he and the other men are there—beyond political duty: 'If I sometimes felt that the scene where I stood or where I sat was a stage set due to vanish the next moment, it was because the players, with their sunburnt faces, were the actors of the moment who were concealing some of the real life in their role as soldiers. But none of them was trying to live up to any heroic image of the soldier; their modesty was one of their most engaging traits.' Herbst then adds that 'Hemingway also wanted to be *the* war writer of his age and he knew it and went toward it. War gave answers that could not be found in that paradise valley of Wyoming where he had fished or even in the waters of Key West when the tarpon struck. What was the deepest reality *there* was in an extreme form *here*, and to get it he had to be in it and he knew it.'

The limits of this engagement are also clear: no psychological analysis or political consequences. 'He seemed to be naïvely embracing on the simpler levels the current ideologies at the very moment when Dos Passos was urgently questioning them.' But this, as Herbst understands, was part of the validating process:

> There was a kind of splurging magnificence about Hemingway at the [Hotel] Florida, a crackling generosity whose underside was a kind of miserliness. He was stingy with his feelings to anyone who broke his code, even brutal, but it is only fair to say that Hemingway was never anything but faithful to the code he set up for himself. . . . Part of his exuberance came from the success of his love affair (with Martha Gellhorn). . . . When you passed Hemingway's room, you heard the busy sound of his typewriter pecking away.

But writers have to validate themselves as men, so Hemingway played the role of reporter, the brave man on the spot, who, with the private eye, had largely supplanted the Mississippi river-boat pilot and the soldier after the American Civil War and with the advent of the national popular press and press photography; a figure unquestioned in authenticity if the reported scene edged validly towards death. The soldier cannot write. Robert Jordan is fully occupied with his war: 'It is not you

who decides what shall be done. You follow orders. Follow them
and do not try to think beyond them.' He is defined: 'My mind
is in suspension until we win the war.' He moves death by
choice, a suicide within what Stephen Crane called both 'the
subtle battle brotherhood . . . a mysterious fraternity' and 'a
moving box', within which Fleming is 'capable of profound
sacrifices, a tremendous death. He had no time for dissec-
tions. . . .' The result in character Fitzgerald neatly drew
together in his letter to Hemingway in December 1927[9]:

> Please write me at length about your adventures—I hear you
> were seen running through Portugal in used B.V.D.'s, chewing
> ground glass and collecting material for a story about boule
> players; that you were publicity man for Lindbergh; that you
> have finished a novel a hundred thousand words long consisting
> entirely of the word 'balls' used in new groupings; that you have
> been naturalized a Spaniard, dress always in a wine-skin with
> 'zipper' vent and are engaged in bootlegging Spanish Fly
> between St. Sebastian and Biarritz where your agents sprinkle
> it on the floor of the Casino. I hope I have been misinformed
> but, alas!, it all has too true a ring.

But Fitzgerald's appreciative irony has to be placed within the
social pressures. In Ellul's words, 'Propaganda played on the
most elementary drives to make a man engage wholeheartedly
in combat.'[10] Paul Hoch's fourth chapter opens with a useful
configuration of citations from Wilhelm Stekel, Henry Miller,
Fitzgerald and Hemingway for 'masculinity as a defense
against impotence!' In Chapter 7 of *Tropic of Cancer*, the
narrator begs Van Norden to give up trying to cure his
impotence on a whore. Hoch does not provide the full context
in Miller—it's one of the finest pieces of counter-propaganda
against masculinity impositions, and one of the few:

> It's exactly like a state of war—I can't get it out of my head.
> The way she works over me, to blow a spark of passion into me,
> makes me think what a damned poor soldier I'd be if I was ever
> silly enough to be trapped like this and dragged to the front. I
> know for my part that I'd surrender everything, honour included,
> in order to get out of the mess. . . . There are some of us so
> cowardly that you can't even make heroes of us, not even if you
> frighten us to death. We know too much, may be. There are some
> of us who don't live in the moment, who live a little ahead, or a

little behind. My mind is on the peace treaty all the time. . . .

    Van Norden seems to have a more normal attitude about
it. . . . It seems to call for a show of mettle—his manhood is
involved . . . not just manhood perhaps, but will. It's like a man
in trenches again: he doesn't know any more why he should go on
living, because if he escapes now he'll only be caught later, but he
goes on just the same, and even though he has the soul of a
cockroach and has admitted as much to himself, give him a gun
or a knife or even his bare nails, and he'll go on slaughtering and
slaughtering, he'd slaughter a million men rather than stop and
ask himself why.

    As I watch Van Norden tackle her, it seems to me that I'm
looking at a machine whose cogs have slipped. . . . He's like a
hero come back from the war, a poor maimed bastard living out
the reality of his dreams. . . . Only between the time he went to
sleep and the time he woke up, his body was stolen.

Stolen, that is, by that other machine: official masculinity
invalidation. Hoch quotes Stekel—'The frigid woman and the
impotent man are the products of a diseased age. Impotence is
a *social* disorder' (*Impotence in the Male*)—and, without quoting
it, cites the pathetic episode in *A Moveable Feast*, 'A Matter of
Measurements', misusing it to infer Fitzgerald's mere obsession
with penis measurements, rather than Zelda's mean inferences
as to his powers. But the obsessions are certainly there in a
general messy way. We need to add the 1936 confrontation
between Miller and Orwell in 1936, recorded in 'Inside the
Whale' (1940).[12] *Tropic of Cancer* appeared when 'the Italians
were marching into Abyssinia and Hitler's concentration-
camps were already bulging', but beneath its apparent political
irrelevance this book 'broke down, at any rate momentarily, the
solitude in which the human being lives'. Orwell understands
clearly that Miller's international readership—and in this he
does move with Hemingway—is partly founded on his recognition of existential solitude and the limits of its dissolution.
Where Hemingway's hero needed an extreme situation and a
small band of fighter followers, Miller's needs male friendship
and a frank examination of the need for heterosexual relationships, both exhilarating and exhausting. Orwell 'felt the
peculiar relief that comes not so much from understanding as
from *being understood*'; Miller 'dealt with the recognizable

experiences of human beings'. If the writing meant exile, the results were liberating, and especially the 'callous coarseness' of the language Miller's characters used, 'a spoken language, but spoken *without fear*'.

But the nature of existential acceptance differs in the two writers. Miller is nearer Whitman's active passivity and unwarlike 'adhesiveness', but still speaking to that majority sense of the fundamentals of existence. Most men do not feel that they are masters of their fate; to them Miller's 'sex and truthfulness' came as relief. But his opposition to war and the Spanish Civil War in particular was not passive at all:

> He merely told me in forcible terms that to go to Spain at that moment was the act of an idiot. He could understand anyone going there from purely selfish motives, out of curiosity, for instance, but to mix oneself up in such things from a sense of obligation was sheer stupidity. . . . Our civilization was destined to be swept away and replaced by something so different that we should scarcely regard it as human.

Miller would have probably approved of Hemingway's going to the Civil War for his own personal needs, and certainly both men adopt a moderately stoic tone when considering the fate of having been born into the twentieth century. Unlike Miller, Hemingway does not regard a man as helpless in war as some kind of daft situation bringing *thanatos* unnecessarily nearer. Both men, though, engage in what Orwell calls a 'non-co-operative' attitude towards the century's disintegrations: it is there in Hemingway's variable sense of the evil of fascism in *For Whom the Bell Tolls* and *Islands in the Stream*. That possibility was and is another source of Hemingway's popularity, a commitment to neither Left nor Right which the ideologue loathes and distrusts. Both these Americans are 'inside the whale', enduring and recording, in Orwell's terms; they are not spuriously engaged in 'more positive, "constructive" lines' against 'world-power'.

Miller's man needs apparently endless lateral engagements with women and men as revolt against the political and social enclosure. Hemingway's needs other victories over self and society, and a different kind of acceptance and revolt pattern is offered, recognizably related to Camus's astonishingly dignified terms in that section of *The Myth of Sisyphus* entitled 'Absurd Freedom'[13]:

> Living an experience, a particular fate, is accepting it fully. ... To abolish conscious revolt is to elude the problem. The theme of permanent revolution is thus carried into individual experience. Living is keeping the absurd alive. Keeping alive is above all contemplating it ... [Metaphysical revolt] is that constant presence of man in his own eyes. It is not aspiration, for it is devoid of hope. That revolt is the certainty of a crushing fate, without the resignation that ought to accompany it.
>
> It may be thought that suicide follows revolt—but wrongly. For it does not represent the logical outcome of revolt. It is just the contrary by the consent it presupposes. Suicide, like the [existential] leap, is acceptance at its extreme. Everything is over and man returns to his essential history. His future, his unique and dreadful future—he sees and rushes towards it ... the absurd cannot be settled. It escapes suicide to the extent that it is simultaneously awareness and rejection of death.
>
> That revolt gives life its value. Spread out over the whole length of life, it restores its majesty to that life. To a man devoid of blinkers, there is no finer sight than that of the intelligence at grips with a reality that transcends it.

This is the fine context for Hemingway's explorations of the necessity of an extreme situation in which to achieve dignified definition (how it places Miller is another matter). His romances of decision to be or not to be authentic refuse *la mauvaise foi*, and therefore must be romances of isolation, as they have to be in Hawthorne and Melville—romances of heroes who are not full patriots or responsible to an ideologically formulated foundation or institution *they have not joined*, as Thoreau would say. The Spanish War became a vehicle for opportunities of self-definition and to find stories through which to become and remain a 'champion',[14] just as Hemingway's last disquisition on the bullfighters, *The Dangerous Summer*, presents the arena as the necessary scene for the maintenance of 'perfect nerves, judgment, courage and art'. In 1960 Lorca's 'Llanto por Ignacio Sánchez Mejías' is mentioned but not the concept of *duende*, a dionysian urge to risk by transcending old forms.[15] The *duende* prevents the repetition of forms, drives artists to 'find something new and totally unprecedented that could give lifeblood and art to bodies devoid of expressiveness'. Hemingway may stand, in Lorca's terms, at 'the very rim of the well . . . the rim of the wound', but he uses old forms, identifying the traditional moves of the bullfight with the art of writing—explicitly the way Ordonez 'always called the *faena* writing'. For all these American conservative anarchists, courage and cowardice are the products of the private isolated man moving within the box of the public evaluation of morality, particularly the pattern of guilt and shame revealed in the extreme situation. Hemingway's sometimes even take the tone of devotional tracts dedicated to the theology of a secularized holy dying, fulfilling something of the requirements of Heidegger's *das Sein zum Tode*, or being in a time process towards a death so anticipated that it appears as a decision, in a sense a suicidal life projected away from the fulfilments of domesticity, politics and ideology. Just as the sexual focus in Miller verges towards Heidegger's concept, so the Nick Adams stories turn on death prevented from suicide by lonely decisions, with a father's suicide as an example to be avoided ('Fathers and Sons' is extended into Robert Jordan's resistance).

But the need to repeat elements of the absurd, in art and in welcomes for the extreme situation, become addictive variants of the same hyperactivity, common in sportsmen, warriors, professional riskers of all kinds, and heroin fixers. Of Santiago, Hemingway writes: 'Now he was proving it again. Each time was a new time and he never thought about the past when he was doing it.' For Jordan the key is the 'now, ahora, maintenant, heute' of the addictive Absurd; bravery is an unsharable power; the repetition of the freedom to kill animals, rather than human beings, is a singular necessity—'Killing is not a feeling that you share' (*Green Hills of Africa*). These are the limits of the leader in the crew or guerrilla band or in any society. The resulting *aficionado* and white hunter are aristocrats of existential differentiation from the mass of men who despairingly adjust to their contingent condition. The only complication in *aficion* is that the ritual of skills should shed the complications of the social and political. The islands in the stream, and the fishing and combat around them and on them, must be clear, as far as possible, clear of social and domestic elements, even nostalgia for elegant wives and fine sons in the mould of their father's ideals. Existential desire must finally stand a part.

But the dream of the tribal in *Green Hills of Africa* was a possible way through, by reducing to a male hunting clan, complete with insignia of scarification. Sensibly, it is rejected: it is as impossible to be a Masai as a White Negro. It is not a tribe the hero needs but a fraternity for immediate action. And, to modify Legman's accusations, women certainly appear condoned as tribal or ritual adjuncts, discardable for the most part when the rites are over, and when they are not Marjorie, in 'The End of Something', and her variants, women of complicated knowledge (it is probably not too remote to ally them with the dark and intelligent women over whom male judges stand in Hawthorne). To Hemingway the complex informed intellect may well move towards the vulnerable, the female in his popular scheme of erotic and behavioural polarities. It is therefore highly male to fear losing innocence and simplicity, which takes the later form of that pared down declarative language which Lillian Ross calls his 'Indian Talk' and his fascination with the Macomber type of boy-man who fears what he considers to be soul fat ('The Snows of Kilimanjaro') that hinders being in a state of sole excitement. The moment of 'pure excitement' ('The Short Happy Life of Francis Macomber') is rejuvenating, a sort of Ponce de Leon fountain of youth, whether in Florida or elsewhere (there is an American literary and cultural history of the search for an elixir of youth). And it is obvious that in the fictions pure means clean which means simplified, a main direction his heroic lives must assume.

Krebs's desire for no complications can be compared to Catherine's remark in *A Farewell to Arms*: 'I wasn't crazy in a complicated manner.' This draws her towards Frederick in staving off the enclosing existential contingency: 'You always feel trapped biologically.' Sex has to be with someone else and can only be useful for 'pure excitement' or the moment of 'now' between Maria and Jordan as they work out their religous names. But the ideal is again Santiago within his romance of a man 'too simple to wonder when he had attained humility', humility being the farther shore of pure and clean.

Being 'spooked', a key expression in *Islands in the Stream*, is akin to Hemingway's other deleterious conditions—feeling bad, feeling nausea, feeling sick, all those moments of moral-physical repugnance, repulsions from those who do not challenge the biological trap, who complicate by thought, cowardice and brutality: and tendencies to such conditions in the hero's own self. Death cannot be risked in a state of impurity. Hemingway's ideal is a warrior ideal in many cultures, the zen-samurai condition of cleansed worth and the state of the warrior in Don Juan Matus's remnants of Yaqui tradition. Ritual gives form to the mess of human existence. Curiously enough, a key formulation of brave confrontation with death, quoted or paraphrased, Hemingway drew from *Henry IV* Part 2 (III.2) (the origin in Milan is given in section 6 of Carlos Baker's biography), part of the Elizabethan nostalgia for a medieval warrior definition. Except that Shakespeare gives the words to Feeble, a poor press-ganged recruit, ideally cleared of cant by his condition:

> By my troth, I care not; a man can die but once; we owe God a death; I'll ne'er bear a base mind: an't be my destiny, so; an't be not, so: no man's too good to serve his prince; and, let it go which it will, he that dies this year is quit for the next.

It is such clarity that supports John's remark to Nick Adams in 'An Alpine Idyll': 'It's no good doing a thing too long.' But the *de la muerte* passage in Chapter 19 of *For Whom the Bell Tolls* is different from Lorca's *duende* because it is superstitious and linked to *nada*. The odour of death was so strong on Manolo 'that it created sickness and fear in others—*Pues nada*. There is nothing to do.' For Pilar it is akin to the dog's ability to sniff out what a man cannot. To Jordan's scepticism she counters the centre of it: the old women of the Puente de Toledo who 'drink the blood of the beasts that are slaughtered'; kiss one, and you will know the odour. It is there, too, in dead chrysanthemums and prostitutes' paraphernalia in a gunny sack on a damp autumn day: 'In this sack will be contained the essence of it all, both the dead earth and the dead stalks of the flowers and their rotted blooms and the smell that is both the death and the birth of man. Thou wilt wrap this sack around thy head and try to breath through it.' This stifling version of the biological trap is nearer the erotics of Bataille's fictions than Lorca, and bizarre and vaguely pornographic compared with his precisions. In Lorca, as we noted earlier, the *duende* emerges from skill in arts practised with peculiar triumphant power which overwhelms the experiencer: 'a power, not a work . . . a struggle, not a thought . . . it is not a question of ability, but of true, living style, of blood, of the most ancient culture, of spontaneous creation.' A pre-Christian daemon is fought for perfection in art: 'he burns the blood like a poultice of broken glass, he exhausts, he rejects all the sweet geometry we have learned, he smashes styles and makes Goya (master of the greys, silvers, and pinks of the best English painting) work with his fists and knees with horrible bitumins. . . . The *duende*'s arrival always means a radical change in forms.'[16] Death to the artists of *duende* is the destruction of old forms. Hemingway invented one form, the declarative sentence: his models were De Maupassant, Stendhal, Flaubert, Tolstoy and other great nineteenth-century fictionists, and Conrad above all.[17] And compared with the *duende* artist, Hemingway is elegiac and stoic rather than active for confrontation with that restructuring that comes, says Lorca, not from the muse or the angel, but from the demon. The muse turns to epitaphs and the angel 'flies in slow circles and weaves, from tears of narcissus and ice, the elegy we have seen tremble in the hands of Keats . . . and Jiménez'. In the bullfight the *duende*'s artist fights both death and 'geometry—measurement, the very basis of the festival'.

Like Hemingway, Lorca identifies 'the moment of the kill' with 'artistic truth', but with this difference: it is not a question of impressing an audience with bravery but with 'a lesson in Pythagorean music' which transcends 'vulgar' performances of courage. Hemingway noted some of this in Madrid in 1923 but insists on placing it within the only convention he had been trained to fit it, tragedy:[18]

> Bullfighting is not a sport . . . It is a tragedy. . . . The tragedy is the death of the bull. It is played out in three definite acts.
> It must all be done gracefully, seemingly effortlessly and always with dignity. The worst criticism the Spaniards ever make of a bullfighter is that his work is 'vulgar'.

It is not unfair to say that this is a vulgarization of the event, however much needed for an available scene of post-war recovery in Hemingway's early resistance movement without

134

written protest texts and counter-ideologies. 'Bravery' he needed, like 'pride', to be cleared of pollution. The two qualities must produce that *pundonor* (Chapter 9 in *Death in the Afternoon*) which relieves death of confusion. But again Hemingway, unlike Lorca (and in view of his *Tauromachia*, we can include Picasso), isolates the arena:

> Bullfighting is the only art in which the artist is in danger of death and in which the degree of brilliance in the performance is left to the fighter's honour. . . . Called pundonor, it means honour, probity, courage, self-respect, and pride in one word. Pride is the strongest characteristic of the race and it is a matter of pundonor not to show cowardice. . . . Having lost his honour he goes along living through his contracts, hating the public he fights for. . . . There is honour among pickpockets and honour among whores. It is simply that standards differ.

The relationship between Thomas Hudson and Honest Lil shows something of Hemingway's meaning here, and the bartender turning into a Feeble for Cantwell in Chapter 6 of *Across the River and Into the Trees*: 'Better to live one day as a lion than a hundred years as a sheep.' Cantwell's version is: 'Better to die on our feet than to live on our knees.' For Jordan it is opposition to 'heroic resignation'. The suicidal hyena eats its own intestines (*Green Hills of Africa*); the Indian husband cuts his throat ('Indian Camp'); Jordan's father commits suicide— 'You have to be awfully occupied with yourself to do a thing like that' (Chapter 30). But then we have the soldier's reduction of the crucified Christ to a death-defying sportsman—'He was pretty good in there today' ('Today is Friday'), and all those Hemingway malingerers including the self-castrated boy in 'God Rest You Merry Gentlemen'. Hyenas and castrates have no brotherhood, nor does Christ. Jordan and Hudson have their fraternal bands. (For all the fraternity between bullfighters in *The Dangerous Summer*, it is a bonding of suicidal *isolatoes*.) Hemingway is explicit on the necessity for such an authenticity (a typical existential term) in *For Whom the Bell Tolls*:

> . . . a feeling of consecration to a duty toward all of the oppressed of the world which would be as difficult and embarrassing to speak about as religious experience and yet it was authentic as

the feeling you had when you heard Bach or stood in Chartres Cathedral or the Cathedral at Leon and saw the light coming through windows; or when you saw Mantegna and Greco and Brueghel in the Prado. It gave you a part in something that you could believe in wholly and completely and in which you felt an absolute brotherhood with the others who were engaged in it . . . your death seemed of complete unimportance; only a thing to be avoided because it would interfere with the performance of your duty.

Hemingway is one of the very few writers who know and say outright that such knowledge of creative art within fraternity is the moral core of society, and not some spurious ideological programmatic coercion, or some temporary terrorism or guru grouping.[19] Jordan's resistance to Goltz's orders is halted when he considers 'you are an instrument to do your duty.' And this includes Maria, just as in *A Farewell to Arms* someone loved is value for Frederick Henry and Count Greffi. The beloved must be objectifiable as instrument in the group. Even Thomas Hudson, who admits his mistakes in the field of love and marriage, still requires his first wife to be objectified in this way. Hemingway edges dangerously near that connoisseurship of women which damns Gilbert Osmond and practically perjures Adam Verver within James's 'communities of doom'.[20] But in fact, at least in this immediate context, he avoids it. It could even be said that Cantwell directs Renata's life just because she is both passionate and intelligent, and needs to be within the security of a dutiful band as a dutiful daughter. Maria and Jordan become 'as one animal in the forest', so that *one* and *now* are the terms for a mutual separate peace: 'there will never be a separable one.' For the cause, the duty, the object, they belong to the guerrilla group, yet Jordan must die as *one*—'each one must do it alone.' Such is Hudson's position of decision within his crew. He and his wife repeat Catherine's description of necessity in *A Farewell to Arms*: 'they love each other and they misunderstand on purpose and they fight and then suddenly they aren't the same one.' Jake Barnes's band is smaller and far less organized, and his wound limits complications of surrender with Brett. Sexual consummation is replaced by a supportive code of duty. Brett does not attempt to rival Jake in the manner of Mrs. Macomber.

Hemingway is disinclined to detail sexual intercourse, the orgasmic moment, but it is still there, intrinsic to love creating the existential *now* which makes *nada* bearable. Equally, he does not detail the fact that it is there with whores too—again the exception, possibly, is Honest Lil, but she is really another objective ideal: the woman as sex object whom the man can use *and* respect but re-create as both an uncomplicated detachment and part of the band.

It is commonplace to say that Hemingway inherits a long recognition that sex and death resemble each other by climaxing in a totalitarian simplicity. The alternative simplicity in politics and religion is a bigotry Hemingway did not commit. *The Fifth Column* shows, according to Hemingway, the necessity of fanaticism. Philip Rawlings, an Anglo-American Communist secret police agent works for the Republicans, but has a philosophical ulterior motive—'We're in for fifty years of undeclared wars, and I've signed up for the duration'—and of the girl who wants to marry him, Dorothy Bridges, Hemingway wrote: 'her name might also have been Nostalgia.' It is not an entirely creditable text, and Edmund Wilson's hefty criticisms are probably correct.[21] He even has Jordan observe, after his sexual acts, 'his mind was much clearer and cleaner on that business. Bigotry is an odd thing. To be bigoted you have to be absolutely sure you are right and nothing makes that surety and righteousness like continence. Continence is the foe of heresy.' Jordan aims therefore at that happy balance which still obsesses Hudson: 'the negation of apprehension that often turned into an actual happiness before action' (Chapter 39). But the ability to achieve it is 'destroyed by too much responsibility for others or the necessity of undertaking something ill planned or badly conceived'. When he and Maria are 'everything', he himself and death are 'nothing': *nada* is subsumed in a simplicity which makes clear decision possible and satisfying.

If Hemingway's fiction now reads as a long act of nostalgia for a world in which, if a man 'has balls', he is a man without prejudicial complexity, the texts continue to take place within a scarcely dying pattern of male needs. He uses 'cojones' partly still for the same reasons that he writes 'mucking' for 'fucking', but partly because he wants to separate a concept—just as he uses *nada* rather than 'nothing'. The sacred castrate, Jake

Barnes, could not be repeated (it is nearly as 'vulgar' as Lawrence's fiddling with Clifford Chatterly). Sexual inability and intellectual creativity in one body is too complicated. 'The lad who sought eunuch-hood' ('God Rest You Merry Gentlemen') is a different proposition—a boy betrayed by the Church into believing an erection to be a sign and source of lust, 'a sin against purity'. His case is an emergency not in Doctor Wilcox's *The Young Doctor's Friend and Guide*, and it takes place on Christmas Day. Systems, especially when they interlock, corrupt absolutely.

2

So the risk of death is life-promoting but suicidal. Hemingway's romances enact the dream of ideal male self-definition released from work and family. The search is for the elixir of youth and for a state of engulfing happiness, however momentary. The writer who spends so much of his life sitting down, creating, writing and revising, composes fictions of parallel activity which fulfils duty and resists social and sexual coercion. The aim is always happiness, as much as it is in the writings of Thomas Paine. The neurosis of killing mammals and fish is said, in *Green Hills of Africa*, to be a state of being 'altogether happy'. Yet the book is nervous and anxious. There appears to be little force in the diagnosis that the fictions mask a need for virility demonstration which amounts, in its persistence, to a fear of homosexuality, because, given the emphasis on male dominances and male bonding in western societies, most men enact this condition automatically, one way or another. When polar masculinity is an ideal which cannot remotely become a fact, and homosexualities are not, for many men, considered to be possible definitions of masculinity, social and personal anxieties are endemic. Hemingway's fictions take place in an interface between social documentation and imaginary idealism which Hawthorne called 'a neutral territory . . . where the Actual and the Imaginary may meet, and each imbue itself with the nature of the other'. Far from being exceptional or even chosen, this ground is the region of our day to day lives, including our sexual programmes and the scenes we enact them in. If art is feared as an unmasculine activity within the false polarizations which assign sexual category to work and profession, the writer may well mask himself in order to work freely in 'neutral territory'. In 'The Snows of Kilimanjaro', the leopard dies the clean death of the socially uncomplicated—the tribal, even—'dried and frozen'; the writer dies a dirty death; the wife is merely superstitiously aggressive—'What have we done to have that happen to us?' (that is, the gangrene leg)—and archaic, using images of medieval chivalry for her husband. The snow is the equivalent of the clean café in 'A Clean, Well-Lighted Place', the snow of the writer's memories of Europe before wealth got to him, the white walls of his family house, and the peak where he will join the animal in legendary death.

In a state of hallucination, the writer is not willing his frozen paradise but recognizing it. He is beyond the hero's usual acts of will to conquer guilt, shame, fear and the sense of waste. He is as clean of ideology as Hemingway in 1935 (the story appeared in *Esquire* in 1936) when he wrote 'Who Murdered the Vets?' for *New Masses*. Like the writer in the story, he has needed both loving admiration and solitude, personal victory and a small society of friends. He is typical of many men and women trained to such consciousness, but he is not typical in one characteristic: apart from elements in the early Indian stories, his masculinity pressures do not include the requirement and assumption that white manhood can be achieved by oppressing the darker man. The dark bull, but not the Negro. Nor can his beasts be called dragons in order to shove them inside the dominance system's archetypes—Theseus, St. George, Perseus, Billy the Kid. . . . As the acceptances of male domination begin to erode in this century, Hemingway plays out war, war between the sexes, hunt and bullfight as a romance to obtain purity of existence. His plots contain such obvious nostalgia that their historicity is clear; hence their popularity. But between suicidal nostalgia desires lies the further stage—the elimination of other cancerous dominances, hierarchies and hegemonies. Hemingway's fictions do not look forward since they yearn for repression, and their historic wars and hunts and sports are, like all such desires, part of history as the return of the repressed. His heroes step outside the competitive machine of 'capitalist democracy' and try for 'the personal life', and then the strains of living up to ideals of archetypal dominance become the substance of his plots. The dominant male is dominated by the role. The result is suicidal nostalgic romance, inviting spectators more than participators, and devoted to paying off debts to the archetypal in order to maintain self-respect and reputation, quite as much, in another mode, a Arthur Miller's tortured men—Willy Loman, John Proctor, Eddie Carbone, Gay Langland and Perse Howland, and Quentin, the lawyer. As they move from youth to middle age or patriarchalism, these men cannot resist risking suicide for 'good name', a term to place with Hemingway's honour and pride in *pundonor*. Pilar, the guerrilla embodiment of the matriarch only becomes the Q-ship of *Islands in the Stream*.

Hemingway, then, explores how to make a life and a work out of the decaying body of the history of male prerogatives. Sometimes it is pathetic, like the idea that bulls are brave, and 'what the hell does a fighting cock like to do?' (A British Tory is on record for opining that if a fox could vote he would vote Tory.) Robert Cantwell can't be well and cants well, dying in Venice, the extreme opposite of war in its commerce, architecture, music and painting—the social value just about present in *Across the River and Into the Trees*. But the continued insistence that ordinary actions as well as the exceptional should be done 'truly' and well fights off incipient mediocrity, the fear that will and skill might degenerate into a life with no bulwarks against social and personal death. Renata is re-born, as her name suggests, but it is temporary. Pride is redemptive within the programme of the book, provided it is the product of rearguard actions for truth and self-awareness: in Santiago's words for his fish, 'You killed him for pride and because you are a fisherman'—and for himself: 'Man is not made for defeat. A man can be destroyed but not defeated.'

But, necessarily, paranoia encroaches on what is essentially an entropic vision of decreased and threatened opportunities. Kept at bay, the enemy is all around, and often only as semi-visible as in *Islands in the Stream*, and it is this novel which of course represents the limits of Hemingway's theatre of survivals. The aims are clear: to 'exorcize guilt with work'; to 'learn how not to get married'; to maintain 'discipline' and the hedonistic calculus in balance; to be alone and yet to control loneliness and not be 'spooked' by it; to make sure your sons inherit skills, the styles of pleasure through training in sport and art; to understand that 'sharks' and 'bad things in the ocean' are always present; to recognize 'luck'—and this covers the unknown and undeveloped elements in Hudson's sons, curtailed by accident and war—is also required for happiness, and that happiness is partly social and partly the ego at its pleasures; that 'good', too, is both social and personal in its feeling processes (Hemingway fortunately never completely relinquished the hedonistic calculus that defines good as feeling good).[22]

Hudson's luck and choice meet in his having made painting his work and still have fine sons. He can afford the 'wonder' (106) of the fishing scene in part 1, Chapter 9, a late victory of style in Hemingway's career (96 ff). Disciplined hedonism is carefully accounted for—painting, fishing, writing. The exaggerations of the boys is countered by gentle, fine training from the men, particularly in David's ordeal—'bloody hand and lacquered-looking oozing feet . . . the welts the harness had made across his back and the almost helpless expression on his face as he turned his head at the last finish of the pull' (119). The disciplines are neither puritan nor stoic but the existential conditions for a non-reductive life. Even if David at one point 'works like a machine, or like a very tired boy performing as a machine' (118), he is not alone 'in the dark and the cold' (116). Nor is his failure tragedy: as Hudson says of Eddy's condition in chapter 11, it is not tragic because he is happy. Eddy and David are simple; Roger Davis is 'more complicated', dogged by 'bad carelessness' (and 'careless' is also a main critical term in Fitzgerald).

If the language of being 'brave and good' (147) does edge into parody, it is because the condition and its terms are tense under the behavioural surfaces of calm, a calm the prose demonstrates at crucial points in the narrative. If the conversation of the men and boys shifts, at moments of tension and unease, into the ritualistic mode, it is because ritual is a repetitive surface of gestures which enclose the dangers of chaos, parallel to the hedonistic control from skills. Their conversational manners ensure community without undue mutual interrogation. Wary mutual explorations avoid hurting each other and becoming too probing. 'Let's not talk about it' infers limits to analysis, as if they were raw and recovering. The car accident to David and Andrew is not, as some imperceptive critics have decided, a Hemingway repetition of disaster caused by women; it is part of the accidental, the chance, the condition of luck, which only the surface of ritual can help to make bearable. The risks of Bimini constitute a safety area, as France and Paris cannot be— Europe rarely is in the fictions (the exceptions are the primitive Abruzzi village and the agrarian Pamplona, special regions of nostalgia).

Part Two moves forward to World War II in the waters between Florida and Cuba to enable Hudson's skills to be employed in Q-boat warfare—a hunt for Nazis rather than fish, although the images of cold darkness, the ocean predators, the existential, irreducible evil, remain. Hudson loses his remaining son, a pilot: 'there isn't any solution', except to learn from the pathetic cat, Boise, how to 'relax awfully well' (180). Hudson's 'love' for Boise is a recognition of the cat's helplessness in semi-domestication, upon which the wild insists on encroaching. *Islands in the Stream* seals in Hemingway's lifelong theme of the destructions human life is heir to, and the need, therefore, to achieve calm, through discipline, relaxation, art, against them. If the books are impregnated with a fear of cowardice and lonely disaster—nervous breakdown, suicide— it is because these states undermine the safety of brave risks. The risks include falling in love—a kind of luck, since women embody the invariable variable which is exciting: mutual courting in Hemingway is a skill among others to enable the ego to enter a society.

But this part of the novel only just holds down nostalgia for happiness. The opportunity for suicide, like an insidious gas, penetrates intolerable conditions against which discipline and relaxation cannot prevail. The arts become part of therapy— Hudson's Gris, for example (208): '*Nostalgia hecha hombre*, he thought in Spanish. People did not know you died of it. Across the room, above the bookcase, was Paul Klee's *Monument in Arbeit* (*sic*). He didn't love it as he loved the *Guitar Player* but he loved to look at it and he remembered how corrupt it had seemed when he first bought it in Berlin.' Outside the room is the sea, the existential Other in nature, like the chestnut tree in *La Nausée*, complete and indifferent, but to Hudson necessary:

'You know you love the sea and would not be anywhere else. . . . She is not cruel or callous nor any of that *Quatsch*. She is just there and the wind moves her and they fight on her surface but down below none of it matters.' On that surface, Hudson has to exert 'so much sense' that the house, the paintings and Boise are nearly a nervous liability.

The other given, or basic data, is the poverty of Cuba, which has none of the nostalgic security of the Abruzzi or Pamplona (215, 219). It is not presented historically but as the datum, part of the world in which Tom is killed, his athletic skills useless in the chance of war as an example of existence. Both are part of that 'grief' which 'doesn't split' (238), of the state of Honest Lil, whom the men respect when they have 'loved her at some time in the last twenty-five years . . . a beautiful smile and wonderful dark eyes and lovely black hair'—and part of the state of Boise and the ball-teams of the 'crazies' and the lepers (241). The conversation between Lil and Hudson again stretches verbal ritual over tensions, a banter of anxiety which moves from English to Spanish when their feelings about Tom need control. Hudson lies to Lil by withholding Tom's death, but this, too, is ritual non-interference. Suicide of Cubans is mentioned several times (247); the existential context is clear and oppressive; Hudson has to give it, again, in Spanish: 'Tell me, Tom. What are you sad about?' '*El mundo entero.*' But it is Lil who seals in the philosophic issue: 'There doesn't have to be a law against things for them to be wrong.' Hemingway never explored precisely named issues of existential law, the law of courts and wars, the law of hunt and manhunt, but inside his melodramas of nostalgia and suicide, law is so emphatically active as to be inspirational. It charges the hedonistic calculus against despair to the point where the pleasure principle fights off reality. Memories of happiness sustain Hudson (251); he tells Lil the story of 'good love with fun', and, like most of Hemingway's scenes of this kind, it is the action of a tourist, abroad, a long time after childhood. Hemingway's fictions actually look ahead to a time when leisure will be not simply a fragment of life exhausted by labour but the main quantity of life—a new ratio which will enable a man to notice his condition, make choices about it, and remain masculine without being damned for not being a worker in the capitalist and marxist senses.

143

Hemingway's heroes are tourists in search of authenticity, perhaps part of what Dean MacCannell identifies as 'the conquering spirit of modernity . . . tourism and revolution . . . the two poles of modern consciousness—a willingness to accept, even venerate, things as they are on the one hand, a desire to transform things on the other.'[23]

Hudson is 'aware of the limitations' of his tense action against the conditions (262) and maintains a basic politics against the corrupt politics of exploitation (263), whose voice is that of a politician at a Havana bar:

> There's no trick like water. You can always get money for the promise to produce water. No politician would destroy a *truco* like that by building an adequate aqueduct. Aspirant politicians occasionally shoot one another in the lowest levels of politics. But no politician would so strike at the true basis of political economy. Let me propose a toast to the Custom House, a lottery racket, the free numbers racket, the fixed price of sugar, and the eternal lack of an aqueduct.

Hudson ironically drinks to that exposition of the *Realpolitik* he despises, and there is no further detail. The surface demonstrates enough of the interior complication. A woman gets out of her car like a film star 'conferring a warm and generous favour to the ground'; bodies make love within a survivalist banter; the 'neutral ground' is documented no further. But the woman is Tom's mother. When she learns of her son's death, she knows the existential ritual: 'I suppose we'll learn how to take it.' It is Hemingway's last understatement of existential necessity and his finest. To the end, he could produce such authentic heartbreak:

> 'Do you remember skiing with him on your shoulders and how we'd sing coming down through the orchard behind the inn in the dusk?'
> 'I remember everything.'
> 'So do I,' she said. 'And why were we so stupid?'
> 'We were rivals as well as lovers.'
> 'I know it and we shouldn't have been. But you don't love anyone else, do you? Now that's all we have?'
> 'No. Truly.'
> 'I don't either really. Do you think we could take each other back?'

'I don't know whether it would work. We could try.'
'How long will the war be?'
'Ask the man owns one.'

Let the academics and reviewers deny Hemingway as they will, no other writer in our time can bring that off any better, and it fully contradicts the lie that he did not realize the nature of his male-female relationships.

But the situation cannot be resolved—as another existentialist concluded: 'Eh bien, nous continuons'; and Hemingway—'we just go on' (284). That, too, is duty (287). In part three, Hudson becomes Hemingway's last warrior leader of a male band in duty. Undoubtedly, this one is 'supposed to be able to think' (294) as well as observe the beach through a painter's eyes, and nurse a pistol at the ready while he rests. But he is supported by an elaborate mutual consideration in the boat society. The crew are deeply concerned for him. Hemingway is a major artist of loyalty; his primary admiration for Conrad is not surprising. The crew are locals, mainly, who know the coasts even better than Hudson, and this keeps his vanity down and reinforces mutuality. Hudson's responsibility interacts with his terrible helplessness as a sensitive man whose sons have been destroyed. Action 'keeps your mind off things' (310) but he remains a haunted and hunted man. The novel sometimes takes on the quality of a romantic guilt and remorse drama without gods. The Furies have to be kept off because they will never turn into Eumenides. The war cannot be made simple or a tragedy (299, 311):

> Why don't you think of them as murderers and have the righteous feelings that you should have? Why do you just pound and pound on after it like a riderless horse that is still in the race? Because we are all murderers, he told himself. We are all on both sides, if we are any good, and no good will come of any of it.
>
> But you have to do it. Sure, he said. But I don't have to be proud of it. I only have to do it well. I didn't hire out to like it. You did not even hire out, he told himself. That makes it even worse.

The crew only see the surface, Hudson driving himself to exhaustion—as one member says, 'that's no reason' (318). But in terms of what now appears as the conclusion of a philosophical career, all this is strategy towards a phrase which summarizes the cores of the fiction series: 'Pride without vanity' (312). It is the key to Hemingway's ethic. The contrasts are Roger Davis and Peters, extensions of Robert Cohen and other failures or partial failures. Davis is a man perpetually impulsive and ashamed (66), a writer who has sold himself to the popular and futilely dreams of reversing his direction, a lover who has been dominated by vulpine women (89), who goes 'out West' for relief (89): 'If he could write the way he fought on the dock it could be cruel but it would be very good' (91). He can help David through his ordeal—'a great fisherman'—but he 'was as beautiful and sound in action as he was unbeautiful and unsound in his life and in his work' (126). In a word, Davis is 'complicated' (142); he 'needs to work well to save his soul' (168), but he will not. Peters, radio operator on the *Pilar*, is falsely guided by his reliance on being an ex-Marine: 'he was proudest of the real discipline without the formalities of discipline which was the rule of the ship. He was the one who took the greatest advantage of it' (319).

Hudson comes to understand, in the existentialist tradition, the nature of his relationship with the nonhuman Other—hermit crabs, a school of mullet, a barracuda, the heron, the yellow sand of the beach, the darkening clouds, in a passage exemplifying the calm movement of accumulative declarative sentences, a paragraphic serenity at the very moment of risk (Chapter 10): 'I love doing it, he thought. I just don't like the end' (330). He recalls Cézanne's bathers, and Eakins, as he notices the crew bathing naked on the stern (333). And here Hemingway introduces his lifelong notion of purity, taking up the riderless horse from that earlier passage (334):

> He had traded in remorse for another horse that he was riding now. So lie here now and feel clean from the soap and the rain and do a good job at nonthinking. You learned to do it quite well for a while.

But the novel finally concentrates on the grim helplessness of human beings in the situations they choose to be in to manufacture an ethic. Its concentrated world of privacy and inwardness, forced before public moral gaze, comes to this (335):

All you have now is a basic problem and your intermediate problems. That is all so you better like it. You will not have good dreams any more so you might as well not sleep.

The world is 'a big crap game' in which Hudson has won 'horrors' and 'the gift of uneasy unpleasant sleep'. Now remembered happiness is fatal—'Remember that, Thomas Hudson, and see how much good it will do you'. His leadership and skills among 'half saints and half desperate men' (346) leaves him 'prisoner' of command. His wound brings 'the feeling of reprieve.' But these are tactics to define duty (363):

> I am really tired finally, he thought. Well, I know what I have to do, so it is simple. Duty is a wonderful thing. I do not know what I would have done without duty since young Tom died. You could have painted, he told himself. Or you could have done something useful. Maybe, he thought. Duty is simpler.
> This is useful, he thought. Do not think against it. It helps to get it over with. That's all we are working for.

As in *The Red Badge of Courage*, the Earth with its creatures continues—'the hunger-ridden impersonality of certain wading birds', flamingoes 'ugly in detail and yet perversely beautiful' (347, 365). The artist's eye goes on appreciating. The double continuity of habit—duty and painter's eye—helps to discard futile worry and thought which cannot alter circumstance—war, love children dead, art, navigation, the skills which make the Absurd bearable from time to time, and which enable the impersonality of history, psychology and Nature to be at least watched. The blowing up of the vine-draped turtle boat, like Jordan's blowing up of the bridge, is a concrete simplicity which brings relief. But afterwards Hudson takes the drink which 'unlocked his memory that he kept locked so carefully now' (387), and his nostalgia for happiness floods in for the last time: 'the time of innocence and the lack of useless money and still being able to work and eat', in Paris with his wife and Tom. He has resisted walking out, betrayal, dishonesty, selling out and pointless death as best he can: the terms summarize the book's ethic and place it in the code of loyalty, as well as within the onward processes of Nature, as Conrad does. Passages of the

147

syntax of calm return, declarative sentences whose 'and' generates a continuous evenness, the serenity of continuity Hemingway admired in Bach and Cézanne, monumental artists whose architectonic surfaces control pleasure as value as impersonally as possible, through intensely personal style (393). The tranquillity of recollected Paris youth meets the captain's ageing life off Cuba; 'nothing' becomes a serene recognition of the process:

> But nothing happened all night long except the movement of the stars and the steady blowing of the east wind and the sucking of the currents past the ship. There was much phosphorescence in the water from the weed that the big tides and the sea made by the wind had torn up from the bottom, and it floated in and out and in again like cold strips and patches of white, unhealthy fire in the water.

Surface and depth: such sentences and their sense of process are concordant with the sea and sky processes in Conrad, the earlier master of that steadying of violations within an even prose which reduces a man to neither Nature nor the imposition of politics finally. Art is the work through which a man manifests his difference (403–4):

> You can paint the sea better than anyone now if you will do it and not get mixed up in other things. . . . life is a cheap thing beside a man's work. The only thing is that you need it. Hold it tight. Now is the true time you make your play. Make it now without hope of anything. You always coagulated well and you can make one more real play. We are not the lumpenproletariat. We are the best and we do it for free.

Work without hope is the instigation of prose both elegiac and exhilarating in its pleasures of skill and intense privacy of observation (Part One, Chapter 4):

> It was dark now and there was a breeze blowing so that there were no mosquitoes nor sand flies and the boats had all come in, hoisting their outriggers as they came up the channel, and now were lying tied up in the slips of the three docks that projected out from the beach into the harbour. The tide was running out fast and the lights of the boats shone on the water that showed green in the light and moved so fast it sucked at the piling of the docks and swirled at the stern of the big cruiser

they were on. Alongside in the water where the light was reflected off the planking of the cruiser towards the unpointed piling of the dock where old motor car and truck tyres were tied as fenders, making dark rings against the darkness under the rocks, garfish, attracted by the light, held themselves against the current. Thin and long, shining as green as the water, only their tails moving, they were not feeding, nor playing; only holding themselves in the fascination of the light.

The voice of a mid twentieth-century man who above all has had enough of the futile politics and wars of his time and who knows that the creativity of the arts and the practice of the skills are primary: that is Hemingway's legacy, a definition of duty far beyond his love for generals and his brave-animal slaughters. This is the source of his popularity—but not, of course, with the onward-going authoritarian system which seeks to evaluate life as military and industrial instruments at the service of the military industrial complex and its agents among the literary establishment.

NOTES

1. Gershon Legman, *Love and Death* (1949; New York: Hacker Art Books, 1963).
2. Edmund Wilson, 'Hemingway: Gauge of Morale' (1939); *The Wound and the Bow* (1941; rev. ed., London: W. H. Allen, 1952).
3. Paul Hoch, *White Hero Black Beast* (London: Pluto Press, 1979).
4. Harold Rosenberg, 'Notes from the Ground Up' (1960); reprinted as part of 'Themes' in *Discovering the Present* (Chicago: University of Chicago, 1973); 'Masculinity: Style and Cult' (1967; ibid., 1973).
5. Jacques Ellul, *Propaganda* (New York: Knopf, 1965).
6. John Killinger, *Hemingway and the Dead Gods* (New York: The Citadel Press, 1960).
7. Lionel Tiger, *Men in Groups* (New York: Random House, 1969).
8. Josephine Herbst, 'The Starched Blue Sky of Spain', *The Noble Savage*, No. 1 (New York: Meridian Books, 1960).
9. Andrew Turnbull (ed.), *The Letters of F. Scott Fitzgerald* (London: Bodley Head, 1963), p. 302.
10. Ellul, op. cit., p. 273.
11. Hoch, op. cit., p. 65.
12. George Orwell, 'Inside the Whale' (1940); S. Orwell and I. Angus (eds.), *The Collected Essays, Journalism and Letters of George Orwell*, Vol. 1 (London: Secker and Warburg, 1968), pp. 493–527.

13. Albert Camus, *The Myth of Sisyphus* (1942; London: Penguin Books, 1975), p. 54.
14. Lillian Ross, 'Portrait of Hemingway', *Reporting* (New York: Simon and Schuster, 1964), p. 196.
15. Federico García Lorca, 'Play and the Theory of the Duende', *Deep Song and Other Prose*, Christopher Maurer (ed.) (New York: New Directions, 1980), pp. 42–53.
16. Lorca, op. cit.
17. William White (ed.), *By-Line: Ernest Hemingway* (1968; London: Penguin Books, 1970), p. 17.
18. William White, op. cit., pp. 102–3.
19. C.f. *Art and Confrontation* (Bruxelles: La Connaissance, 1968; London: Studio Vista, 1970): essays provoked by the Paris uprisings of 1968 which unite the existential need to create with the duty of the artist to rebel against 'the totalitarian machine', 'a confrontation of the entire machine, a condemnation of its existence'.
20. Henry James, preface to *The Wings of a Dove*.
21. Hemingway, preface to *The Fifth Column and the First Forty-Nine Stories* (London: Cape, 1939); Edmund Wilson, op. cit.
22. In the Penguin edition of *Islands in the Stream* (London, 1971), the relevant passages are to be found on pages 5, 6, 12, 171–72, 90–1, 16 (74, 78), 71, 84 (105, 135), 85 and 133 respectively.
23. Dean MacCannell, *The Tourist* (New York: Schocken, 1976), p. 3.

8

Hemingway the Intellectual: A Version of Modernism

by BRIAN WAY

To speak of Hemingway as an intellectual is to risk a calculated, even a provocative gesture. Intelligence is the last quality which those who dislike his work would be willing to allow him, and even his admirers tend to see him as a natural who acquired a marvellous ear for a certain rather simple kind of good writing early in his career, and then lost it just as it was fully matured. This opinion is strengthened by accounts of Hemingway's own behaviour, especially the pose of swaggering and often offensive anti-intellectualism which he cultivated after 1930. More significantly, it is a view which appears to be confirmed by several characteristic features of his actual writing. In his best work, he almost always avoids the explicit presentation of ideas and arguments, and of that give and take of cultural allusion which so often does more than anything else to place a writer as an intellectual. When he deviates from this principle (as in his attempts to define Robert Jordan's war aims in *For Whom the Bell Tolls*) the results are so unfortunate as to emphasize his supposed incapacity for serious thought. Again, his insistence that he writes only of what he knows at first hand—his apparent allegiance to the cult of raw experience—seems a radical disengagement from any notion of an intellectual tradition. His prose style, finally—simple, direct, declarative (or so it seems)—is aggressively non-literary: if it is not entirely self-generated, it points only to the work of authors like Mark Twain, who are as anti-intellectual as Hemingway himself.

This picture has the character of a mischievous half-truth: like a bad photograph or a crude likeness, it blurs all the finer lines and subtler gradations which give distinction to the portrait. Even on a superficial reading, it is too simple a view. Hemingway was clearly capable of analytical modes of thought, and his recently published letters are full of shrewd literary and political comments—not only sharp, off-the-cuff judgements, but sustained passages of exposition. As one instance among many, one might mention his letter to John Dos Passos on the appearance of *Nineteen Nineteen*, in which he mingles judicious praise of the latter's achievement with warnings as to where his ideological commitments seemed to be taking him.[1]

In the novels themselves, Hemingway sometimes devises large and complex narrative structures which indicate still more impressively a capacity for sophisticated thought-processes. The retreat from Caporetto in *A Farewell to Arms* is one such episode. Another, even more germane to my argument, is the narrative of Andrés's journey through the Spanish Republican lines in *For Whom the Bell Tolls*, during which he carries Robert Jordan's message urging General Golz to call off the attack. This brilliant sequence of chapters gives a wonderfully precise sense of the anomalous character of a great army—how the bold conceptions of strategic planning and political intention are lost in the confused detail of human fallibility and error. Hemingway's success reflects not only his powers of observation, but his ability to learn from the masters of the European novel. He frequently expressed his admiration for Tolstoy and Stendhal as writers of war, and his narrative is an extension, in no way derivative, of their methods—of Tolstoy's treatment of the Battle of Austerlitz in *War and Peace*, and of Stendhal's account of Waterloo in *The Charterhouse of Parma*. In the former, Nicholas Rostov rides about the field all day trying to deliver a dispatch to the Russian Commander-in-Chief. In the latter, Fabrice Del Dongo, participating in the chaotic actuality of battle, cannot believe that he has really fought at Waterloo, since with the passage of time Waterloo has become merely a name—that is to say, acquired the delusive clarity of a historical event. Hemingway's sequence of chapters re-creates the complicated inner logic of these scenes while remaining absolutely faithful to the unique conditions of the Spanish War—the psychopathic Anarchist militiamen who delay Andrés at the front line; the negligent and cynical regular officer who wastes his time at a command post; the paranoid commissar who nearly has him shot and the mere traffic chaos and general disorganization incidental to any big attack.

The case for Hemingway's intellectual status, however, cannot rest upon occasional successes of this kind, remarkable as they are. It is necessary to look for qualities which are not merely peripheral but integral to the achievement of his best work, and since his fiction contains none of that conspicuous intellectual paraphernalia which is so evident in the writing of Norman Mailer, say, one must invoke the idea of a mode of intelligence which shows itself in the special operations of the artistic process and nowhere else. The nature of what I am suggesting here may be illustrated by reference to certain non-verbal art-forms such as acting, music and the dance: it is well known that practitioners of these arts often display a consummate intellectual control in their performances, while giving no other signs of intelligence. Hemingway's fascination with the figure of the bullfighter can be accounted for very largely in these terms. The latter, it is true, possesses the heroic virtue which Hemingway values most—courage in the face of death—but, more important still, he is an artist, whose patterns of work offer close analogies at a number of points to Hemingway's own.

This preoccupation is reflected in the best of his bullfighting stories, 'The Undefeated': like so much modernist writing, its ostensible subject is a partial disguise for the author's deepest concerns—the nature of art and the artist. Manuel Garcia, the main character, has this double significance: he is a poor, unsuccessful and ageing matador; he is also a pure artist—a man whose unique qualities are revealed only in the performances he gives in the arena. Outside the ring, he is inarticulate, little more than a cipher: he cannot bargain effectively with the impresario Retana, and the two waiters in the café, after a casual question or two, discuss him and the Madrid bullfight scene over his head, as if he weren't there. With a bull in front of him, he instantaneously becomes the master of subtle processes of thought: his long experience, his intuitive sense of how a *faena* should go, his inborn gift for the one thing he knows how to do—all these are fused in a comprehensive feeling of certainty about himself and his art:

> He thought in bullfight terms. Sometimes he had a thought, and the particular piece of slang would not come into his mind, and he could not realize the thought. His instincts and his knowledge worked automatically, and his brain worked slowly and in words. He knew all about bulls. He did not have to think about them. He just did the right thing. His eyes noticed things, and his body performed the necessary measures without thought. If he thought about it, he would be gone. Now, facing the bull, he was conscious of many things at the same time.

This intuitive understanding, which Manuel never formulates clearly even to himself, appears in his occasional moments of brilliance, and even more prominently—paradoxical as it may seem—in the nature of his failure. He could very easily have cheated at the end, killing the bull safely and ingloriously, but his refusal to settle for anything less than perfection reveals the purity of his instincts and the completeness of his understanding of the art he is practising. By comparison, the bullfight critic who is covering the corrida for a Madrid newspaper, knows nothing and sees nothing: his report is a string of vulgar sporting clichés, and the more he exploits his dismal fluency with words, the more he demonstrates the depths of his ignorance.

From this story, the outlines of Hemingway's conception of the artist begin to emerge. The latter's ability to talk about art is clearly unimportant, even suspect, and the quality of his achievement is not a decisive criterion in itself. Manuel Garcia is not a great bullfighter, but he is a true one, and his genuineness appears in the way he sets about his work. Similarly, the essential truth or falsity of any artist is to be seen in the manner in which he approaches the task of creation. With this notion of artistic truth, although it is expressed obliquely and in an unexpected quarter, Hemingway places himself unobtrusively within one of the main currents of the modernist aesthetic.

In this connection, two strongly contrasted tendencies can be observed in literary modernism. On the one hand, there are writers for whom the new modes of literary sophistication involved an interest in ideas—an opportunity not merely to create art in new ways, but to reflect directly in their work upon the ferment of intellectual innovation which was taking place all around them. Thomas Mann is a pre-eminent example of this kind of artist: the discussions of music and aesthetics in *Doctor Faustus*, and the debates on politics and culture in *The Magic Mountain*, are not only integral to the success of these novels as works of art, but of fundamental importance for the understanding of twentieth-century civilization. On the other hand, there are writers for whom ideas are a distraction from, a betrayal of, their art. In this spirit, T. S. Eliot said of Henry James 'he had a mind so fine that no idea could violate it'[2]; and Marcel Proust, in an equally uncompromising sentence declared, 'We reason, that is, our mind wanders, each time our courage fails to force us to pursue an intuition through all the successive stages which end in its fixing, in the expression of its own reality.'[3]

This latter quotation is taken from the very long passage in *Time Regained* in which Marcel describes how he finally arrived at a true notion of the methods and subject-matter of his art. However unlikely it may seem, his account gives a particularly precise and detailed statement of the aesthetic which is implied by those features of Hemingway's writing we have considered so far. Manuel Garcia, in the non-verbal art of bullfighting, proceeds directly from his intuitive certainty to the execution of his finished purpose in the arena. Similarly, in the literary art analysed by Proust, the writer, impelled by the same intuitive certainty, transforms his experiences, his memories, his impressions, into the completed work of fiction. The kind of intellectual activity which manifests itself in the formulation of concepts, or in ratiocination, can only produce a blurring and confusing effect when it intervenes in this process—just as Manuel would be confused if he allowed any words (except the special bits of bullfighting slang which are integral to his art) to come between him and his work:

> For the truths which the intelligence apprehends through
> direct and clear vision in the daylight world are less profound
> and less necessary than those which life has communicated to
> us unconsciously through an intuition which is material only
> in so far as it reaches us through our senses, and the spirit of
> which we can elicit. In fact, in this case as in the other, whether
> it was a question of impressions given me by a view of the
> Martinville belfry, or memories like those of the two uneven
> paving stones or the taste of the madeleine, it was necessary to
> attempt to interpret them as symbols of so many laws and
> ideas, by trying to think: that is, by trying to educe my sensa-
> tion from its obscurity, and convert it into an intellectual
> equivalent. And what other means were open to me than the
> creation of a work of art?

As well as describing the imaginative processes which lead up
to the act of composition, Proust here suggests the notion of a
certain kind of good writing. It is a mode of fiction based on
memories and impressions which have lodged themselves
deeply in the novelist's unconscious, so that when they emerge
from their obscurity they have an incalculable force and a
complex meaning. For this reason, he must 'attempt to interpret them as symbols of so many laws and ideas'—in other
words, properly handled, they are not descriptive details, but
significant indicators of an underlying reality.

Proust's sense of the creative process and of the nature of
good writing seems to me to correspond at all points with what
we find in Hemingway's best work. Despite this underlying
similarity in their aesthetic assumptions, however, their novels
could hardly be more different, since, while Proust spells out
the significance of his memories in enormous detail, Hemingway's prose is spare and economical, and his hidden meanings
are implied rather than stated. It is as if he took the business of
converting his impressions into symbols just far enough to
enable his readers to complete the task for themselves.
Hemingway's own account of this process appears in *Death in
the Afternoon*, in what is undoubtedly the most celebrated statement he ever made about his methods as a writer. Using the
simile of an iceberg, he asserts that fiction should be an art of

implication: only one-eighth of the iceberg is visible above water, and yet we infer the presence of the other seven-eighths: in the same way, the apparently meagre surface detail of a novel or story should suggest a world of buried meanings. We see a particularly subtle instance of this method in his description of the remembered landscape which Nick Adams re-enters in 'Big Two-hearted River':

> Ahead of him, as far as he could see, was the pine plain. The burnt country stopped off at the left of the range of hills. On ahead, islands of dark pine-trees rose out of the plain. Far off to the left was the line of the river. Nick followed it with his eye, and caught glints of the water in the sun. There was nothing but the pine plain ahead of him until the far blue hills that marked the Lake Superior height of land. He could hardly see them, faint and far away in the heat-light over the plain. If he looked too steadily they were gone, but if he only half looked they were there, the far-off hills of the height of land.

Nick Adams has returned to this familiar landscape from the War, in a state of inner tension, if not incipient disintegration. It is a stretch of country he knows so well that it seems an integral part of his own identity, and in re-entering it, he hopes to recapture the sense of wholeness which he associates with the relatively untroubled world of his boyhood. As he looks out across the pine plains, the unbroken pattern of an intimately remembered scene takes shape around him. Hemingway does not tell us this in so many words: he does not have to, since every detail of his description is charged with a weight of implication. Without appearing to do so, he shows us not only what Nick sees, but how he sees it, so that the country becomes a mirror of his mental state. Nick has no need to look at the view in order to know that it is there: He cannot see the distant hills if he gazes at them too fixedly, but if he looks away, they reappear, clearer in the eye of memory than to his physical sight. He experiences a great sense of peace as the landscape establishes its order around him and within him, as if the fragments of his shattered psyche were somehow re-assembled within the framework of the known.

This subtle and unobtrusive style is characterized exactly in Proust's dictum: Authentic art does not proclaim itself, for it is produced in silence. The silence of the artist—his willingness to efface himself except as a kind of ghostly presence haunting the shadows of his own work—is not an end in itself: it is essential as a precondition for attaining that quality of authenticity which is the supreme criterion of artistic success. Hemingway constantly asserts that writing is a form of truth-telling, but in this regard he has rarely been credited with the sophisticated self-awareness of literary modernism. He is usually thought to have been stating nothing more than a naïve belief in a crude equivalence between words and experience, a view summed up in the cliché to which he himself admittedly gave currency—'that is the way it was.' That such a notion involves a complete misreading of his fiction, however, can be seen even in a relatively uncomplicated story like 'Fifty Grand'. As the boxer Jack Brennan trains for what is to be the last fight of his career, his sparring partner Jerry Doyle comments on the way in which the newspapermen have discussed his prospects: 'I don't care who they are . . . what the hell do they know? They can write, maybe, but what the hell do they know?' At first sight, this seems a typical piece of man-on-the-spot anti-intellectualism, but it is entirely validated by the effect of the story as a whole. Jerry, the fictional narrator, does show a knowledge of the worlds of sport and gambling which is not easily come by. His understanding begins where most people's ends, and he takes the mere technicalities of boxing—the stock-in-trade of the sporting columnists—so completely for granted that he never even mentions them. He knows what a boxer worries about when he prepares for a fight he cannot win; he knows how big fights are fixed, and how the spectators are deceived by a pretence of sportsmanship; and, sitting in his corner of the ring, he hears what the contestants actually say to each other. By the end of the story, we are made to feel that we should not want to read anything about boxing which told less of the truth than Jerry Doyle does here.

The case of Krebs in 'Soldier's Home' is a more complex one. Returning from the War where he had proved himself to be brave and efficient in combat, he nevertheless falls into the habit of lying about his experiences. He does this in quite an innocent way, simply to draw attention to himself in his home town or to establish a friendly rapport with other old soldiers, but the effect is totally destructive. 'Krebs acquired the nausea in regard to experience that is the result of untruth or exaggeration', and, in the process, all his most worthwhile memories, the most authentic elements of his inner self, 'lost their cool valuable quality, and then were lost themselves'. Krebs's situation, on a modest scale, is an image of the predicament of the artist: anyone who undertakes to turn his innermost experiences into art, is committed to a complex network of responsibilities, in which the penalty for failure is not simply the production of bad writing, but the destruction of his own identity.

This is a recognizable version of the morality of art, a fundamental element of the modernist aesthetic. At the same time, Hemingway's insistence on the importance of what is known—on what is, in the deepest sense, true—establishes a connection between his modernism and something older, something more specifically American, in his work. He acquired his modernism in Paris from writers who were either expatriates or Europeans, but, through Mark Twain and Sherwood Anderson, he had access to a tradition of American writing which, however unexpectedly, seemed to point in the same general direction. These writers, in fact, anticipated in their fiction all the modernist traits we have been considering: in particular, they claimed for their work that special quality of truth which is conferred by memory and experience. Hemingway's debt to Anderson was enormous, though his acknowledgement of it was almost always disingenuous and grudging.[4] He was more willing to praise Twain, since even his competitiveness could not turn the latter into a rival; and in his correspondence and in *Green Hills of Africa*, he singled out *The Adventures of Huckleberry Finn* as the most authentic book in American literature. For him, the American novel was born when Twain discovered how to recapture the life of Huck and Jim on the raft. Hemingway felt that the most valuable gift a writer could possess was this ability to re-create the atmosphere of a specific time and place—to render not merely the mechanical detail of a landscape or the course of an adventure, but to suggest through these elements the pattern of emotion which alone makes them memorable. As he put it in *Green Hills of*

Africa, 'We have been there in the books and out of the books, and where we go, if we are any good, there you can go, as we have been.' It is clear from the immediate context of this sentence that he learnt as much from Turgenev and Tolstoy as from Twain but the latter, since he was an American predecessor had a special symbolic value for him, and, besides, the America in which Nick Adams grew up, is not vastly different from that of Huck Finn.

Twain developed the style which Hemingway admired in the process of remembering his early days as a river pilot. The moment when he realized the significance of his own deepest memories was also the moment when he found himself most completely as an artist—a situation which implies a seemingly remote but nevertheless fundamental analogy with the case Proust describes in *Time Regained.* Marcel, too, discovers his vocation as a writer at the point when the meaning of the past becomes clear to him. Leo Marx gives an illuminating account of what went into the making of Twain's style in his analysis of the well-known passage from *Life on the Mississippi*—the chapter in which Twain describes the same stretch of river twice over, first as a man of letters would see it, and then as a pilot would see it.[5] The former looks at it with a painterly eye, in terms of masses of colour, and contrasts of light and dark; the latter reads it like a chart in code, a series of hazards to navigation— places where a steamboat might founder, or signs that the river is changing its course. Twain's mature style, as it emerges in *Huckleberry Finn,* is an amalgam of the two. The sophistication of the man of letters is present in Twain's power to take a comprehensive view of his material and give it form. The special knowledge of the pilot is not wholly explicit, but absorbed into the texture of the writing. It is transformed into a subtle rhetoric in which every detail functions as a silent affidavit, an unspoken guarantee of the authenticity of the whole.

The celebrated opening to Chapter 19 of *Huck Finn* is the best known—and probably the best—of such writing in Twain's work, and while it is unnecessary to quote so familiar a passage or analyse it extensively, it is worth indicating briefly the presence of the stylistic elements we have been considering. The note of authenticity is provided through Huck's sense of detail: only someone who knows, who has really been there, could tell us whether the steamboat on the other side of the river is a side-wheeler or a stern-wheeler; or that the small dark spots far off over the water are trading scows, while the long black streaks are rafts. These facts do not simply document the scene: they also act as stylistic devices, which give a rhetorical emphasis to the implicit claim that nothing here is either extraneous or derivative—everything has been uniquely remembered by the artist himself.

One can often detect a similar aim in Hemingway's use of detail, and a particularly fine instance occurs in the opening sentences of his story 'The End of Something':

> In the old days Hortons Bay was a lumbering town. No one who lived in it was out of sound of the big saws in the mill by the lake. Then one year there were no more logs to make the lumber. The lumber schooners came into the bay and were loaded with the cut of the mill that stood stacked in the yard. All the piles of lumber were carried away. The big mill building had all its machinery that was removable taken out and hoisted on board one of the schooners by the men who had worked in the mill. The schooner moved out of the bay toward the open lake carrying the two great saws, the travelling carriage that hurled the logs against the revolving, circular saws, and all the rollers, wheels, belts and iron piled on a hull-deep load of lumber. Its open hold covered with canvas and lashed tight, the sails of the schooner filled and it moved out into the open lake, carrying with it everything that had made the mill a mill and Hortons Bay a town.
>
> The one-storey bunk houses, the eating-house, the company store, the mill offices, and the big mill itself stood deserted in the acres of sawdust that covered the swampy meadow by the shore of the bay.
>
> Ten years later there was nothing of the mill left except the broken white limestone of its foundations showing through the swampy second growth as Nick and Marjorie rowed along the shore. . . .
>
> 'There's our old ruin, Nick,' Marjorie said.
> Nick, rowing, looked at the white stone in the green trees.
> 'There it is,' he said.
> 'Can you remember when it was a mill?' Marjorie asked.
> 'I can just remember,' Nick said.
> 'It seems more like a castle,' Marjorie said.

There is one item in this description which arrests the eye more than everything else put together—the broken white limestone foundation of the old sawmill. Hemingway mentions it twice and it stands out as the one sharply etched object in what is otherwise a landscape of memory. It also provokes a rare conversational exchange between Nick and Marjorie. Like the visual detail in Twain's evocation of the Mississippi, it functions as a touchstone by which the genuineness of their feelings, and of the scene itself, can be judged. For Marjorie, who is a romantic, the stones are 'our old ruin'—more like a castle than an abandoned sawmill. Her view is coloured, and to a degree vitiated, by her desire to impose an emotional tone on her evening with Nick. Nick himself has just decided that he no longer loves her. He is, in consequence, sick of associations and memories. He is trying to see his situation as clearly as he can, and this affects the way he looks at the fragment of white stone: 'There it is', he remarks laconically in response to Marjorie's enthusiasm. He refuses to concede anything more, except to admit grudgingly that he can just remember the mill which stood there. For the moment, he inhabits a bleak and empty landscape: his double loss—of Marjorie, and of the innocent pre-adolescent world of boyhood experience which he had already sacrificed when he began to love her—has drained the scene of its associations and therefore of its meaning. The narrator, on the contrary, implicitly lays claim to a wide and comprehensive understanding: for him, the white stones are as full of significance as the dark specks on the river were for Mark Twain. Through them, he conjures up the vision of a vanished world—the noise and activity of the lumber town and, beyond that, the primeval forest which the town itself destroyed. But these recollections are themselves no more than an involuntary record of layer upon layer of loss: they create the effect of a prolonged and infinitely receding perspective in which Nick's personal predicament has an added richness of implication—lost love, lost youth, vanished town, vanished wilderness.

The white stones in 'The End of Something' play much the same role as the almost invisible Lake Superior hills in 'Big Two-hearted River', but by analysing the two stories in quite different ways, I have tried to show that two seemingly dissimilar literary traditions converge in Hemingway's best writing—one derived from his modernist contemporaries, the other from his American predecessors. Only his earliest work, however—*In Our Time, The Sun Also Rises,* and *Men Without Women*—gives evidence of this marvellous synthesis in its fullest perfection. With the publication of *A Farewell to Arms* in 1929, his mastery already seems incomplete, and after 1930, it only reappears in a handful of short stories and occasional episodes in the novels. Most of the critics who share this view of Hemingway's development, have attempted to explain his sudden decline in purely biographical terms.

In particular, they have drawn attention to the harmful influence of the Papa Hemingway persona which the author adopted as he became an international celebrity: the overbearing tone and wooden posturings of his public manner soon began to invade his fictional style, destroying the delicate resonances and associations which had given it distinction. There is undoubtedly an element of truth in this theory, but it has the disadvantage of keeping us at a greater distance from the actual writing than is either desirable or necessary. A possible line of explanation which is free from this defect may be found in an important letter which Hemingway wrote to Maxwell Perkins in December 1926. It was a decisive moment in his career: *The Sun Also Rises* had just appeared, and in his letter he pauses to take stock of his position. He clearly feels the reality of his success, but is nevertheless disturbed by some of the adverse comment which the book has received—especially the suggestion that its subject-matter is too limited and its main characters too unworthy to merit the attention of a serious artist. Out of these uncertainties, he tries to set his course for the future, and in the process seems to me to lay the groundwork for a disastrously wrong analysis of the real nature of his genius. If this is true, then the deterioration in his writing is not the result primarily of any external factor such as the pressure of publicity, or the damaging effect of an unsuitable life-style, but of a crucial miscalculation in his thinking. Like Manuel Garcia, it appears, he is lost from the moment he starts thinking about his work instead of thinking through it. The precise nature of his confusions can be seen in the following quotation:

> There really is, to me anyway, very great glamour in life—and places and all sorts of things and I would like sometime to get it

into the stuff. People aren't all as bad as Ring Lardner finds them—or as hollowed out and exhausted emotionally as some of the Sun generation. I've known some very wonderful people who even though they were going directly toward the grave (which is what makes any story a tragedy if carried out until the end) managed to put up a very fine performance enroute. Impotence is a pretty dull subject compared with war or love or the old lucha por la vida. I do hope though that the Sun will sell a tremendous lot because while the subject is dull the book isn't. Then maybe sometime, and with that impetus to go on, we'll have a novel where the subject won't be dull and try and keep the good qualities of this one. Only, of course, you don't have subjects— Louis Bromfield has subjects—but just write them and if God is good to you they come out well. But it would always be much better to write than to talk about writing.[6]

This letter is interesting for the distinction Hemingway draws between what he calls 'subjects' and 'writing'. The former term is self-explanatory: the latter, though not elaborated upon, seems to imply all those subtle interrelations between memory and symbolism, concrete detail and latent significance, which we have been considering. At times, Hemingway seems quite clear in his own mind that only writing, in this ample sense, really matters, and that a fictional subject—some predetermined plot, theme or character—has no particular value or even meaning apart from the writing in which it is expressed: a second-rate author like Louis Bromfield has subjects; a true artist 'just writes'. Nevertheless, Hemingway has a nagging suspicion that perhaps subjects have a crucial importance after all—that *The Sun Also Rises*, for instance, might have been a better novel if it had had a great theme like love or war rather than the 'pretty dull subject' of impotence. These doubts reveal a degree of uncertainty about the nature of his own talent: in Proustian terms he is beginning to reason about his writing from the outside, instead of following his instinct. His true bent had led him to create people who were 'hollowed out and exhausted emotionally': the sensitive and vulnerable Nick Adams; Jake Barnes, with his nightmares and his cynicism, his canny hedonism and his odd sense of humour; Lady Brett Ashley damaged by life, and destructive to all around her. No one could ask for more interesting characters than these, and yet Hemingway evidently feels that he ought to force himself to write about tragic situations and exalted emotions. The effects of this false diagnosis were ultimately disastrous, as he tried, more and more insistently, to give his work a specious value— commenting portentously on contemporary history in *To Have and Have Not* and *For Whom the Bells Tolls*, and infusing a bogus epic solemnity in *The Old Man and the Sea*.

It is only with hindsight and in the context of Hemingway's whole career that one can see his letter to Perkins as the first step in a totally wrong direction. At the time, it has more the air of an incipient confusion about what he should do next, and this view of the case is confirmed by his second novel, *A Farewell to Arms*. In many ways, this new work retains the strengths of the old. To an even greater degree than Nick Adams or Jake Barnes, Frederick Henry is an authentic anti-hero. As a soldier, he is a failure, and Hemingway goes to considerable lengths to strip his military adventures of every scrap of glamour. His wound, though dangerous, is inglorious, received while shelter-ing in a dugout eating cheese and pasta. He recuperates luxuriously in Milan, missing the whole of the gruelling sum-mer offensive in the mountains, and returning to the front just in time for the retreat from Caporetto. In the retreat itself, he is unable to keep his men together, or bring his ambulances through; and when he shoots the sergeant who refuses to help him push a stalled vehicle, his behaviour seems brutal and overbearing—no better than that of the battle police who try to shoot him at the crossing of the Tagliamento. When he deserts, he tries to justify his conduct at first as the making of 'a separate peace', but he soon comes to see it himself as an act of truancy— an evasion of the historical realities of the time.

Evasion of responsibility is in fact the keynote of Henry's personality. He is a rich expatriate, a student of architecture caught in Rome when the war begins. In Milan, he goes to the races with Meyers, a semi-underworld character who cannot return to the United States for unspecified reasons; and he is always able to escape the unpleasantnesses consequent upon being a deserter and a refugee by cashing another sight-draft on his wealthy grandfather. In general he is either self-indulgent or self-pitying: he continually whines that a mysterious 'they' always try to punish you for having a good time. He emerges finally as a hedonist who is nevertheless a sneaking puritan at heart.

As an anti-hero, he is a memorable figure and in some ways, Hemingway clearly conceived of *A Farewell to Arms* as a consciously anti-heroic book: in a well-known passage, he repudiates the resounding words 'glorious', 'sacrifice' and 'in vain', which have been devalued by the carnage of the War; and in his correspondence he expresses the hope that his novel will supplant Erich Maria Remarque's *All Quiet on the Western Front* as the leading anti-war novel of the 1920s.[7] But in his evocation of Henry's love-affair with Catherine Barkley, and especially in the portrayal of Catherine herself, there is a false romanticism, a contrived nobility of sentiment, of a kind which had never disfigured Hemingway's writing before. The sentimental vacuity of his compliant heroines has been remarked upon too often for the point to need arguing here. For my purpose, it is only necessary to observe that with the presentation of Catherine Barkley, a 'subject', in the damaging sense indicated by Hemingway's letter, makes its appearance in his fiction for the first time.

From this point of view, *A Farewell to Arms* represents a significant moment of transition in his development. He had singled out love and war as the two greatest subjects which an author could attempt, and in this novel love is certainly given the sort of treatment such a notion would imply. Apart from the romantic unreality of Catherine herself, Henry's feelings are enobled beyond anything he is genuinely capable of experiencing, and the story is freighted with narrative implausibilities like the lovers' escape by boat through a storm in which their craft would not have survived ten minutes. By contrast, the war scenes convey that atmosphere of complete authenticity which characterizes Hemingway's earliest work, since in them he is not in search of a subject but simply writing—again in the special sense suggested by his letter. The War is always a wholly credible element in the inner landscape of Frederick Henry's memories. He remembers only those things which, given what he is, he would be likely to remember: the War, instead of being a grandiose theme dragged in from outside because of its objective importance, is his war—the very texture of his fears, guilts, anxieties and obsessions. Thanks to this, *A Farewell to*

Arms, though seriously flawed, is a remarkable novel, containing much of Hemingway's best writing.

Hemingway could not remain long in this anomalous position, suspended as he was between two mutually antagonistic conceptions of art, and by the time he wrote *For Whom the Bell Tolls* a decade later, the process of change was complete. 'The amoeba-like little Spanish girl Maria', as Edmund Wilson calls her,[8] is more unreal even than Catherine Barkley: she is a sexual fantasy, not a woman, a kind of succubus who floats into Robert Jordan's sleeping-bag at night, like the celluloid images of Jean Harlow and Greta Garbo. If Maria is a banal sex-symbol, Robert Jordan is a conventional war hero: war, like love, has become a subject, and the process of romantic simplification is complete. The Spanish conflict itself is presented blankly as a portentous historical event, and often with that air of hectoring self-importance which is epitomized in W. H. Auden's 'Spain, 1937'. It is brought to life only intermittently in the adventures of minor characters like Andrés and Pilar, and it certainly never sets up those complex vibrations in Robert Jordan's consciousness which we observe in the minds of Nick Adams or Frederick Henry.

Jordan is, in fact, dead at the core, and his peculiar woodenness is especially evident in his mental processes. A representative instance occurs when he reflects on the nature of his feelings after his briefing with General Golz:

> All the best ones, when you thought it over, were gay. It was much better to be gay and it was a sign of something too. It was like having immortality while you were still alive. That was a complicated one. There were not many of them left though. No, there were not many of the gay ones left. There were very damned few of them left. If you keep on thinking like that, my boy, you won't be left either. Turn off the thinking now, old timer, old comrade. You're a bridge blower now. Not a thinker.

Even in a quotation as short as this, the tiresome repetitions and heavily facetious tone produce a lifeless effect. In the novel as a whole it soon becomes apparent that this vein of prolix rumination is to be Hemingway's sole resource for rendering the unique texture of his thought. An inner landscape as lifeless as this must end by casting its blight on the external world as well, particularly when we consider that so much of the action is presented from Jordan's point of view. This weakness is most immediately obvious in Hemingway's descriptions of the outer physical landscapes—the actual Spanish scenery—through which Jordan moves. As we have seen, the landscapes in his early fiction are delicate indicators of the states of mind of the characters who perceive them, but in *For Whom the Bell Tolls*, country is merely country. When Jordan goes with Anselmo to look at the bridge he has been ordered to destroy, he sees only a bridge, rocks, a mountain torrent, patches of snow: it is a scene without inner resonance, as empty of meaning as the mind which observes it. Certainly there is no trace of those subtle correspondences between exterior fact and hidden emotion which make the minds of Nick Adams, Jake Barnes and Frederick Henry such interesting places to visit. Since this is Hemingway's sole technical resource for evoking the mental processes of the characters he creates—giving them the necessary sharpness of focus, bringing them to life—Robert Jordan has, strictly speaking, no mind at all.

Hemingway's failure here seems to me the primary reason for the intellectual incoherence which is so marked a feature of *For Whom the Bell Tolls*—the muddled sense of what Robert Jordan is fighting for and why. It is not that his conflicting ideas about the Spanish Civil War cannot be reconciled: it is possible to hate war in general, and yet to believe that the best thing to do in a particular war is to fight it quickly, efficiently, ruthlessly even; again, it is possible to take sides in an ideological war for sound non-ideological reasons. These positions can be resolved logically: the trouble is that they are not resolved in Jordan's mind. They hardly could be, since the mind in which they jostle for pre-eminence has not begun to exist in any meaningful fictional form. Hemingway is not one of those writers who can make an intellectual debate itself the ground on which to bring a character to life. In *The Magic Mountain*, Settembrini and Naphta live for us through their arguments and their intellectual antagonism. Similarly in *Absalom, Absalom!*, Quentin and Shreve are dramatic embodiments of a process of inquiry into the nature of Southern history. But this method does not work for Hemingway. He is the kind of artist described in *Time Regained*, one for whom ideas and arguments are the most dangerous of all distractions. Proust maintains that the worst thing that can happen to such a writer is for him to be betrayed into the pursuit of false notions of significance. Marcel had felt the pressure to write about great themes and great events such as the Dreyfus affair and the War, but he had recognized that for him these were only an evasion of the true responsibilities of the artist. His business was to decipher the secret book of memories and experiences hidden within his own consciousness: 'The artist must at all times follow his instinct, which makes art the most real thing, the most austere school in life, and the true Last Judgement. That book, which is the most arduous of all to decipher, is the only one which reality has dictated, the only one printed within us by reality itself.' Hemingway was diverted from this high sense of vocation by his mistaken conviction that the Spanish War was an epic subject offering unlimited possibilities of artistic achievement, whereas it was, approached in this way, wholly inimical to the operation of his truest creative powers.

The most unfortunate consequence of Hemingway's decision was that he created a situation for himself in which it was impossible for the functioning of memory to be more than a marginal element in his novel. People, events and landscapes, as a rule, only acquire resonance and complexity in his fiction when they are remembered. This is clearly the case as we have seen, in the Nick Adams stories where the act of remembering— or sometimes of trying not to remember—is an explicit and major preoccupation. Similarly Jake Barnes and Frederick Henry, because they are first person narrators, establish a distance between themselves and what they describe, so that their stories, too, embody a process of recollection. In *For Whom the Bell Tolls*, Hemingway adopts a structural principle which makes any such effect impossible. By presenting the action as a blow-by-blow account of the events of three days, he abolishes the space between Robert Jordan and his experiences, with the result that no interesting reverbations are set up. The effect on the reader may be compared to that of listening to music from a single source instead of hearing it in stereo.

Hemingway made two attempts in his late fiction to resuscitate the dead art of memory, but without very much success. *Across the River and Into the Trees* it is true, makes a promising start, and Colonel Richard Cantwell is probably the most authentic character Hemingway created after he abandoned short story writing in the 1930s. As Scott Donaldson has pointed out, Cantwell is a kind of failed *miles gloriosus*,[9] and the style of aggressive reminiscence which is inseparable from this role might well have developed into an interesting variation on the process of remembering. The opening pages, in which the Colonel ruminates grumpily over his thirty years of soldiering, and bullies his army driver, are very good indeed, but the moment his mistress Renata appears, the novel falls to pieces; Hemingway's heroines seem to grow worse by geometrical progression, and since Renata becomes the sole recipient of Cantwell's memories, her effect on what might have been an oddly distinguished novel is correspondingly disastrous.

The posthumously published *Islands in the Stream* fails for somewhat different reasons. Its main character, Thomas Hudson, unlike Colonel Cantwell, never becomes a real dramatic presence in the work—indeed he displays much of the wooden anonymity of Robert Jordan. More seriously, in Hudson's case, the act of remembering is no longer a genuine psychological process in which past and present are subtly interfused. His mind seems rather to be a kind of lumber-room from which he emerges at intervals with a dusty photograph or a bundle of old newspapers. A similar situation can be observed in a much earlier—and equally unsatisfactory—work, 'The Snows of Kilimanjaro', where the dying writer, Harry, mechanically sorts over the material he never put into his fiction.

Having acknowledged that Hemingway's career after 1930 is clouded by a sense of anticlimax if not of outright failure, it is nevertheless necessary to put this fact in the right perspective. One should not see his decline primarily as a biographical problem: it is not a manifestation of underlying barbarism, nor a surrender to the forces of publicity, nor the result of alcoholism or brain damage (though all these may have played their part). It is first and foremost a question of art, a striking instance of the predicament of the modernist writer: working in an experimental and innovative manner, with no clear signposts from the past to guide him, he still has to assess the real nature of his talent and may easily be mistaken. To risk making such mistakes, is a part of the intellectual process, not a denial of it, and on this showing even Hemingway's failures are those of a man who lived the life of the mind in the privacy of his art however he may have lived elsewhere. But in conclusion, it is his success and not his failures that one would wish to emphasize—that quality of fine and unobtrusive intelligence which appears in the novels and stories of the 1920s and is the truest mark of his genius.

NOTES

1. Ernest Hemingway, *Selected Letters*, Carlos Baker (ed.), (London, 1981), p. 354.
2. T. S. Eliot, 'Henry James' (1918), reprinted in Philip Rahv, *Literature in America* (New York, 1957), p. 223.
3. All the quotations from Marcel Proust, *Time Regained*, are taken from the translation by Andreas Mayor (London, 1970).
4. See e.g. *Selected Letters*, p. 385.
5. Leo Marx, *The Machine in the Garden* (New York, 1964), 321 ff.
6. *Selected Letters*, p. 238.
7. Ibid., pp. 297, 307.
8. Edmund Wilson, 'Hemingway: Gauge of Morale', *The Wound and the Bow* (London, 1961), p. 213 fn.
9. Scott Donaldson, *By Force of Will: The Life and Art of Ernest Hemingway* (New York, 1977), 139 ff.

9

Hemingway and the Secret Language of Hate

by FAITH PULLIN

> His authentic work has a single subject: the flirtation with
> death, the approach to the void.
>
> —Leslie Fiedler

> Not Hemingway—a really dishonest man, the closet-every-
> thing. . . .
>
> —Truman Capote

In an essay called 'Place in Fiction' written in 1956, Eudora
Welty provides a basic insight into the problems of relationships, particularly sexual ones, which are endemic in Hemingway's work. The crucial difficulty is that people are pain-
givers; only places can create the balm that this hurt requires:

> whatever the scene of his work, it is the *places* that never are
> hostile. People give pain, are callous and insensitive, empty and
> cruel, carrying with them no pasts as they promise no futures.
> But place heals the hurt, soothes the outrage, fills the terrible
> vacuum that these human beings make.[1]

This leads inevitably to a situation in which 'fishing streams
or naming over streets becomes almost something of the
lover's secret language—as the careful conversations between
characters in Hemingway bear hints of the secret language of
hate.' It has often been said that Hemingway is not a novelist

at all since he isn't concerned with the novel's essential material in respect of social background, money or human relations—'all the prose of life' as Dwight Macdonald puts it in *Against the American Grain* (1963). What Hemingway seems to pursue in his writing is the physical epiphany in which the 'event' is the sensation itself and the people—if present at all—are merely part of the background. As Malcolm Cowley points out, Hemingway was much more of an intellectual and much more interested in ideas than he or anyone else wanted to admit, but

> He was most at ease in describing natural scenes and activities. He made everything palpable, so that a landscape was suggested by hills to be climbed with aching muscles or by the feel of hemlock needles under bare feet, all remembered with a sense of precarious joy.[2]

Miss Welty's perception focuses on the precariousness of that joy which is a palliative rather than a good in itself: a compensation for a failure in human communication and love rather than a positive achievement. The fact is that Hemingway's sense of the relationships between people, and particularly between men and women, is that they are invariably destructive. Sometimes, this destruction is actual and physical, rather than emotional or metaphoric. As Judith Fetterley rightly contends in her feminist essay '*A Farewell to Arms*: Hemingway's "Resentful Cryptogram" ':

> The message to women reading this classic love story and experiencing its image of the female ideal is clear and simple: the only good woman is a dead one.[3]

Considering the 'ideal' with which Hemingway makes Nick Adams set off on his voyage into the sexual life, it isn't surprising that both are doomed to disappointment. Trudy Ojibway, an Indian adolescent, is the standard from which all later American partners of the Hemingway protagonist fall away:

> Could you say she did first what no one has ever done better and mention plump brown legs, flat belly, hard little breasts, well holding arms, quick searching tongue, the flat eyes, the good taste of mouth, then uncomfortably, tightly, sweetly,

173

moistly, lovely, tightly, achingly, fully, finally, unendingly, never-endingly, never-to-endingly, suddenly ended, the great bird flown like an owl in the twilight, only in daylight in the woods and hemlock needles stuck against your belly.[4]

In contrast to this somewhat undemanding encounter and grateful companion, American women (according to Wilson in 'The Short Happy Life of Francis Macomber') are, 'the hardest in the world; the hardest, the cruellest, the most predatory and the most attractive.'[5] Trudy, on the other hand, is simply a fantasy figure whose vague exoticism makes her easy to dismiss; contact with her involves no taint of the biological trap ('Make plenty baby what the hell'). This easy irresponsibility is in striking contrast to the resentment or strong ambivalence expressed by Nick when he has to leave skiing in Switzerland to return to America because his wife is pregnant. The servant girl also is pregnant and hostile to George and Nick who are 'happy', 'fond of each other' and would much prefer to 'just bum together . . . and not give a damn about school or anything'. Renata, in *Across the River and Into the Trees* is a sophisticated, updated version of Maria in *For Whom the Bell Tolls* and Maria is an older Trudy. It's axiomatic that the landscape that Colonel Cantwell (significantly named) loves and the scenes of duck-shooting are more accurately and truthfully realized than anything in the supposedly pain-wracked encounters between the two lovers. At her first entrance, Renata manifests herself like something out of *Vogue*:

> Then she came into the room, shining in her youth and tall striding beauty, and the carelessness the wind had made of her hair. She had a pale, almost olive-coloured skin, and a profile that could break your, or anyone else's heart, and her dark hair, of an olive texture, hung down over her shoulders.[6]

At this point, the Colonel seems to have forgotten his own aphorism (which comes out of an attitude of similar senti-mentality but differently angled): 'He only loved people, he thought, who had fought or been mutilated' (55). Love is perhaps too strong a term, even for the relationships between fellow-fighters or fellow-mutilated in Hemingway's fiction. The fact that Hemingway's fictional women are not *people* explains the occasionally vicious note that creeps into the

soap-opera conversations of Renata and the Colonel, splinter-
ing their ludicrous nature. As Leslie Fiedler has it:

> In his earlier fictions, Hemingway's descriptions of the sexual
> encounter are intentionally brutal, in his later ones uninten-
> tionally comic.[7]

The problem is that Hemingway merely asserts a conviction of
the importance and the value of the sexual relationship
without in any sense demonstrating it convincingly: it's a
matter of gesture rather than feeling and the falsity of the
gesture is proved by the falsity of the language:

> The Colonel said nothing, because he was assisting, or had
> made an act of presence, at the only mystery that he believed in
> except the occasional bravery of man.[8]

Later, we are back to Trudy and Nick's 'great bird' which
this time around 'had flown out of the closed window of the
gondola'. In the Colonel's mawkish conversations with Renata's
portrait, we have an overt statement of the striking differences
between charming foreign girls (unreal, fantasy figures) and
American bitches—Renatas versus Texans:

> With us, if a girl is really beautiful, she comes from Texas and
> maybe, with luck, she can tell you what month it is. They can all
> count good though.
> They teach them how to count, and keep their legs together,
> and how to put their hair up in pin curls. Sometime, portrait, for
> your sins, if you have any, you ought to have to sleep in a bed
> with a girl who has put her hair up in pin curls to be beautiful
> tomorrow. Not tonight. They'd never be beautiful tonight. For
> tomorrow, when we make the competition. . . .
> I see [Renata] in the street with the lovely long-legged stride
> and the wind doing anything it wants to her hair, and her true
> breasts under the sweater, and then I see the nights in Texas with
> the pin curls; tight and subjected by metallic instruments.[9]

The unreality of this is plain. Renata, as a sophisticated,
aristocratic Venetian girl is cast in the same role and as the
same type as Trudy, whereas Texan girls are totally artificial,
mere man-trapping objects. This is a case of a character
serving the emotional needs of the author: the reality of the
novel consists in its travel-book qualities and constitutes a
vindication of those editors who rejected Hemingway's early

short stories on the ground that they were 'anecdotes, sketches, contes'.[10] Hemingway's *forte* is the encapsulation of an emotion in a symbolic landscape: he is the most formidable exponent of Eliot's technique of the objective correlative. He himself expresses this concretely in the description in *A Moveable Feast* of his early attempts to build up his stamina in the direction of novel writing:

> I knew I must write a novel. But it seemed an impossible thing to do when I had been trying with great difficulty to write paragraphs that would be the distillation of what made a novel. It was necessary to write longer stories now as you would train for a longer race. . . .
>
> What did I know best that I had not written about and lost? What did I know about truly and care for the most? . . . When I stopped writing I did not want to leave the river where I could see the trout in the pool, its surface pushing and swelling smooth against the resistance of the log-driven piles of the bridge. The story was about coming back from the war but there was no mention of the war in it. (59–60)

Colonel Cantwell's Venetian landscapes are repositories of his true feelings about war: all the novel's moving elegiac quality is contained in its natural description beside which the scenes of 'Papa's' and 'Daughter's' mutual love are an impertinence. The facile and unrealistic characterization of Renata means that the novel is inevitably destroyed on a human level. Renata's only significance is as a symbol of youth and physical perfection to be duly contrasted with the age and mutilation (and wisdom) of the Colonel. However, there is more to it than this. The duck-shooting obviously functions as some kind of purification ritual, comparable to Nick's fishing-trip in 'Big Two-hearted River'. The colonel isn't just dealing with the fear of his own death but with a burden of residual guilt:

> He feels bound to suffer, for, allied to his physical disabilities, he has inherited a mental burden, because he has accepted sole spiritual responsibility for losing three battalions in combat through decisions which were not his own.[11]

Renata is the drug with which he tries to suppress the pain of this psychological mutilation; inevitably she is compared favourably with Cantwell's wife, a journalist and therefore an equal and competitor ('She had more ambition than Napoleon and about the talent of the average High School Valedictorian'). The wife is the pain-giver; Renata the medication for the wound, but the real flirtation is between Cantwell and his death which he meets, like a lover in the back seat of the car.

In *For Whom the Bell Tolls*, the protagonist is seen actively engaged in combat and, in the process, achieving a social education; again, Hemingway makes the attempt to embody, in the relationship between Jordan and Maria, the positives of the action—in this case, enlarging it to encompass the concepts of solidarity and social love. But, as in the grosser case of the Colonel and Renata, this ambitiously social *and* transcendental emotion is not worked for or proved in the text. The scenes in the sleeping bag with 'rabbit' provoke in the reader not empathy but a snigger. It's hard to disagree with Fiedler that in *For Whom the Bell Tolls* Hemingway has written 'the most absurd love scene in the history of the American novel'.[12] The erotic world is perfectly unknown to Hemingway. The only other female character in the novel is Pilar and she is a fake man. The convincing evidence of 'love' that Hemingway comes up with in the book is the affection that Jordan feels for the old man Anselmo; this genuine camaraderie and concern is in sharp contrast to Jordan's response to Maria (trained by Pilar to service him) which can be switched on and off at will:

> As he knelt to put on his rope-soled shoes, Robert Jordan could feel Maria against his knees, dressing herself under the robe. She had no place in his life now.[13]

The essential elements in the situation are lack of time and the romantic inevitability of death. Jordan, like Frederick Henry, is saved from what he thinks he wants most. Catherine is punished by her own biology (truly her destiny); Maria (like Brett Ashley a boy/woman with her cropped hair) will never actually be in a position to make boring, quotidian demands. What is presented as a threnody is in fact a welcome escape:

> Not time, not happiness, not fun, not children, not a house, not a bathroom, not a clean pair of pyjamas, not the morning paper, not to wake up together, not to wake and know she's there and that you're not alone. No. None of that. (153)

It's the foreshortening of the experience that gives it its value:

> I did not know that I could ever feel what I have felt, he thought. Nor that this could happen to me. I would like to have it for my whole life. You will, the other part of him said. You will. You have it *now* and that is all your whole life is; now. There is nothing else than now. There is neither yesterday, certainly, nor is there any tomorrow. (154)

The other side of this coin is repellent actuality: 'Why not marry her? Sure, he thought, I will marry her. Then we will be Mr. and Mrs. Robert Jordan of Sun Valley, Idaho' (150). Jordan's imagining of that potential life—Maria as the Spanish wife of the university instructor—supposedly tinged with savage bitterness for its inevitable loss and with cruel irony at the unbearable gap between *that* and reality actually contains a hidden charge of secret hatred for her, the unconscious perpetrator of this pain:

> And when I get my job back at the university she can be an instructor's wife and when undergraduates who take Spanish IV come in to smoke pipes in the evening and I have those so valuable informal discussions about Quevedo, Lope de Vega, Galdós and the other always admirable dead, Maria can tell them about how some of the blue-shirted crusaders for the true faith sat on her head while others twisted her arms and pulled her skirts up and stuffed them in her mouth. (150)

Timeliness[14] and its corollary—the inability to sustain anything—seem crucial both to Hemingway's world-view and to his fictional technique. The humdrum continuity of a relationship bears no part in this sense of things—only the intensity of a doomed sexual relationship or the intense commitment of comrades in the moment of action is of concern to the Hemingway protagonist who is, by definition, an *isolato*. Jordan's isolation is temporarily broken by the non-threatening association with 'rabbit' to whom he can play the gentle tutor ('Where do the noses go? I always wondered where the noses would go'). However, the essential feature of this *affaire* is that it is not to lead to 'a home'. Again, the value of Maria is that she provides an experience of pure sensation, comparable to the physical pleasures of fighting itself: this apart, she is pure

stereotype. Jordan is embarrassed, as was Frederick Henry, by
the hypocrisy of noble words:

> At either of those places you felt that you were taking part in a
> crusade. That was the only word for it although it was a word
> that had been so worn and abused that it no longer gave its true
> meaning. (210)

Jordan is shown as disillusioned with war and with the
treachery of both sides, but unlike Henry, he's unable to make
a separate peace. What impresses the reader is not Jordan's
political or social awakening but Hemingway's conviction that
the only truth is in physical sensation. The only value to be
found in life is in extremes of feeling:

> You learned the dry-mouthed, fear-purged, purging ecstasy
> of battle and you fought that summer and that autumn for all
> the poor in the world, against all tyranny, for all the things that
> you believed and for the new world you had been educated
> into. You learned that autumn, he thought, how to endure and
> how to ignore suffering in the long time of cold and wetness, of
> mud and of digging and fortifying. And the feeling of the
> summer and the autumn was buried deep under tiredness,
> sleepiness, and nervousness and discomfort. (211)

Neither Frederick Henry nor Robert Jordan ever appear to
gain any valid experiential knowledge other than the reality of
the physical life; other kinds of knowledge are perceived as
disturbing, repellent and, above all, difficult:

> He would write a book when he got through with this. But
> only about the things he knew, truly, and about what he knew.
> But I will have to be a much better writer than I am now to
> handle them, he thought. The things he had come to know in
> this war were not so simple. (222)

Yet again, the most compelling emotion is felt by Jordan in
preparing for his own death and exorcising the cowardice (as
he sees it) of his father's.

> It is as though death in some subtle fashion has not only
> twisted itself about love but has become a secret forbidden
> attraction that the Hemingway hero finds hard to resist.[15]

In fact, the heroism with which he handles the final parting
with Maria and its sacramental pretensions, is merely a

179

prelude to the important business of concentrating on dying: *God, that was lucky I could make her go.*

As has often been noticed by critics, Hemingway's compelling desire to write 'the one true sentence' actually led, more often than not, to a technique of evasion, if not actual lying. As he himself said, 'It is not *un-natural* that the best writers are liars. A major part of their trade is to lie or invent.'[16]

Sometimes Hemingway seems to become confused about the nature and impact of what he wants to say (as in the self-regarding interior monologues of Colonel Cantwell); for instance, in the soliloquy at the end of *To Have and Have Not* in which Harry Morgan's wife expresses her despair at the loss of his virile attentions:

> I couldn't go to the funeral. But people don't understand that. They don't know how you feel. Because good men are scarce. They just don't have them. Nobody knows the way you feel, because they don't know what it's all about that way. I know. I know too well. And if I live now twenty years what am I going to do? Nobody's going to tell me that and there ain't nothing now but take it every day the way it comes and just get started doing something right away. That's what I got to do. But Jesus Christ, what do you do at nights is what I want to know. (190)

As Edmund Wilson remarks in *Hemingway: Gauge of Morale*, 'there is a choral refrain of praise of his *cojones*.' My point is that this sensual lament is not what it seems to be at first sight; it actually reveals great animus against women and a sadistic delight in the prospect of a wife deprived of physical pleasure. A more credible and vicious comment on sexual relations is expressed earlier in this book by Richard Gordon's wife:

> Love is just another dirty lie. Love is ergoapiol pills to make me come around because you were afraid to have a baby. Love is quinine and quinine and quinine until I'm deaf with it. Love is that dirty aborting horror that you took me to. Love is my insides all messed up. It's half catheters and half whirling douches. I know about love. Love always hangs up behind the bath-room door. It smells like lysol. To hell with love. Love is you making me happy and then going off to sleep with your mouth open while I lie awake all night afraid to say my prayers

even because I know I have no right to any more. Love is all the dirty little tricks you taught me that you probably got out of some books. All right. I'm through with you and I'm through with love. (137)

Women, poor things, may end up as bitches without even realizing it ('maybe I'm one now. I suppose you never know when you get to be one. Only her best friends would tell her') owing to the strain of 'trying to be a lot of wives yourself'.

Educated women fare just as badly: Dorothy in *The Fifth Column*, a Vassar girl (and therefore above herself to begin with), is treated with great antagonism by Philip and reduced to the level of 'commodity'; predictably, before the final renunciation we hear that they won't marry ('even lying in the night I know we won't'). Dorothy is rejected and punished in the name of all 'equal' women ('the trouble is I *love* him') and the way is made clear for a resumption of relations with the Moorish tart.

We know from his *Paris Review* interview of 1962 that Evelyn Waugh admired Hemingway's language experiments in *The Sun Also Rises* (in particular, the way he made drunk people talk). I want to suggest that, like Waugh, Hemingway has no real interest in character and therefore no genuine comprehension of, or expertise in, the fictive treatment of human relationships. Like Waugh, he regarded writing 'not as investigation of character but as an exercise in the use of language'; like Waugh he had no 'technical psychological interest'. Like Waugh, he consistently arranges and rearranges the same basic elements, 'drama, speech, events', throughout his fictional career. As Judith Fetterley claims, almost all of Hemingway's materials are present in the early story 'Indian Camp', and specifically that material that relates to sex and women:

> in that story a little boy watches his doctor-father perform a contemptuous and grotesque Caesarean section on an Indian woman while her husband in the bunk above slits his throat. . . . The lesson reflected in the double mirror of the two fathers, is one of guilt—guilt for the attitudes men have toward women and guilt for the consequences to women of male sexuality.[17]

In *A Farewell to Arms*, both guilts have been projected on to Catherine herself—it is her sexuality that is the enemy and she, as the scapegoat figure, who has to bear the burden of

Frederick's sins and die of them. 'Indian Camp' has its own overt meaning but *A Farewell to Arms* contains an inside narrative which subverts all that Hemingway's *Romeo and Juliet* intends to say.

In spite of the surface idealization of Catherine, it's clear that hostility is not far below the surface and the ending (inevitable as it is) releases Frederick for further adventures, freed of the trammels of 'home' and 'mother'.

The opening paragraph of *A Farewell to Arms* is preeminently elegiac; it is a landscape that in and by itself encapsulates regret. 'Death is the mother of beauty' and Catherine's death, together with the failure of Frederick's romantic hopes of war, creates the emotional pressure in the passage:

> In the late summer of that year we lived in a house in a village that looked across the river and the plain to the mountains. In the bed of the river there were pebbles and boulders, dry and white in the sun, and the water was clear and swiftly moving and blue in the channels. Troops went by the house and down the road and the dust they raised powdered the leaves of the trees. The trunks of the trees too were dusty and the leaves fell early that year and we saw the troops marching along the road and the dust rising and leaves, stirred by the breeze, falling and the soldiers marching and afterwards the road bare and white except for the leaves.[18]

All ethical and aesthetically pleasing standards in *A Farewell to Arms* are identified with the priest and the cold, clear, dry and pure area of the Abruzzi; in comparison, Catherine represents everything that is confusing, ambivalent and threatening. The Abruzzi is a masculine retreat, safe from the problems of sex and a place where there is 'good hunting'. Abruzzi is the ideal which Frederick Henry can't achieve; he tells the priest that he had wanted to go, but 'we did not do the things we wanted to do; we never did such things': in the following famous paragraph Hemingway juxtaposes the cold, clean, celibate masculine world with the confusions and distortions of life caused by drink, women and general self-indulgence:

> I had wanted to go to Abruzzi. I had gone to no place where the roads were frozen and hard as iron, where it was clear cold

and dry and the snow was dry and powdery and hare-tracks in the snow and the peasants took off their hats and called you Lord and there was good hunting. I had gone to no such place but to the smoke of cafés and nights when the room whirled and you needed to look at the wall to make it stop, nights in bed, drunk, when you knew that that was all there was, and the strange excitement of waking and not knowing who it was with you, and the world all unreal in the dark and so exciting that you must resume again unknowing and not caring in the night, sure that this was all and all and not caring. Suddenly to care very much and to sleep, to wake with it sometimes morning and all that had been there gone and everything sharp and hard and clear and sometimes a dispute about the cost. Sometimes still pleasant and fond and warm and breakfast and lunch. Sometimes all niceness gone and glad to get out on the street but always another day starting and then another night. I tried to tell about the night and the difference between the night and the day and how the night was better unless the day was very clean and cold and I could not tell it; as I cannot tell it now. But if you have had it you know. He had not had it but he understood that I had really wanted to go to the Abruzzi but had not gone and we were still friends, with many tastes alike, but with the difference between us. He had always known what I did not know and what, when I learned it, I was always able to forget. (14–15)

The initial encounter between Frederick and Catherine involves a hidden ingredient of sadism on his part:

> This was better than going every evening to the house for officers. . . . I knew I did not love Catherine Barkley nor had any idea of loving her. This was a game, like bridge, in which you said things instead of playing cards. Like bridge, you had to pretend you were playing for money or playing for some stakes. (27–8)

This hostility is continued when Frederick falls in love with Catherine and is thereby trapped by her. Even so, there is little real advance in his emotional attitude to her: he doesn't fulfil the terms of the priest's definition of love: 'When you love you wish to do things for. You wish to sacrifice for. You wish to serve' (60). Catherine is just a more available sex-object who, unlike the whores in the Villa Rossa, doesn't have to be shared with the other officers. When Catherine comes to the hospital in Milan, she is in a perfect position to fulfil all Frederick's needs as nurse and lover, 'when I saw her I was in love with her.' Before her coming, he had shown himself hostile to any woman in any position of authority, undermining and humiliating them as the occasion presented itself. Any real affection, in which bullying and exploitation do not play a significant part, is shown in Frederick's response, not to any woman, but to the priest and Rinaldi. The reality of the Catherine/Frederick liaison is to be found in its precursor, 'A Very Short Story', where Nick is rejected for an Italian major. Luz is punished for this betrayal by the failure of the Italian to marry her and for the lack of response to her letter to Chicago about it. Nick shows the extent of his revulsion from romantic love by contracting 'gonorrhea from a sales girl in a loop department store while riding in a taxicab through Lincoln Park'.[19] The relationship between Frederick and Catherine works only on the basis of the total abnegation of her personality: 'There isn't any me any more. Just what you want.' When Catherine announces her pregnancy, she has to do it in the most placatory manner possible: 'It doesn't worry me but I'm afraid to worry you.' The announcement is met by Frederick's dictum about the biological trap. From this point on, Frederick's reactions reveal an increasing insensitivity to Catherine's needs and a developing antagonism to her. A significant point is reached in the scene in the hotel when Catherine feels like a whore. Frederick 'had not thought it would be like this'. Catherine's problem is that Frederick needs her to be both pure and whorish simultaneously and certainly not to *fail* him in a crucial way by committing the crime of getting pregnant. Of course, Catherine hardly exists as a human being since she is crippled by self-hatred and by the sexual nausea that pervades the novel as a whole. Frederick is also a cipher: the value of the novel, then, consists in the exact and detailed reporting of the experience of sensations of an extreme kind, painful physically or emotionally. There are a series of set-pieces throughout the book—extended insights which in themselves function like mini-short stories. The description of Frederick and his companions being hit by a shell in the dug-out; the magnificent account of the retreat from Caporetto—these elements in the novel support the contention of Jed Kiley that Hemingway is not a fiction writer; 'he's a reporter of emotions.'[20]

War naturally simplifies the relationship between the sexes, by removing surfaces and revealing the basic power situation. Catherine confuses the Italians because they don't want nurses at the front, only whores; on the other hand, to be a nurse is in itself to be de-sexed, or rather, to be cast in the role of mother. Catherine's mistake is that she is to be a mother to a real child, thereby removing herself from a position of total subservience to the infantile demands of Frederick. To Catherine, sex seems to be something extraneous to herself, an abstract possession which can be used to please Frederick but not, apparently, herself.

Hemingway's completely unsatisfactory attempt to whip up the reader's emotion over the bitter-sweet fate of the star-crossed lovers is revealed in all its inadequacy by the totally apt, laconic reporting of the following passage:

> Aymo lay in the mud within the angle of the embankment. He was quite small and his arms were by his side, his puttee-wrapped legs and muddy boots together, his cap over his face. He looked very dead. It was raining. I had liked him as well as anyone I ever knew. I had his papers in my pocket and would write to his family. (167)

In Hemingway's own terms this description is 'true' and 'clean' in a way that the narrator's adolescent philosophizing on the nature of life and death is not:

> If people bring so much courage to this world the world has to kill them to break them, so of course it kills them. The world breaks every one and afterward many are strong at the broken places. But those that will not break it kills. It kills the very good and the very gentle and the very brave impartially. If you are none of these you can be sure it will kill you too but there will be no special hurry. (193)

> That was what you did. You died. You did not know what it was about. You never had time to learn. They threw you in and told you the rules and the first time they caught you off base they killed you. (252)

Betrayal is one of Hemingway's major themes: Frederick is betrayed by the sordidness and futility of war and by women and biology.

As the priest is the hidden hero in *A Farewell to Arms*, so Romero is the focal character of *The Sun Also Rises*. He is the type of the dedicated man whose adherence to his art is paramount and admirable. Women exist to serve him but they can't be allowed to sully the purity of his vocation. Women, in the figure of Brett, are presented as purely destructive and there is a similar kind of subdued revenge present in Jake's inability to satisfy her as in Harry Morgan's absence reducing his wife to a frenzy of unfulfilled desire. Fear of women predominates in *The Sun Also Rises* combined with a repellent desire to punish them. Jake presents himself as someone carefully working out an ethical system by which to live and, in the course of it, acknowledges possible wrongs done to Brett:

> I had been having Brett for a friend. I had not been thinking about her side of it. I had been getting something for nothing. That only delayed the presentation of the bill. The bill always came. That was one of the swell things you could count on.[21]

However, the natural scheme conveniently allows for injustice as far as the sexes are concerned: 'I thought I had paid for everything. Not like the woman pays and pays and pays.' In any case, 'I did not care what it was all about. All I wanted to know was how to live in it.' However, if there are any positives in the novel, they don't reside in Jake's self-regarding philosophy but in Romero's dedication and artistry; Jake comments on his purity of line:

> Romero never made any contortions, always it was straight and pure and natural in line. The others twisted themselves like corkscrews, their elbows raised, and leaned against the flanks of the bull after his horns had passed, to give a faked look of danger. Afterward, all that was faked turned bad and gave an unpleasant feeling. Romero's bull-fighting gave real emotion, because he kept the absolute purity of line in his movements and always quietly and calmly let the horns pass him close each time. (139)

Like a priest, Romero practises his vocation and discusses it objectively with no egotism: 'He talked of his work as something altogether apart from himself.'

Hemingway is always supremely interested in how things

are *done*: his other pre-eminent concern is with the transience of life. The bull-fight combines these two elements in the stylization of violent death. This is the art that Brett must not be allowed to contaminate and the corrupting process that she has begun as a result of her predatory association with Romero must be, and is, halted:

> The fight with Cohn had not touched his spirit but his face had been smashed and his body hurt. He was wiping all that out now. Each thing that he did with his bull wiped that out a little cleaner. (183).

Brett's destructive urge is thwarted and the novel ends with the undermining of the hypothesis of a fulfilled love between Brett and Jake. Romantic passion depends upon the concept of non-consummation but, even so, no relationship between these two could have compared with the male companionship of the fishing-trip. Neither Brett nor Jake are capable of sexual love and this is why Cohn, with his stubborn persistence in its existence and value, antagonizes them and the other characters in the novel so radically. Both love and sex fail in *The Sun Also Rises*. Romero is the only character to survive with integrity and some measure of hope.

Brett functions as a boy/woman finally saving Romero from herself by practising a masculine code of self-denial and self-restraint. In the early stories of *In Our Time*, Hemingway shows women denying reality rather than affirming and accepting it. Marjorie in 'The End of Something' has to be forced to acknowledge that 'it isn't fun any more' (presumably no helpful clues have been supplied to her): subsequently ('The Three Day Blow'), it seems that it might be fun again and Nick might 'get back into it again'. Marjorie's views are uncanvassed and obviously irrelevant. Krebs ('Soldier's Home') has discovered that 'you did not need a girl unless you thought about them.' 'He did not want them themselves really. They were too complicated. Vaguely he wanted a girl but he did not want to have to work to get her.'[22] His mother embarrasses him with inconvenient talk about love. However acceptable Krebs's reaction to this emotional blackmail may be, the accurate comments on Krebs's attitude to women as mere objects is rather chilling: nevertheless, it is the underlying attitude of all Hemingway's male protagonists throughout the rest of his work. A similar irritation appears at the refusal of the doctor's wife to face brutal motives in human behaviour ('I really don't think that anyone would really do a thing like that'). The story 'Mr. and Mrs. Elliot', though extending its irony to both the male and female characters, focuses attention on the lesbianism of the women and the sterility of the man/woman relationship. 'Cat in the Rain' describes a more compatible but equally unsatisfied couple—the 'kitty in the rain' symbolizing the wife whose needs are not met or acknowledged by her husband. In 'A Canary For One' it's the woman herself who behaves brutally in separating her daughter from the man she loves. The canary symbolizes the loneliness (for which there seems no real reason, except the conditions of life itself) experienced by all the characters, including the narrator himself who confides in the last line of the story that he and his wife 'were returning to Paris to set up separate residences'.

There is no doubt that Hemingway is essentially ill-at-ease when dealing with sexual matters and the assumed air of wry cynicism which his narrator often adopts seems to cover a kind of provinciality of moral attitude. As has been said by Harry Levin:

> the world that remains most alive to Hemingway is that stretch between puberty and maturity which is strictly governed by the ephebic code: a world of mixed apprehension and bravado before the rite of passage, the baptism of fire, the introduction to sex. Afterward comes the boasting, along with such surviving ideals as Hemingway subsumes in the word *cojones*.[23]

So, in 'The Sea Change' the man's attitude to the fact that the girl intends to have a lesbian affair is self-consciously stoical but basically self-regarding:

> Couldn't you have gotten into something else? Couldn't you have gotten into some other jam?[24]

When he allows the girl to go, he feels that he has been initiated into the world of 'vice' and that he will never look, or be, the same again. In 'Hills Like White Elephants', the Hemingway protagonist is finding another pregnancy difficult to cope with and refuses to understand that his relationship with the girl will be radically impaired, whether he persuades her to have an abortion or not. This story which consists solely in one line dialogue between the two participants ends with a short passage of description in which the underlying antagonism and hysteria of the couple are marked by the simple actions performed by the man at the end, attention being directed to other people—those not involved—'waiting reasonably for the train':

> He picked up the two heavy bags and carried them around the station to the other tracks. He looked up the tracks but could not see the train. Coming back, he walked through the bar-room, where people waiting for the train were drinking. He drank an Anis at the bar and looked at the people. They were all waiting reasonably for the train. He went out through the bead curtain. She was sitting at the table and smiled at him.[25]

Sexual relationships in 'The Short Happy Life of Francis Macomber' and 'The Snows of Kilimanjaro' are complicated by the issue of money. In 'Macomber', the wife has been bought and in 'Kilimanjaro', the husband. 'Kilimanjaro' is the more autobiographical, even containing a rehash of the famous Hemingway/Fitzgerald conversation about the rich:

> The rich were dull and they drank too much, or they played too much backgammon. They were dull and they were repetitious. He remembered poor Julian and his romantic awe of them and how he had started a story once that began, 'The very rich are different from you and me.' And how someone had said to Julian, Yes, they have more money. But that was not humorous to Julian. He thought they were a special glamorous race and when he found they weren't it wrecked him just as much as any other thing that wrecked him.[26]

In 'Kilimanjaro' Harry has destroyed himself as a writer and is a kind of moral suicide; he veers between blaming his wife and her money and seeing her merely as an instrument by means of which he has engineered his spiritual death (a situation described in *Green Hills of Africa* as the fate of many American writers). The many vicious statements made to Helen clearly express Harry's true feeling as opposed to 'the familiar lie he made his bread and butter by'; yet Hemingway also indicates that this is a projection of the writer's self-hatred for having betrayed himself by not completing his work: 'It was not her fault that when he went to her he was already over. How could a woman know that you meant nothing that you said; that you spoke only from habit and to be comfortable?' The gangrene that is eating Harry up is a symbol of the loss of his artistic integrity; Helen is a participant in this moral and physical decay but not the originator of it. The grave poignancy of the story lies in the sense of waste that oppresses Harry as he relives significant episodes of his past life and remembers all the stories he will now never have time to tell. The naturalistic ending is a *tour-de-force*, the reader realizing, with Harry, that his journey is not to Arusha but to 'the House of God'. Much of Hemingway's success in this story comes from his insistence on physical detail and the use of concrete images (the vulture, the hyena) in a literal as well as a symbolic sense. The pathos of the story is in Harry's human failure, but there is also integrity in his resolute facing of the truth about himself and his career. His wife is seen as secondary, as an adjunct, whose role is to support and not to quarrel and 'to do everything he wanted to do'. Basically, Harry despises her because she's rich and therefore not to be taken seriously and because she has no work of her own: it's a double-bind situation—had she a profession, then she would be of no use to him.

The 'Macomber' story exemplifies in microcosm all Hemingway's strengths and is the best example of his particular talent. Oddly, in spite of the great emotion engendered by the failed marriage, both Francis and his wife remain caricatures; Hemingway seems concerned with the essence of the situation, rather than with the characters as people. Structurally, the story falls into two parts, in the second of which Francis retrieves his integrity and experiences a rebirth into a life of courage and manhood. The rather specialized form of this initiation, with its emphasis on a particular type of physical courage stands for something much larger, really the strength to be one's self and realize all one's human potential. One reading of the story would be that the wife has to destroy her husband when he is freed from fear and therefore from his dependence on her. However, it's not clear that we are intended to take over Wilson's analysis of the situation:

> 'That was a pretty thing to do,' he said in a toneless voice.
> 'He *would* have left you too. . . . Why didn't you poison him?
> That's what they do in England.'[27]

Nevertheless, the narrator has told us that 'Mrs. Macomber in the car, *had shot at the buffalo* with the 6.5 Mannlicher as it seemed about to gore Macomber and had hit her husband about two inches up and a little to one side of the base of his skull.' The ambivalence is part of the story's meaning since a large area of it is based on the shifting allegiances of the sexes, the wife's sexual betrayal of her husband being followed by the retaliatory comradeship between Wilson and Macomber when Macomber has been freed of his fear ('he had seen men come of age before and it always moved him. It was not a matter of their twenty-first birthday'). In spite of the antagonism shown to women in general by the comments of both men, due regard is paid to the wife's genuine fear and anger at significant points in the narrative. Wilson expresses typical Hemingway views on the cruelty of American women ('They govern, of course, and to govern one has to be cruel sometimes') and on the worthlessness of the idle rich, but the crucial element in the story is in the extremes of emotion expressed and the way in which Hemingway is able to increase tension to an unbearable extent and to give a sharp sense of the panic and exhilaration of hunting. Hunting, in itself is a test of spiritual, mental, emotional as well as physical skills.

Hemingway's material, like Jane Austen's, was severely limited: the physical life provided him with metaphors for truth-telling and for the investigation of extremes of feeling and sensation. Characterization is irrelevant to this kind of concern and to a great extent Hemingway's fiction shows that he is uninterested in the complexities of personality and, by extension, in the relationships between people, except in so far as they embody his major themes. His work reveals a progressive repudiation of people in general and of women in particular. The Hemingway protagonist is the archetypal loner fighting against a hostile world and an indifferent nature; the fact that some of the locations of his fiction are 'exotic' makes no difference to the essentially American mystique.

NOTES

All references to Granada editions of Hemingway's works unless otherwise stated.

1. Eudora Welty, *The Eye of the Story* (1977), pp. 131–32.
2. Malcolm Cowley, *And I Worked At the Writer's Trade* (1979), p. 30.
3. Judith Fetterley, *The Resisting Reader* (1978), p. 71.
4. 'Fathers and Sons' in *Winner Take Nothing* (Granada, 1977), p. 174.
5. Ibid., p. 12.
6. *Across the River and Into the Trees*, p. 62.
7. *Love and Death in the American Novel* (1970), p. 295.
8. *Across the River and Into the Trees*, p. 113.
9. Ibid., p. 131.
10. *Green Hills of Africa*, p. 64.
11. Jeffrey Walsh, *American War Literature 1914 To Vietnam* (1982), p. 128.
12. *Love and Death in the American Novel*, p. 295.
13. *For Whom the Bell Tolls* (1976), p. 237.
14. 'You told what happened and, with one trick and another, you communicated the emotion aided by the element of timeliness which gives a certain emotion to any account of something that has happened on that day' (*Death in the Afternoon*, p. 8).
15. Melvin Backman, *Hemingway: The Matador and the Crucified* in *Modern American Fiction*, A. Walton Litz (ed.), (1967), p. 209.
16. Unpublished fragment, Kennedy Library MS 845.
17. *The Resisting Reader*, p. 46.
18. *A Farewell to Arms* (Penguin, 1975), p. 7.
19. *In Our Time* (1955), p. 85.
20. *Hemingway, A Title Fight in Ten Rounds* (1965), p. 77.
21. *Fiesta (The Sun Also Rises)*, (Pan, 1949), p. 122.
22. *In Our Time*, pp. 92–3.
23. 'Observations on the style of Hemingway', *Kenyon Review* XIII (Autumn, 1951), 607.
24. *The First 49 Stories* (1962), p. 327.
25. Ibid., p. 223.
26. Ibid., p. 71.
27. Ibid., pp. 39–40.

10

Stalking Papa's Ghost: Hemingway's Presence in Contemporary American Writing

by FRANK McCONNELL

To Seymour L. Gross

In 1944 the Second World War was virtually over, the Axis will and neck all but terminally broken, Paris retaken, and Ernest Hemingway a picturesque but faintly absurd epiphenomenon of the tidal wave rolling toward Berlin. The most important American novelist of his time (but that time was passing), a sometime war correspondent (but his war correspondence was muddled), and a self-styled soldier on behalf of the civilized world altogether (though the civilized world, at that crucial moment, had very much larger things to worry about), he was lurching between bravery and silliness in a way that boded ill, indeed, for the remainder of his career. Carlos Baker records, in *Ernest Hemingway: A Life Story*, that by the middle of the year, 'after nearly a week of sticking his neck out, said Ernest, his only present war aim was "to get to Paris without being shot".' It was a singularly unglorious ambition for a man who had made the profession of risk, the role of *miles gloriosus*, nearly the distinctive American mask of the '20s and '30s.

And it is also the story of the decline of Hemingway's reputation. For, just as the First World War virtually made Hemingway a serious writer—second only to T. S. Eliot as the chronicler and anthem-writer of a whole generation's despair— so the Second World War effectively marked the end of Hemingway's moment: or, at least, appeared to do so. 1944, the year of Allied victory and Hemingway foolishness was also the year of a new and startling talent in American letters. For while Hemingway was hoping to get into Paris without getting shot, Saul Bellow was publishing his first novel, *Dangling Man.* It is the fictionalized journal of 'Joseph', a Chicago-based intellectual and agonized draft-resister, a sensitive man who cannot even decide if he should enter the war to which Hemingway gave himself so enthusiastically. And it begins with what is essentially a refutation of the entire Hemingway mystique:

> There was a time when people were in the habit of addressing themselves frequently and felt no shame at making a record of their inward transactions. But to keep a journal nowadays is considered a kind of self-indulgence, a weakness, and in poor taste. For this is an era of hardboileddom. Today, the code of the athlete, of the tough boy—an American inheritance, I believe, from the English gentleman—that curious mixture of striving, asceticism, and rigor, the origins of which some trace back to Alexander the Great—is stronger than ever. Do you have feelings? There are correct and incorrect ways of indicating them. Do you have an inner life? It is nobody's business but your own. Do you have emotions? Strangle them. To a degree, everyone obeys this code.

In retrospect, there is something a little *too* cruelly parodic about this sendup of the 'tough boy'. Much of our contemporary sense of Hemingway, after all, is precisely the sense of how far from 'tough' he really was, all along. Philip Young was probably the first critic to demonstrate compellingly what an ocean of self-doubt and vulnerability underlay that charade of gusto. But we do not, now, even need Young: we have the suicide. And in the glare of the suicide we can see that Nick Adams, Jake Barnes, Frederick Henry, Robert Jordan and the whole Hemingway crew were always, in one way or another, weak men overcompensating desperately for their weakness.

Bellow goes on, in the passage I have cited, to observe that the hardboiled writers tend to be deficient in the finer senses of despair and possibility. They are unpractised in introspection, he writes, 'and therefore badly equipped to deal with opponents whom they cannot shoot like big game or outdo in daring'.

Badly equipped, yes: but one wonders about that word, unpractised. Is anyone *well* equipped to deal with the monsters inside, as opposed to outside the head? And isn't the man who quests obsessively for beasts in view, for clear and evident monsters to kill, perhaps also the man who understands best how unkillable are the monsters within?

To ask such questions is, of course, to re-romanticize Hemingway, to return him—man and style—to the arena of melodrama he himself felt most comfortable in. But that itself might not be a bad thing to do. In the twenty-odd years since his death, Hemingway has been subjected to much more blatant, and much less understanding, kinds of parody than Bellow's treatment in *Dangling Man*. And most of the worst of it has come from the literary critics.

He was a sad man. His bluster, his bullying, his loud adventurism were a mask for a deep-seated insecurity. He was, as I have said, a *miles gloriosus*, a braggart soldier who could be taken as a mere, absurd figure of fun. So much is true, and is eminently acceptable as an attitude to strike toward Hemingway in the American academy. For so much is, to put it bluntly, reassuring. One needn't fear the braggart soldier, just because he *is* only a braggart: we know that by the last act he will be revealed to be a coward, like us.

But, I want to suggest, Hemingway managed to be all those absurd, laughable things, and also to be something else, something permanently valuable for American letters. He managed to be a hero of consciousness, a writer and a stylist who made his cowardice, and his knowledge of his cowardice, the very stuff of his heroism and his endurance. This is, again, a cliché of a certain strain of romanticism: the Byronic. And yet the evidence of American fiction after Hemingway is that he, like Lord Byron, was the kind of truly great clown whose special talent is for making that kind of cliché vital and serviceable.

Bellow perceptively identifies the hardboiled pose as 'an American inheritance . . . from the English gentleman—that curious mixture of striving, asceticism, and rigor'; although it would have been even more perceptive to substitute 'English dandy' for 'English gentleman'. Both Byron and Hemingway were dandies: ostentatious, elegantly vulgar men who made their insecure egotism the subject of their art. Hemingway's most lasting importance, indeed, may be that he was the first great American dandy of this century (only Whitman and Twain come to mind from the nineteenth century); and that, like all the truly valuable members of the sect (e.g. Byron, Baudelaire, Wilde, T. E. Lawrence), he shows us something of the cost, as well as the value, of the dandy's pose.

Francis Jeffrey wrote what is probably the definitive analysis of the literary dandy, in his review of Byron's *The Corsair*; and his analysis applies with striking appropriateness to the Hemingway persona, also. Why all this fascination, in a civilized country, with violence, adventure, and deep melancholia, he asks. Because the very civilization with which we have surrounded ourselves puts us out of touch with certain primal instincts, rages, and passions that are necessary to our souls. So that Byron's 'primitivism' is not primitivism at all, but the very sophisticated nostalgia of an over-complex victim of the modern age. Furthermore, he writes:

> Our modern poets . . . have borrowed little more than the situations and unrestrained passions of the state of society from which they have taken their characters—and have added all the sensibility and delicacy from the stores of their own experience. They have lent their knights and squires of the fifteenth century the deep reflection and considerate delicacy of the nineteenth.

One might say the same, *mutatis mutandis*, of Hemingway's Spanish peasants, Cuban fishermen, and safari guides. He is not only definitively in the Byronic tradition, he is one of the greatest manipulators of its masks and postures.

For a pose is what it is. The dandy values style above substance precisely because he finds the world of substances empty, void, a sham. This is the Byronic abyss of cynicism, this is Lawrence's profound despair at politics, and this is Hemingway's celebrated *nada*. The dandy confuses the life and the work: to the degree that his heirs or his successors must laboriously separate the life from the work, in order to see the work afresh. The dandy loves to show off; loves to be sketched or photographed in the various poses and costumes of his dandyism: see the portrait of Byron in Albanian garb, or the photos of Hemingway, smiling over dead buffalo, in his white-hunter slouch hat and khaki.

And the dandy loves war. He loves war for the same reason he loves stylized brutality, because war *is* stylized brutality, the absolute triumph of technique over value and therefore the permanent, the true condition of humankind. Patton and Montgomery are two dandies *manqués*—neither wrote well—in that they both seemed to understand war as theatre, as a riotous backdrop for their own performing selves.

But the dandy loves war as he loves everything else: ironically. 'Abstract words such as glory, honour, courage, or hallow were obscene beside the concrete names of villages, the numbers of roads, the names of rivers, the numbers of regiments and the dates.' That, of course, is Frederick Henry in *A Farewell to Arms*: one of the most often-quoted, and one of the most crucial of Hemingway passages. Byronic romantic that he was, Hemingway believed in this wounded emptiness before he ever saw it manifested in the War (think about his jejune parody of Anderson's sentimentality in *The Torrents of Spring*). But he welcomed the War—and became its chief elegiac voice—just because it was the manifestation of the *nada* he carried inside himself.

And that gift of irony, that sublime hollowness, is his bequest to later American writers. Harold Bloom has recently observed, in *Agon*, that the chief genius of the American writer is for loneliness, for an isolation from his fellows and from the great tradition either imposed upon or earned by him, but that is nevertheless, in either case, both his triumph and his cross. Bloom does not discuss Hemingway in this connection—the meeting of that writer and that critic would be a fascinating one to observe—but the observation seems nowhere more pointed than in Hemingway's case.

For if every strong novelist must struggle against his strong precursors; if every artist, in good Freudian fashion, must kill or castrate his artistic father before he can begin to function on his own; then Hemingway can be taken as the symbolic father of almost all American novelists to come after him, the dreaded

and revered, heroic parent against whom our best living writers
must wage family war in order to emerge. The man who was
called—and who liked to be called—'Papa' could certainly
expect his share of literary-filial rebellion. Bellow's satire is
significant, in this respect, not so much because it is vicious, but
just because it is as wise as it is. An heir who attacks his father as
cannily as all that, we must believe, is an heir who will thrive
and prosper: and so Bellow has.

But if the '50s belonged to the rebellious sons of Hemingway,
the two succeeding decades belonged largely to his more
faithful inheritors. The dandy—the American dandy—may
have gone temporarily out of favour. But give us a good, silly
war; give us a real national moral vacuity; give us a mass-
marketed *nada* adequate to express the full adriftness of the
national life: and watch dandyism reassert itself, rear again its
handsome, ironic, smiling head. So, at any rate, it proved to be
with Hemingway, Vietnam, and the years just after mid-
century.

I said that the dandy confuses his life and his art to such a
degree that they become inseparable. Only another and a later
dandy can successfully distinguish them from one another.
Bellow, obsessed as he is with moral earnestness, could not in
Dangling Man, and has not since, differentiated the Hemingway
style of public performance from the Hemingway style of
perception. So that the figure of the manic, enthusiastic, over-
achieving writer in Bellow's fiction becomes an almost invariable
figure of fun and contempt. For Bellow, whatever else he may
be, is certainly not a dandy: dandies (Hemingway himself
excepted) tend not to win Nobel Prizes.

But in the Patriarchal Plot, from the story of Isaac, Esau and
Jacob through the parable of the Prodigal Son and beyond,
there is a regularity. The patriarch should have *two* sons, one of
whom betrays or dupes or subverts his father's values and
succeeds, and the other of whom accepts, assimilates, and tries
to perpetuate those values and fails—but fails spectacularly. 'It
will soon be time to mourn for my father', reflects Esau in
Genesis 27:41, 'and then I will slay my brother Jacob.'

Generally descriptive as that rivalry for sonship may be of the
whole complicated business of literary inheritance, it is particularly appropriate to Hemingway's presence in American

letters. The faithful son, the one who attempts to carry on Papa's ways, is of course Norman Mailer. And Mailer's career-long quarrel with Bellow is only part of the heavy cost of his discipleship to Hemingway; which is to say, part of his torturous, if brilliant, achievement.

It has often been remarked how all of Mailer's central characters, from Lt. Hearn of *The Naked and the Dead* to the re-created 'Gary Gilmore' of *The Executioner's Song*, are existential orphans cut off through accident and through choice from their past. That, of course, is an archetypal American situation, incarnated best in that book Hemingway was fond of calling the central American novel, *The Adventures of Huckleberry Finn*. But Mailer's orphans share a desperation, a deep insecurity about their own flamboyant style, that obviously derives from, and illuminates certain dark corners of, the Hemingway hero.

Here is Mailer, in the early '60s, reviewing Morley Callaghan's memoir of Hemingway, *That Summer in Paris*. Callaghan relates how he once knocked Hemingway down in a boxing match refereed by F. Scott Fitzgerald. And Mailer defends Hemingway's chagrin at the knockdown, writing:

> It is possible Hemingway lived every day of his life in the style of the suicide. What a great dread is that. It is the dread which sits in the silences of his short declarative sentences. At any instant, by any failure of magic, by a mean defeat, or by a moment of cowardice, Hemingway could be thrust back again into the agonizing demands of his courage. For the life of his talent must have depended on living in a psychic terrain where one must either be brave beyond one's limit, or sicken closer into a bad illness, or, indeed, by the ultimate logic of the suicide, must advance the hour in which one would make another reconnaissance into one's death.

If Bellow is a little cruel in his parody of the 'tough boy', Mailer is surely a little fulsome in his avowal of that physical and psychic vanity. But what is significant is the way both writers use Hemingway—the image of the man as well as the image of the books—to define their own stylistic identity. Bellow's suave disdain for the cult of the literary bully is virtually a précis of the wry, humane academicism that marks all his best fiction. And Mailer's outrageous romanticism (cf.

the agonizing demands of his courage), his rhetorical pumping for Papa, is not just a defence but an *assumption* of the Hemingway voice. 'What a great dread is that', he writes. The sentence is clumsy, inelegant; until we realize that Mailer is writing *Hemingwayese*. For it is just the sort of thing one of the peasants in *For Whom the Bell Tolls*, or Santiago in *The Old Man and the Sea*, might say. When in doubt, teaches the aesthetics of dandyism, write awkwardly.

For awkwardness is not just the earnest of sincerity (if, after the recent plague of deconstructionism, we still choose to use that word); it is also the badge of the improviser. It is the shoestring catch, the nearly perfect veronica, the almost—but not quite—flawless jazz solo whose very failure of elegance is a new kind of elegance of its own. Byron may well have invented this transcendental clumsiness in the headlong improvisation of *Don Juan*. But Hemingway turned it into the very basis of his style, and Mailer, his most faithful son, has made it a *lingua franca* in postwar American writing.

An example: in *The Armies of the Night*, Mailer reflects long and lovingly over a chance phrase he hears from a Southern G.I.: 'Man, I just took me a *noble* shit!' Where else, wonders Mailer, but in southern-redneck-Army culture would you come across the completely unself-conscious and completely poetic collocation of those last two words? The meditation obviously has little to do with ideas of deliberate utterance (that, Mailer might say, would be Saul Bellow's province), but everything to do with the idea of utterance, the idea of writing, as a totally adequate response to the shifting, chaotic demands of the present moment; everything to do with the idea of style as survival mechanism in a universe of social and personal fragmentation. And it becomes more rather than less compelling when we realize that its origin is literary. For, in its tone and its resonance for Mailer's book, it is really a reprise of that passage in *For Whom the Bell Tolls* when Robert Jordan, hearing one of his loyalist cohorts observe that he is very bored, thinks to himself that only in Spanish could a peasant unself-consciously use the word, 'bored'.

Spanish peasant speech or southern-U.S. patois: in both cases what is being presented is an idea of style both innovative and deliberately vulgar, both poetic and anti-poetic in its response to life. If Hemingway invented the code-hero whose measured hedonism was an island of sanity and control in a mad world, Mailer invents (or at least patents) the hipster as the logical extension of the code-hero. The difference—and it is a serious difference—is that the hipster chooses to live much closer to the ragged edge of neurosis, that very edge the code-hero spends so much of his time evading. There is no equivalent, in recent American fiction, to the bitter but lyrical pastoralism of 'The Big Two-Hearted River' or, even, of *Islands in the Stream*. Perhaps the closest approach to that is Mailer's *Why Are We In Vietnam?* where the narrator, 'D.J.', a manic and scatological Nick Adams, tells us of his crazy hunting expedition before his enlistment in the Army. But here the solaces of nature have all turned ugly, parodic: Mailer may trust the irony of the Hemingway voice, but he cannot bring himself to trust its capacity for limited joy.

And this itself is an irony about the inheritance of Hemingway. For while Mailer assimilates the bluster, the toughness, the outrageousness, and the suicidal risk of the style, it is Bellow—Bellow the anti-'tough boy'—who seems to have assimilated most successfully the hopefulness that runs through Hemingway's work right through to the end. When Herzog cries out, in the midst of the novel named after him, 'We owe the void a human life', it is difficult not to hear echoes of *The Old Man and the Sea* (Man may be destroyed, but never defeated) and any number of earlier, similar utterances against *nada*.

The point of all this is that Hemingway—as writer and as presence—broods with a particular urgency over the writers who come after him. I have said that the literary dandy confuses his life and his art. In Hemingway's case that confusion has been unusually productive, and unusually indicative of shifts in the national self-consciousness. We can take Hemingway as the first successful American romantic after Walt Whitman, the first man to identify a style of writing with a style of being in the world, and to make the identification popular. He *was*, largely, the Byron of his age: so much so that 'Byronic' and 'Hemingwayesque' are the only two terms we normally apply as adjectives to the word, 'hero'.

The examples of Bellow and Mailer allow us to see how suggestive that idea of hero may be for later writers. In Bellow it is all but obscured by the demands and considerations of ordinary, intellectual, urban-quotidian existence: although Bellow's one novel featuring a non-Jewish hero, *Henderson the Rain King*, is set, significantly enough, in Africa, that continent that Hemingway made his own in American letters. In Mailer, on the other hand, the idea of the existential hero (for that, after all, is what the Hemingway hero really is) is not obscured at all by ordinary considerations, but in fact becomes the centre of the storyteller's obsession.

Not that Bellow and Mailer alone are the important American writers of the post-war years. And not that they are the most visibly influenced by Hemingway. If Hemingway is the American Byron, we might expect that his influence and his presence would be, like Byron's, both blatant and subtle. And so it has been. Indeed, like Byron, Hemingway has had at least as important an influence on so-called 'popular' culture as he has had on so-called 'serious' writing. His very short story, 'The Killers', from *In Our Time*, has provided a title and at least the bare bones of a script for two excellent gangster films (one directed by Robert Siodmak, 1946; one directed by Don Siegel, 1963). But beyond this explicit influence, it is also evident that Hemingway and the Hemingway style have exercised a strong, probably determinative, effect on the whole course of the American detective story in both film and literature.

Dashiell Hammet and Raymond Chandler are usually credited with being the originators of the American or 'hardboiled' style of detective writing. But, as the phrase itself, 'hardboiled' may indicate, both Hammett and Chandler—and their contemporary heirs, Ross McDonald, John D. MacDonald, Lawrence Sanders, and Stuart Kaminsky—would not really be possible without Hemingway. Indeed, the Hemingway hero is, by and large, the classic American hardboiled private eye; and the prose style that goes along with that peculiar figure is, by and large, the prose style Hemingway developed for a very different kind of character: i.e. the wounded, disillusioned veteran of the First World War.

'Doctors did things to you and then it was not your body any more', thinks Frederick Henry in *A Farewell to Arms*, returning to the Front. 'The head was mine, and the inside of the belly. It was very hungry in there. I could feel it turn over on itself. The head was mine, but not to use, not to think with, only to remember and not too much remember.'

'Only to remember and not too much remember': that may be the distinctive definition of the Hemingway style. For at its best it is a style that places a screen of words, a screen of short, ritualistically declarative sentences between the narrator/perceiver of the action and the horrendous, tragic quality of the action itself. Jake Barnes *is* impotent; Frederick Henry *does* fail to make 'a separate peace'; Robert Jordan *does* die needlessly; Santiago *does* fail to catch and bring back the great fish. It is a universe of defeat and disillusionment, and yet that telegraphic style—what Mailer calls the 'dread' sitting in his short declarative sentences—almost reconciles us to the horror, since it all but masks the horror within an ironic, primitive, unremembering articulation.

This is to say that the Hemingway style is a direct equivalent of the celebrated 'code' of the Hemingway hero; for both are deliberate reductions of the flux of life to the dimensions of an elaborate game—the one in the world of behaviour, the other in the world of utterance. And that, of course, is precisely the tone of the classic American detective story, whether in film or in literature. It is a deliberate unremembering: a recapitulation of the violent past that filters the horror of the past—the horror of betrayal, of failure, of psychic impotence—through the obsessive detail of its descriptive style. In American film this is the tradition of the *film noir*, from classics of the '40s like *The Maltese Falcon* and *Double Indemnity* to recent attempts at recapturing that special tone like *Chinatown*, *The Godfather*, and *Body Heat*. What all these disparate films have in common is their celebration of a certain tender cynicism, a certain conviction that, rotten at the core and inevitably entropic as human history may be, there is a kind of existential toughness, a bullet-biting disengagement that can survive the ravages of time with something like dignity.

That is the Hemingway tradition at its most popular—and perhaps also at its most dangerous. The self-advertising 'toughness' deliberately eschewed by a Bellow and self-consciously reassumed by a Mailer can also be adopted at its most vulgar and arrogant pitch of *machismo*. No one, for example, could seriously argue that the popularity of the Hemingway hero is

directly responsible for the obscene bullyism of America's
venture into Vietnam. But, on the other hand, one could argue
that the Hemingway vision is symptomatic of a certain strain of
irresponsibility, of cruelty, of dangerously arrested adolescence
that is a permanent flaw in human character and a fatal flaw of
empires. We know that Richard Nixon authorized the invasion
of Cambodia after watching the film, *Patton*, numerous times:
intimation, if not proof, that warrior-dandyism is a severe
intoxicant for the wrong minds. And we also know that one of
the men Hemingway most admired was his friend Gary Cooper;
but not the Gary Cooper of history—an aesthete, a sophisticate,
and rather a careerist—rather the Gary Cooper of his films, the
laconic, stoical, almost parodically manly man. Indeed, only
John Wayne among film stars comes closer than Cooper to
incarnating the Hemingway hero's mask. And Hemingway
probably never befriended Wayne for the simple reason that it
was not until the very late '40s that Wayne became a major star.

In a century where it is a commonplace to mourn the split
between the art novel and the popular novel, Hemingway's
career is an anomaly. Not only a 'best seller', but a best seller
who was actually *read* by his buyers, he was a writer whose
genius was precisely his ability to catch and reflect with uncanny accuracy and great art the neuroses and daydreams of his
time and culture. A sickly, introspective boy who transformed
himself, by sheer act of will, into an athlete, soldier, and meta-
physician of the active life: it may be an indication of Hemingway's special intimacy with the American mythology that that
description applies equally to himself and to Theodore
Roosevelt.

But, as I have said, there are dangers to incarnating the myth
too well. Hemingway's irony ensured that his own books never
became the cruel cartoons of toughness they might have been;
and ensured that writers like Hammett and Chandler would
retain, under his influence, that saving irony. But here is
Mickey Spillane, another heir to the hardboiled tradition,
describing the final shoot-out in *One Lonely Night*:

> There was only the guy in the pork-pie hat who made a crazy
> try for a gun in his pocket. I aimed the tommy gun for the first
> time and took his arm off at the shoulder. It dropped on the floor

next to him and I let him have a good look at it. He couldn't believe it happened. I proved it by shooting him in the belly. They were all so damned clever!

It could almost be a satire of Hemingway, the prose is so unmistakable in its provenance. And the very great moral ugliness of the passage is an indication of one of the risks of the style. For here to remember and not too much remember means to be, effectively, an ethical moron. The 'dread' has departed from the silences between the sentences, that dread that indicates the tension of irretrievable loss. And what is left in its place is human emptiness. The style devised as a shield against *nada* has become the voice of *nada*.

What are we to make, then, of Hemingway's ongoing presence in our writing? I have called him a hero of consciousness, and have said that his measured, ironic despair shines—or darkles—through all his major successors. And I have also said that the cruder aspects of his vision can—and have—become components of a childish mythography of moral irresponsibility. Where is the final shape of the man then?

According to Leslie Fiedler, at least, writing in the early '60s, the final shape of the man was precisely the shape of that contradiction. Fiedler's *Waiting for the End* is a dazzlingly intelligent survey of American fiction of the '50s and early '60s, and over all the survey broods the shadow of Hemingway as both prophet and fool. Fiedler, of course, is not only one of the most perceptive of American critics, but probably also the American critic closest in tone, spirit, and style to 'Papa' (his own novels are remarkably Hemingwayesque exercises). Writing of the suicide, he can be even more romantic and more outrageous than Mailer:

> One quarry was left him only, the single beast he had always had it in his power to destroy, the single beast worthy of him: himself. . . . With a single shot he redeemed his best work from his worst, his art from himself, his vision of truth from the lies of his adulators.

Eloquent, one thinks: but is not this kind of prose itself the prose of 'one of his adulators'? A glance back at 1944, and Bellow's sardonic comments on the cult of the hunter-dandy, can remind us how contagious and how misleading the hardboiled style of perception can be. *No* suicide, to speak bluntly, ever 'redeems' anything.

Nevertheless, Fiedler is spendidly right about Hemingway's importance for the generation of 'apocalyptic' young writers who were just beginning to emerge in the early '60s. If Mailer was the godfather of sensibilities like Robert Coover, Kurt Vonnegut, and Thomas Pynchon, then Hemingway was their great-godfather. These then-young men were all, in one way or another, influenced not just by the American literary tradition, but by the American adventure in Vietnam, that nightmare of misguided honour and misdirected heroics which may prove to be the single most important psychic event of American life in the twentieth century. And Fiedler, writing in 1963—before he or anyone could have known what Vietnam would ultimately mean—described its meaning, and its relevance to the Hemingway vision, perfectly:

> We inhabit for the first time a world in which men begin wars knowing that their avowed ends will not be accomplished, a world in which it is more and more difficult to believe that the conflicts we cannot avert are in any sense justified. And in such a world . . . all who make what Hemingway was the first to call 'a separate peace' . . . become a new kind of anti-heroic hero.

Well, not particularly a 'new' kind of anti-heroic hero, but certainly an important kind. What Fiedler suggests here is of some importance: that that callow, frightened, diffidently-revolutionary youth movement of the Vietnam years may have been, one and all, the spiritual heirs of Frederick Henry and Jake Barnes. And this in the midst of the very war that also seemed such a grotesque exaggeration and obscene reduction of the Hemingway idiom.

The draft resisters and the generals, the underground novelists and the writers of State Department White Papers, the freakouts and the company men: they were all, during the '60s and '70s, pursuing one version or another of the central irony of the twentieth century: the irony of the discovery that public expediency and private morality may be, not only unparallel, but actually contradictory: the irony that, in America, Hemingway made his own.

'Only to remember and not too much remember': of course

public expediency and private morality have never been necessarily congruent, at least since the dilemma of Achilles in the *Iliad*, and that is one of the things the Hemingway vision does not remember—or conveniently forgets. But there is something more significant in that observation than mere historical ignorance: there is historical ignorance *by choice*. It is not too much to say of Hemingway that he invented a whole new way of, a whole new justification for, hating and fearing history.

And here again Hemingway's archetypal Americanness is evident. For hating and fearing history has always been a salient American disease: Tocqueville isolated and identified the strain virtually before there was an American literature, and American literature and American foreign policy since Tocqueville have, by and large, only reinforced his diagnosis. For all Hemingway's major characters, history is the arena of defeat and the architecture of despair, and their styles of being and articulating themselves are ways of escaping its central horror. (Hemingway is here, perhaps more than anywhere else, the twin of that other great American lyricist of the wasteland, Eliot.)

But if this studied forgetting, this fear of history, has its debilitating and cynical consequences, it also has its peculiar—and peculiarly spiritual—rewards. Hemingway forgot history, escaped from history, to make 'a separate peace', which is the separate peace of his vision and most specially of his ironic style. His great countertype in early twentieth-century American literature, William Faulkner, contemplated no such escape. Obsessed as he was by history and by the inescapability of guilt, Faulkner's mythic landscape and narrative style are so perfectly the opposite of Hemingway's that it is difficult not to regard the two writers as manifestations of some deep-seated dichotomy in the human mind.

Sartre said of Faulkner that, in his work, time was 'amputated at the head': time was so labyrinthine in its repetitions, in other words, that the possibility of a future, of an escape from time, simply did not exist. The gorgeously baroque complexity of the Faulknerian sentence, forever returning to its major premise and forever frustrating our attempts to see it as a completed proposition, is a perfect reflection of this entrapment.

'Only to remember, and too much remember' might be taken as the slogan of the Faulknerian vision. And if Hemingway's middle-aged and old men are, for all their bruising experience, still in one way or another orphaned children, then Faulkner's troubled young men (Quentin Compson, Ike McCaslin) are prematurely old men.

For all the awesome power of his best work, though, Faulkner has not been the perennial presence in later writing Hemingway has. One might have expected that the '60s and '70s, from Vietnam and Watergate on beyond, would have had the effect of a newly historicized sensibility for our best storytellers. But it has not been so. The Frederick Henry vision of the separate peace, the code-aesthetics of the dropout and the deserter, the dandy's solution of style as a counterpoint to the horror of history: these have been, in one way or another, the shape of the best American fiction of those years. Whether or not it has been, on a cosmic scale, the most responsible or the most mature, is of course a matter to be decided only from a cosmic perspective. But we can say that it has produced some of the best American fiction of the century.

Kurt Vonnegut, the most accessible and the most 'popular' of the young novelists to emerge in the '60s, is also the most recognizably Hemingwayesque. His best books—*The Sirens of Titan, Slaughterhouse-Five, Breakfast of Champions,* and *Jailbird*— are all bitter little parables about the brutality of human beings, the impermanence of love, and the impossibility of any meta-physical solution to the ultimate *nada*. But against that gloomy prognosis, Vonnegut poses the solace of an often childishly simple style, and childishly simple pity for the human condition, that is not without its grace and its effect. Vonnegut is fond of inserting himself, as narrator, into his fictions: commenting on his own reactions to the plot in what at first looks like the manner of Thackeray or the early Dickens. But after a while we realize that this technique owes less to the Victorians than it does to the urge to remember, but not too much remember. For Vonnegut has really transformed *himself* into the sensibility of Nick Adams in 'The Big Two-Hearted River'. That is, wounded and saddened by the chaos of his age, Vonnegut retreats to *fiction* the way Nick retreats to the pastoral of nature. His simplicities are disingenuous simplicities, and all the more affecting for that, since they are chosen and ferociously held *precisely* to make a separate peace with a disgusting century.

Slaughterhouse-Five, perhaps his finest novel, is not only an exceptionally original war novel, but an extraordinary re-creation of the *spirit* of Hemingway's response to war. As Vonnegut tells us in the Introduction (which is, of course, an essential part of the fiction itself), the novel is written to allow him to come to terms with his own personal experience of apocalypse, his witnessing, as a prisoner of war, the Allied fire-bombing of Dresden at the end of the Second World War. He frankly admits that he feels incapable of any adequate response to the horror he witnessed; and then invents an elaborate, absurdist science-fiction plot to encompass that horror. Many critics have faulted *Slaughterhouse-Five*—and Vonnegut in general—for 'frivolity' in his tales. But, as this and his other novels make clear, the frivolity is precisely the strong moral point of the work. It is a frivolity *chosen*, as the reductive-ness of the Hemingway style is chosen, because any attempt to confront the unspeakable in terms of conventional 'moral seriousness' is foredoomed to trivialize the enormity of horror by its very pretence to 'explaining'. It is, in other words, dandyism; and dandyism of the most desperate sort.

Other important writers of the same period reflect the same escape into style, and the same deep sense of style as a last resort against chaos. I have mentioned Robert Coover; and Donald Barthelme, John Barth, John Gardner, and even the poet John Ashbery may be added to that list of literary dandies. It is unusual, of course, to regard something like the immense, self-conscious fictions of Barth or the tantalizingly gnomic riddles of Ashbery as 'Hemingwayesque'. But in the context we have been describing, I think it is possible to see how that is, indeed, the case. Other 'influences'—eighteenth-century English fiction, studies in comparative mythology, continental theories of the 'new novel'—are surely more evident in works like *The Sot-Weed Factor* or *Houseboat Days* than the Hemingway influence. But, as with Vonnegut and as with the later work of Norman Mailer, the Hemingway presence here goes beyond ordinary considerations of literary influence. All these writers have assimilated the *writerly* persona of Hemingway; that is, the ironist, the dandified stylist of chaos, the storyteller as survivor of history. And none—excepting, of course, Mailer—has approached the public persona; that is, these writers are remarkably anonymous except in their books, remarkably shy about the sort of high visibility Hemingway made so much a part of his career.

If indeed there are two Hemingways, the self-aggrandizing man and the writer who was a hero of consciousness, it may be fair to say that his heirs have learned an important lesson that he never learned: how to keep the two separate. And they have learned it, of course, from his example. His presence grows increasingly analogous to Byron's presence in the nineteenth century: a sensibility and a style impossible to ignore, and a personality impossible to emulate.

The work of Thomas Pynchon is the best and richest place to track Hemingway's ghost. Pynchon's two massive novels, *V* and *Gravity's Rainbow*, and his novella, *The Crying of Lot 49*, may be the most important fictions produced in America after the Second World War; they are certainly the most apocalyptic. Pynchon's vision is of an absolutely paranoid universe, presided over by giant cartels and international war machines whose grand design is to turn human beings into mere mechanisms. It is a vision of plastic entropy very like Joseph Heller's vision of the War in *Catch-22*, except that its grimness is more unrelenting and its comedy even blacker. And it is, of course, a vision directly inherited from Hemingway. In the same paragraph where Jake Barnes reflects on not too much remembering, he meditates on the surgery that has been performed on his knee:

> Valentini had done a fine job. . . . It was his knee all right. The other knee was mine. Doctors did things to you and then it was not your body any more. The head was mine, and the inside of the belly. It was very hungry in there.

This very famous passage might almost be the epigraph for all of Pynchon's fiction: for all the recent fiction we have been examining. Life is increasingly encroached upon by the technologies of war and healing, both of which have the effect of robbing life of its vitality, and the only escape from that warfare is into the Switzerland of 'the head and the inside of the belly'. Pynchon's heroes more than any we have examined are the contemporary reincarnations of this mode. Benny Profane in *V*, Oedipa Maas in *Lot 49*, Tyrone Slothrop in *Gravity's Rainbow*—they are all weaklings, wounded and put-upon losers who are shocked into rebellion and a separate peace by the discovery that they are being turned into *someone else's* creation.

Their retreat is into style, into canniness—what Mailer would have called 'hip'—and into the kind of bitter, end-of-the-world charity that also characterizes the best of Hemingway throughout his career. In *V* the jazz musician McClintic Sphere articulates, in a brief scene, what may be the summary statement of the dandy's ironic humanism: 'Keep cool, but care.' And in the toughness and tenderness of that short line one hears echoes of all the sensibilities we have been examining, but with Papa at the centre.

No final assessment of the Hemingway presence can really be made, of course. This has been a century of the triumph of partial visions, all of which have left their mark on what comes after. But Hemingway more than any American novelist of the age represented and lived the vocation of art as *risk*, as a deliberate gamble with one's chances for sanity in a mad world. And in that he became a paradigm—something much larger and subtler than an 'influence'—for the most serious American writers of the post-War years. His ghost, the ghost of his finest perceptions and strongest acts of literary courage, is a very unquiet ghost indeed. And its rumblings are an inescapable part of the splendid dissonance that is contemporary American fiction.

Notes on Contributors

ANDREW HOOK is Bradley Professor of English literature at Glasgow University. His American interests are reflected by his book, *Scotland and America 1750–1835* (1975), as well as by articles on Anglo-American literary relations.

JAMES H. JUSTUS, Professor of English at Indiana University, has written on such American authors as Charles Brockden Brown, Hawthorne, Kate Chopin, Faulkner and other twentieth-century writers of the American South. His most recent book is *The Achievement of Robert Penn Warren* (1981).

A. ROBERT LEE teaches American studies and literature at the University of Kent at Canterbury. He writes mainly on the American Renaissance and Afro-American literature. He is Editor of the Everyman *Moby-Dick* (1975) and two other Vision collections, *Black Fiction: New Studies in the Afro-American Novel Since 1945* (1980) and *Nathaniel Hawthorne: New Critical Essays* (1982). He has published recent articles on Melville, George Eliot, Robert Penn Warren, Kingsley Amis, Mark Twain, Hawthorne, and a B.A.A.S. pamphlet, *Black American Fiction Since Richard Wright* (1983).

FRANK McCONNELL is Professor of English at the University of California at Santa Barbara. He is the author of *The Spoken Seen: Film and the Romantic Imagination* (1975), *Four Postwar American Novelists* (1977), *Storytelling and Mythmaking* (1979) and *The Science Fiction of H. G. Wells* (1981) among numerous other books and articles.

ERIC MOTTRAM is Professor of American literature at the University of London. He has published books on Kenneth Rexroth, William Burroughs, Paul Bowles, William Faulkner, Allen Ginsberg and others, and, with Malcolm Bradbury, edited and contributed to *The Penguin Companion to American Literature* (1971). He has written widely on nineteenth- and twentieth-century America. His last three books of poetry were *1980 Mediate, Elegies* and *A Book of Herne*.

Notes on Contributors

COLIN E. NICHOLSON is Lecturer in English and American literature at the University of Edinburgh. His published work includes essays on Alexander Pope, William Faulkner and Thomas Pynchon.

FAITH PULLIN taught English and American literature at the University of Ibadan before taking up her present post at the University of Edinburgh. She is Editor of *New Perspectives on Melville* (1978), has written on D. H. Lawrence and Afro-American literature, and is currently engaged on a critical study of three contemporary women novelists, Rosamund Lehman, Elizabeth Taylor and Barbara Pym.

DAVID SEED teaches American literature at the University of Liverpool. Among his recent publications are articles on Henry James, Thomas Pynchon, I. B. Singer, Fenimore Cooper and Henry Roth.

WILLIAM E. WASSERSTROM is Professor of English at the University of Syracuse, and has published widely on American literature and social issues. Among his books are *Heiress of All the Ages* (1952), *The Time of The Dial* (1963), *A Dial Miscellany* (1963), *Civil Liberties and The Arts* (1964) and *The Legacy of Van Wyck Brooks* (1971).

BRIAN WAY, until his death in 1982, was Senior Lecturer at the University College of Swansea. His publications include a short study of *Moby-Dick* (1977), *F. Scott Fitzgerald and the Art of Social Fiction* (1980) and numerous articles and reviews, mainly on the American novel.

213

Index

Index

Index